SPEED QUEENS

SPEED QUEENS

The Secret History of Women in Motorsport

RACHEL HARRIS-GARDINER

PEN & SWORD
HISTORY

AN IMPRINT OF PEN & SWORD BOOKS LTD.
YORKSHIRE – PHILADELPHIA

First published in Great Britain in 2023 by
PEN AND SWORD HISTORY
An imprint of
Pen & Sword Books Ltd
Yorkshire – Philadelphia

ISBN 978 1 39906 521 4

A CIP catalogue record for this book is available from the British Library.

Typeset in Times New Roman 12/15 by
SJmagic DESIGN SERVICES, India.
Printed and bound in the UK by CPI Group (UK) Ltd.

Pen & Sword Books Limited incorporates the imprints of Atlas, Archaeology,
Aviation, Discovery, Family History, Fiction, History, Maritime, Military,
Military Classics, Politics, Select, Transport, True Crime, Air World, Frontline
Publishing, Leo Cooper, Remember When, Seaforth Publishing, The Praetorian
Press, Wharncliffe Local History, Wharncliffe Transport, Wharncliffe True Crime
and White Owl.

For a complete list of Pen & Sword titles please contact
PEN & SWORD BOOKS LIMITED
47 Church Street, Barnsley, South Yorkshire, S70 2AS, England
E-mail: enquiries@pen-and-sword.co.uk
Website: www.pen-and-sword.co.uk

Or
PEN AND SWORD BOOKS
1950 Lawrence Rd, Havertown, PA 19083, USA
E-mail: Uspen-and-sword@casematepublishers.com
Website: www.penandswordbooks.com

Contents

Introduction

May 2019

W Series hit television screens worldwide in 2019. Eighteen female racing drivers from Europe, Asia and America took to the track in Formula Three cars for the first time. The media interest was huge; publications that would never normally cover a junior racing series such as Formula Three were sending reporters to Hockenheim. Their features all described the W Series as 'ground-breaking' and 'unique'. In their copy, one or two female drivers from the past were name-checked, but then discussed as if they were anomalies or outliers; brave lonely Amazons unable to make much of a difference on their own. We have short memories.

The story of women in motorsport is not one of a constant steady rise, but it is not one of a few plucky individuals either. Going from the W Series backwards, all the way to the first stirrings of motorsport itself while Queen Victoria was still on the throne, women have been there. Not always the most successful nor the most famous, but almost never alone in their fight to win, to be taken seriously or even to race at all.

This book is subtitled 'A Secret History', not because these stories have been deliberately suppressed but because they seem to have slipped through the net of history's narrative.

It is widely believed that women were officially banned from competing in all sorts of places, when this was only the case in some countries and in some circumstances. These intrepid racers more often than not found a way around all manner of rules.

Sometimes we are told that women are not included because they did not take part, but more often, their contributions are simply overlooked. Perusing old newspapers and motoring magazines and even watching old newsreels, women are there. When Kay Petre and Gwenda Hawkes duelled for the Brooklands Outer Circuit Record in 1934, Pathe News was there to cover it. Rally driver Sheila van Damm had her own newspaper column in the 1950s. Divina Galica, a skier turned racer in the UK in the 1970s, was a favourite with the press of the time. They seemed captivated by her lofty ambitions, aristocratic connections and cut-glass speaking voice.

Their reputations just seem to have faded over time in a way that those of their male counterparts did not. As a story gets older and further from the origin, it gets simplified. We lose colour and detail and in the case of motorsport, that means the women.

Speedqueens aims not only to give female drivers back their own history but to explore it as a continuous story with highs and lows, triumphs and tragedy, rivalry and friendships. It also serves to bring some fabulous characters from the past back into the public consciousness where they belong. With this book, I wanted to explore the connections between different drivers and how their careers intersected. It is all very well to celebrate the first woman to achieve something, but for every first woman, there is at least one other who could easily have been the first, be she a rival, a friend or both. It is not just 'first ladies' who deserve to be celebrated.

Each chapter has its own theme, a particular answer to the old question of 'how does a woman compete in motorsport?' The chapters are arranged in a rough chronological order, although some themes run through longer time periods than others.

It is not a complete history. To chronicle the entire history of women's involvement in motorsport would take several volumes. Not just drivers, but rally co-drivers, team owners, mechanics and engineers have enough stories between them for a whole book. More research is needed on the women who competed in the African American speedway leagues in the mid-twentieth century and on competitors from the African continent itself. There were women involved in the nascent motoring scene in the last days of imperial Russia who are currently just names on lists. Maybe this book will inspire more investigations into their stories and put faces to their names once more.

I mentioned W Series at the beginning of this introduction, but I decided not to cover it in any detail. The careers of the women involved are still ongoing and not ready to be discussed as history just yet, like many other Speedqueens still in action and making their own history.

List of Abbreviations

AA	Automobile Association
AAA	American Automobile Association
ACO	Automobile Club de l'Ouest
BARC	Brooklands Automobile Racing Club
BRDC	British Racing Drivers' Club
BSCC	British Saloon Car Championship
BTCC	British Touring Car Championship
CART	Championship Auto Racing Teams
FIA	Federation Internationale de l'Automobile
IMCA	International Motor Contest Association
IMSA	International Motor Sport Association
JCC	Junior Car Club
LAC	Ladies' Automobile Club
LCC	Light Car Club
MC	Motor Club
MSA	Motorsport Association (UK)
MSUK	Motorsport UK
NASCAR	National Association for Stock Car Auto Racing
RAC	Royal Automobile Club
WASA	Women's Automobile and Sports Association
WGGTS	Women's Global GT Series
WRC	World Rally Championship

Chapter 1

The Showgirls

Championnat des Chauffeuses, Longchamps, June 1897

Who would we expect the earliest female racing drivers to be?

The title of this chapter gives away the fact that they were French. This is unsurprising, given that France is the spiritual home of motor racing and the location of the first official races in 1894 – just three years before the Championnat.

'*Chauffeuses*' is a title worth considering. The modern French for 'racing driver', *pilote*, did not yet exist in 1897. This is because the aircraft pilots who first took the title did not yet exist, and would not come into being for a few years yet. 'Chauffeur' is a familiar word for 'driver' to English speakers, but its literal translation is not 'driver' but 'stoker', an idea borrowed from the world of the steam locomotive.

To return to the subject, who were these Frenchwomen who lined up for the first women's motor race?

We might expect them to be a group of serious and earnest *sportives*, tired of bicycles and ballooning and looking for a new challenge; a chance to prove themselves to be every bit as brave and skilled as the men. They could easily be a group of *comtesses* keen to take advantage of all the joys of the new hobby of motoring. They could be early women's suffragists making a political point, or male drivers' bored partners amusing themselves.

We do not expect them to be a group of actresses and other female theatre employees, taking part in a public sports day for showbusiness figures.

The Course des Artistes began in 1893 as a series of cycle races for 'artists', including theatre performers, and, in its first year, painters. Initially, only men's races were staged, but women's events

1

soon followed. The first Course was organised by a French cycling magazine, *Le Véloce-Sport*.

Public appetite for watching celebrities performing unfamiliar activities is nothing new, and certainly not a product of the twenty-first century, along with *Strictly Come Dancing* or *Celebrity Masterchef*. Every year, spectators gathered in one of Paris's large parks to watch dancers, singers, actors and other theatre people take part in sports. The bicycle races seem to have been the most popular, with races for tandems and solo machines.

Naturally, as the new sport of motor racing took off, it was added to the bill for the Course des Artistes, in order to keep up with public tastes and keep audiences coming back for something new. Some of the participants must also have jumped at the chance to try this exciting, dangerous innovation – for personal satisfaction as well as the extra publicity it generated.

Eleven intrepid showgirls were scheduled to take part in the first Championnat des Chauffeuses, held at Longchamp racecourse in June. Contemporary newspaper reports stated to which theatre, if any, each 'chauffeuse' was attached.

> Jane Boié (Palais-Royal)
> Léa (or Léo) Lemoine, a costume designer
> 'Godefroy'
> 'Myrianne'
> Ellen Jouanny (Eldorado)
> Marcelle Delisle (les Variétés)
> Hélène Darbell
> 'Bossu'
> 'Helbé'(or Hellé)
> L. de Grandval
> Germaine Deverne (Cigale)

This list comes from a report in *L'Auto-Vélo*, a sporting publication of the time.

Of these 'chauffeuses', Ellen Jouanny attracted a lot of attention, including photographs. She was a vaudeville performer and musical comedy actress, who worked at the Eldorado theatre. Jane Boié enjoyed a similar career, at the Palais-Royal theatre. The 1897 Course was not her first; she had ridden in bicycle races in previous editions. The same was true of Madame de Grandval and Léa Lemoine. Léa Lemoine, whose name is sometimes given as Léo, was a *costumière,* either a wardrobe mistress or a costume designer, rather than a performer.

The other racers are more obscure. 'Bossu'('hunchback') is clearly a *nom de plume*; there is no reliable record of who she actually was. 'Hellé', also spelled as 'Helbé', likewise. Hélène Darbell and Marcelle Delisle seem to have become equated somewhere as Hélène Darlile, although the contemporary reports have them as two separate people.

The drivers were given petrol-driven tricycles to race. Later Championnats allowed cyclecars. Léa Lemoine's tricycle had a Clément chassis, and like the others, was powered by a De Dion-Bouton engine. The tricycles are sometimes described as being identical, but details of the chassis or engine of those of the other chauffeuses are so vague, it is hard to tell. Reports do not say where these machines came from; whether they were owned by the ladies concerned, loaned by other racers or by the manufacturer, or supplied by the sponsor. The Lemoine Clément-framed machine appears in later races, so we may assume that it belonged to her, or to a personal sponsor, employer or someone else close to her.

Predictably, much was made of the women's appearance. Each driver wore a different colour, to allow them to be differentiated by officials and spectators. Ellen Jouanny's ensemble, which included a full-length skirt and a corset, was described as 'daffodil yellow', and finished with a sailing cap. Unusually for the time, the other ladies were hatless. Léa Lemoine wore tartan, as did de Grandval. The pair had been winners in the ladies' tandem cycle race earlier, and had perhaps matched on purpose. Although highly impractical by today's standards, the chauffeuses' attire was quite sober and functional for its time, and did not include the trailing duster coats or extravagant veiled hats which would soon become associated with early motorists.

Lemoine and de Grandval were not the only ones to have raced bicycles as well; Jane Boié and Germaine Deverne had both taken part in the women's solo cycle event.

On the day itself, only eight ladies took part in the race. There were three heats, of one 3km lap each, and a final, which ran over two laps.

Heat 1
1. Léa Lemoine
2. Ellen Jouanny
3. Jane Boié

Heat 2
1. 'Bossu'
2. Germaine Deverne
3. Hélène Darbell

Heat 3
1. De Grandval
2. 'Hellé'

Final
1. Léa Lemoine
2. De Grandval
3. 'Bossu'

No mishaps were reported for the race, and all the drivers managed to finish. All were awarded prizes: Léa Lemoine's was a bracelet donated by the Baron de Zuylen; de Grandval's, a bicycle provided by the *Paris Echo*; and Bossu's, a silver medal from the French Automobile Club.

After the serious competitive part of the Course was over, the parades, concours and *batailles fleuris*, concours-style contests for cycles decorated with flowers, could begin.

The Championnat was covered quite extensively in the papers, and most reports were broadly supportive of the women involved. Not everyone was convinced, however, although for one outlet, it was the noise of the tricycle motors, rather than the sex of their riders, that was so objectionable.

A writer in the *Gil Blas* newspaper admitted to enjoying the spectacle, although he felt the need to comment 'not very aesthetic, however, and not very suitable for displaying the charms of a pretty woman.' The tricycles themselves were as much at fault as their riders; he described them as 'those heavy tricycles, with a scent and a noise devoid of pleasure'.

The periodical *La vie au grand air* rather mockingly described the sounds made by the machines as 'teuf-teuf'.

Another Championnat was held in 1898. It was sponsored by the *Paris Echo* newspaper.

Heat 1
1. Léa Lemoine
2. Isabelle de Bury
3. Hélène Darbell

Heat 2
1. Bossu
2. Jane de Lancy

Final
1. Léa Lemoine
2. Hélène Darbell
3. Bossu
4. Isabelle de Bury

With Blanche de Nevers as her partner, Léa Lemoine also won the tandem race. She was then third in the 'Patincycleuses' event, which appears to have been a rollerskating race.

In between, the idea of female racing drivers was slowly expanding, away from a sideshow novelty and into something more competitive. Just weeks after the Championnat des Chauffeuses, Léa Lemoine became the first woman to take part in a mixed motoring competition, when she entered the Coupe des Motocycles, driving her De Dion tricycle. This event was organised by *La France Automobile*, and was

100km long. The route ran between Saint-Germain and Ecquevilly, and back, repeated five times. The competitors were released in groups of three. Despite being called the Coupe des Motocycles, it was open to motorcycles, tricycles, quadricycles and voiturettes (lightweight, small-engined cars).

Léa surprised everyone by finishing fifth overall, completing the course in three hours, thirty-one minutes and forty-eight seconds. She was also the first De Dion finisher. The winner was Leon Bollée, in a light car of his own design.

In January 1898, another woman entered a De Dion tricycle into mixed competition. Madame Laumaillé took part in the Marseilles–Nice race. Little is known about Madame Laumaille, even her given name. She took part in the Marseilles-Nice race on her tricycle, completing the 227km course in twelve hours, fifty-two minutes and twenty-nine seconds. This was enough for twenty-seventh place overall, fourth place in her class. Mme Laumaillé had led her class after the first day and was lying second overall, but rain on the second day, and gear troubles, dropped her down the leader board. Still, she fared better than her husband, on another De Dion tricycle. He was thirty-first, almost an hour behind his wife. Newspaper reports suggest that Mme Laumaillé entered at least one other race that year, but fell off her tricycle on a bumpy road and did not finish.

The third edition of the Championnat des Chauffeuses was bigger than ever, and still sponsored by the *Paris Echo*.

Heat 1
1. Léa Lemoine/Madame Ollier (dead heat)

Heat 2
1. Henriette de Limoges
2. Emma Montigny

Heat 3
1. Isabelle de Bury
2. Amélie Girou

Final

1. Léa Lemoine
2. Henriette de Limoges
3. Emma Montigny

DNF: Mlle Laurency

This year's final was the first to have a non-finisher; Mlle Laurency overturned her vehicle on a bend, and had to retire. She was not seriously injured.

Another change this year was the introduction of small cars to the Championnat, although the start lists do not say who drove what. The exception to this is Léa Lemoine, who is said to have used her usual De Dion-engined Clément tricycle.

By 1899, the Championnat had a rival, in the form of the Fête des Automobiles, held at the Bois de Boulogne. This good-natured automotive get-together staged its own ladies' events, under the auspices of the French Automobile Club. Léa Lemoine entered, as did a group of other adventurous women, who were not just from the world of the theatre this time. These included Renée Richard, driving a Marot-Gardon, Claire Price, in a Stanley steam car, and a Mlle Braun, who drove a Peugeot. The events of the Fête included a road race of 100km between Paris and Rambouillet, a motor gymkhana, a motorised quadrille with cars driven in cotillion figures, Concours d'Elégance and a Concours de Direction. Photographs show Léa Lemoine standing on the passenger seat of a moving light car, decked in flowers, reaching up to pick up a ring from the arbour above her. This was one of the novelty races that made up the gymkhana.

The Championnat in that form was shelved for the 1900 season, but its introduction of women into the world of motorsport, particularly in France and the US, set the tone and created a context for the female driver that would last at least thirty years.

The idea of the female racing driver went pan-European in 1899.

Mme Laumaillé and Léa Lemoine had already made the first steps in mixed competition, and in 1898, Hélène Rothschild de Zuylen, using the pseudonym 'Snail', became the first woman to drive in a cross-border race. She entered the Paris–Amsterdam Trail, alongside her husband, who was using the name 'Escargot'. The model of her car is never mentioned, but she was almost certainly the first woman to compete in a major race on four wheels, as opposed to three. She did not finish the race, and seems to have dropped out quite early on. Hélène would race again in 1901, in a Paris to Amsterdam trail. This was not the more famous Gordon Bennett race between Paris and Amsterdam, but a different event, with a diverging route and entrants. Hélène was part of a team, again with her husband, and also some other lady drivers, including a Madame Gobron.

At the same time as automobile gymkhanas and flower parades provided enjoyment and accomplishment for many female motorists, a few determined women were pressing to be included at the highest levels of motorsport. At the turn of the twentieth century, this meant the city-to-city *grands épreuves,* shortly to be formalised as the Gordon Bennett races.

Camille du Gast is probably the best known of the Belle Epoque lady racers; in France, she is a celebrated national figure with a street in Paris named after her.

Born in 1868, she married Jules Crespin, heir to the Dufayel department store. They had one daughter. Camille had an adventurous spirit and had always been sporty and fun-loving, described as a tomboy when she was a child. Jules Crespin seems to have rather admired this side of his wife, and encouraged her in her pursuit of both thrills and sporting excellence. Ballooning was one of her early exploits.

She first appears as a public figure of this sport in 1895, when she became the first woman to make a parachute jump. The jump was undertaken from the gondola of a hot-air balloon, from 2,000 feet. Her parachute was emblazoned with 'Dufayel'. Throughout her career, Camille always went by her own family name, with the blessing of her husband. Some say that they wanted to swerve suspicion that Camille's exploits were purely publicity stunts for Dufayel, and some that she wanted to avoid accusations of nepotism. At this stage of her public life, she retained something in common with the tricycling showgirls who preceded her.

Jules Crespin died in December 1895, suddenly, at the age of 27. Camille became not only a widow but a very wealthy woman. After the correct mourning period was observed, she soon returned to Paris social life, and her appetite for adventure was undimmed. Among her early feats was her crossing of Morocco on horseback. She would retain an affection for both horses and North Africa throughout her lifetime.

Camille learned to drive in 1898 and was the second French woman to receive her *brevet*, or licence. It is said that she first became interested in motor racing in 1900, whilst watching the road race which ran between Paris and Lyon that year.

This may have been so, but it is tempting to imagine that Camille may have been in the crowd for the Championnat des Chauffeuses. She lived in Paris, and was part of the sideshow daredevil world into which the Course des Artistes fitted. Her parachute jumps were public spectacles of a similar nature. She was also musical, and later performed as a pianist and singer – another potential point of connection.

Among the cars that she owned were a Peugeot, which may have originally belonged to Jules, and a De Dietrich. For her first race, she acquired a 20hp Panhard et Levassor tourer, which had been prepared by the factory. Despite this fact, it was not a racing car, but a road-going model, and considerably less powerful than most of the other cars of the time. For example, her rival Henri Fournier's Mors had 60hp.

In June, she entered the Paris–Berlin Trail, organised by the Automobile Club de France (ACF). She was the only female starter in the main trail, although a sister event was held that year, in which Hélène de Zuylen took part. She ran the Panhard in the 'Heavy Car' class for vehicles over 650kg. Her riding mechanic was Hélie de Talleyrand-Périgord, the Duke of Sagan. Like Camille, he was a habitué of the Paris social scene. The pair were close friends and possibly lovers.

The trail was a road race of 1,105km, run in three stages. Camille and the Panhard ran well, finishing in thirty-third place overall, twenty-ninth in the Heavy Car class. There were relatively few dramas on the way.

Motor racing was still quite new in 1901, so the Paris–Berlin race was her only event that year. She does not seem to have entered any of the hillclimbs or speed trials that were starting to appear across Europe. Camille's activities for 1902 are not completely certain; some French sources claim that she entered the Paris–Vienna race, but she does not appear on any entry list I have found. It is possible that she attempted to start, but her entry was not accepted. This was the case with the New York–San Francisco race that was held the same year. The burgeoning motorsport authorities in the US were never keen on female drivers, as Joan Newton Cuneo would find out.

It is sometimes written that Camille spent much of 1902 on an 'extended cruise' somewhere, although the destination is not mentioned. What is certain is that she spent some of this year clearing her name in the French courts, after it was claimed that she was the model for a painting by Henri Gervex, *La Femme au Masque*. The 1885 picture, which does look somewhat like Camille, is of a woman naked apart from a Venetian mask. The accusers appear to have been family members, and the case went on for a long time, despite Gervex and the model herself, Marie Renard, giving evidence. The purported cruise was probably an attempted cover for the court case.

Camille's family appear to have been at odds with her after the death of her husband, and perhaps even before. The reasons for this are not at all clear, and there is no real suggestion that her motor racing was anything to do with it. Money is a more likely bone of contention.

Her next *grand épreuve* was the 1903 Paris–Madrid race, driving a De Dietrich prepared by the factory. The trail was halted at Bordeaux after a string of fatalities to both drivers and spectators. She was doing well in this 'Race to Death', and had been running as high as sixth in her 30hp De Dietrich. Unfortunately, a stop to rescue her teammate Phil Stead after an accident dropped her to seventy-seventh. He was trapped under his car, and Camille helped to free him.

Her drive impressed the Benz factory team enough to offer her a seat in a works car, but women were barred from competition by the ACF in 1904, so nothing became of it. The dreadful publicity that came with the Paris–Madrid deaths probably had a part in this; the public outrage over the death of a female driver would be considerable. The

ACF had one eye on protecting the future of motorsport, although one eye was clearly on keeping women 'in their place'. The reason given for the ban was 'feminine nervousness'.

After her four-wheeled career came to its abrupt end, Camille turned to racing motor boats, mostly around France. Her battling performance in the 1904 Toulon–Algiers boat race, which was abandoned due to atrocious conditions, lived up to her nickname in her native France: *l'Amazone*.

It is sometimes claimed that Camille made a return to terrestrial motorsport in 1905, taking on Dorothy Levitt in a match race, as part of the Brighton Speed Trials. In the available documentation, there is no mention of Camille taking part, although Dorothy and several other women appear on the entry lists. Any race that they had must have been organised privately. Since Camille was racing one of her boats at the time, reporting of the two female protagonists at two separate events may have become confused.

After her enforced retirement from high-speed activities, she trained horses, gave piano recitals and founded the French equivalent of the RSPCA, as well as a charity that provided healthcare to disadvantaged women and children in both France and North Africa. She retained an affinity with the region, and travelled there extensively, sometimes writing about her experiences.

This new, socially conscious Camille still enjoyed action and danger, however. In 1930, she organised a protest against a bullfight at Melun, in which a group, co-ordinated by Camille, jumped into the bullring, blew whistles and set off smoke bombs.

Earlier, in 1910, she had been involved in action and danger of a less welcome kind, involving a flare-up of hostilities with her immediate family. Her own daughter, now a young adult, tried to have her murdered for financial gain. She survived unscathed.

It is the charitable part of her life that is most remembered in France, although her sporting activities are still recognised.

She died in 1942, and her last feat of heroics was to do with helping women and children affected by German occupation in Paris. She is buried in the Crespin family tomb in Père Lachaise cemetery in Paris.

Neither Camille's forced retirement from motor racing, nor her death, was the end of the story for women in motorsports. The ACF's formal prohibition on women entering its sanctioned events was a major stumbling block, but other opportunities arose, and they took inspiration from the *chauffeuses* of 1897.

Overlapping with the career of Camille was that of 'Madame Bob Walter', a theatrical lady in the style of Léa Lemoine. She became famous as a dancer and sometimes incorporated lion taming as part of her act, performing a modern dance in front of watching lions. She also sang and acted.

She had been interested in cars from their first appearance, apparently riding in a steam car with Leon Serpollet in 1886. Her racing career began in 1902, when she was in her forties. The newspapers enthusiastically reported her exploits in the Deauville speed trials, where she drove at speeds of up to 56mph over a kilometre in her Vinot-Guignard. Among her other appearances was another trial in the Bois de Boulogne, where she would have been competitive had she not stopped to wave to the Shah of Iran who was the guest of honour. She also took on the Gaillon hillclimb and challenged motorcyclist Madame Jolivet to a match race for the prize of a tract of land near Deauville.

'Bob', born Baptistine Dupre, ran her own garage and even a fast-car hire firm for eloping couples.

The situation in France was mirrored by that in the US, albeit with a time lag. Organised speed events were slow to get started in America, partly due to the quality of roads there. The biggest automotive events were reliability trials, known as 'Tours'. The best known of these was the Glidden Cup, a reliability trial on extremely rough roads, which was at least a thousand miles long and got progressively longer each year. Joan Newton Cuneo, an adventurous New York socialite who had learned to drive a few years previously, was its premier lady competitor. She entered three times: in 1905, 1907 and 1908. On her first attempt, she managed to swerve her White steam car into a stream while avoiding another car, right in front of assembled press photographers. She fared better in the 1907 and 1908 editions, which she finished, but was usually denied official recognition due to her non-membership of an official motor club. Very few of these clubs admitted women as full members, but the Chicago Motor Club accepted her in in 1908, and as a consequence, her perfect score in the trial was recognised.

Joan also raced on circuits. These were often based at fairgrounds, or were temporary tracks on beaches. She switched her focus to this side of motorsport in 1909, racing a Knox Giant and winning two races outright: the Amateur Championship and the Klaxon Signal 10 Mile race. She broke her own women's speed record twice.

The Association of American Automobile Clubs (AAA) was never very supportive of including women. Unfortunately for Joan, the AAA was the leading sanctioning body for US motorsport at the time. Facing pressure from rival associations and some opposition to competition driving in general, it elected to bar women completely from its sanctioned events. This was partly due to simple sexism, but Elsa Nystrom has argued convincingly that the AAA was trying to protect American motor racing itself from the publicity disaster that a female racing death would cause.

Joan Newton Cuneo was not alone as a female racing driver in 1900s America: her rivals had included Alyce Byrd Potter, a beach racer; Mrs Clarence Cecil Fitler, a race winner on sand; and a Mrs Ernest Rogers. Twelve women, headed by Joan in a Lancia, took part in the 1909 New York–Philadelphia–New York Women's Run.

An avenue for competition opened itself not long afterwards. The AAA may have been the biggest motor club in the US, but it was not the only one to organise competitions. Promoters of fairground and dirt-track racing were sharp to the publicity value of women drivers, and began to put on events for them. These were usually speed trials rather than wheel-to-wheel races, and it was in these events that Joan Cuneo drove her Knox Giant in 1909 and 1910.

By 1915, the foremost of these promotional bodies was IMCA, (International Motor Competition Association). Formed in 1915 by promoter J. Alex Sloan, IMCA allowed women to enter its events, and promoted a number of match races between female drivers. The focus of IMCA was squarely on motor racing as spectacle and entertainment.

Harking back to the earliest days of the French ladies' races, women drivers added drama and a touch of glamour to these meetings, which were sometimes enlivened by a degree of stage-management.

One of the earliest female IMCA drivers may have been Helen Pyott, in 1916, who was pictured with a racing car, and certainly raced later in the 1920s, under the name 'Mrs Oliver Temme'.

Elfrieda Mais was certainly one of IMCA's first female stars. In 1916, she did a 1-mile exhibition run at Westside Speedway, Wichita, using a Mais Special built by her husband, Johnny. Elfrieda was normally engaged to do speed runs, but also enjoyed rivalries with other female racers, including Ora Holben in 1916, and later, Joan LaCosta.

In the 1920s, female drivers were increasingly used by IMCA promoters as exciting and controversial figures who would draw in audiences. Zenita Neville was one of the first to play the media in this way in 1920, engaging in a series of disputes with IMCA's 'Dean of Racing', Bill Endicott, over whether women should be allowed to race. These rows were played out in syndicated articles in local papers and were often resolved through match races, often in Miss Neville's favour.

Neville was undoubtedly a skilled driver who handled a number of cars well, but her story was not quite what it seems. She was a former actress from Chicago who neglected to mention during her serialised spats with Endicott that they were in fact married to each other. Their apparent disagreements were storylines of the kind seen in pro wrestling.

Zenita Neville disappeared from the tracks in 1922. Two years later, Jane Stanage made something of a name for herself, both through racing a Rajo Special against other women and for her off-track conduct. In October 1924, she is said to have punched a man in a cinema whom she caught trying to touch her leg. The story received several illustrated column inches, although the importunate man was not injured and no charges were brought.

Joan LaCosta's career followed a similar arc to that of Elfrieda Mais, but with far more off-track drama and intrigue. Joan posed as a French girl of rather mysterious origins, when she was almost certainly an American from Memphis, named Marion Martins. A Marion Martins definitely raced against Elfrieda Mais in Canada in 1925, shortly before Joan LaCosta burst on to the scene.

Joan was mainly booked for demonstrations and speed trials, but she did have some memorable match races, including one in 1926 against Louis Disbrow, who had pronounced himself against women in motorsports (although he had got his start in motor racing through Joan Newton Cuneo, as her riding mechanic). Joan was the victor. She is most famous for leaping from her burning car on Daytona Beach in 1926, captured on film. Unfortunately, her career quickly declined, and in 1929 she was convicted for robbery, having stolen jewellery from another woman's hotel room. After this, she disappeared from public life.

The IMCA was not the only promoter who saw the value of female drivers as a promotional tool. Omar Toft organised two race meetings in 1918, featuring 'The Speederettes', a group of female racers. The first event, in February, was held at the Ascot Park dirt track. The event was part of a 'Carnival of Femininity', and featured a fly-past by the aviatrix, Katherine Stinson, as well as other entertainment. Mrs C. H. Wolfeld won the feature race, in a Stutz.

The event proved very popular and lucrative, so a second Speederettes meeting was organised at Stockton Park in March. It was billed as a 'World Championship' for women drivers. At least two of the original Speederettes, 18-year-old Ruth Wightman and Italian-American Nina Vitaglioni, were involved. Sadly, it all went very wrong, when Nina Vitaglioni crashed a Stutz on the first corner, killing herself, her riding mechanic and three spectators. A tyre blowout and entering the bend at too high a speed were the probable causes. The Speederettes were quietly retired.

Elfrieda Mais's career also ended in tragedy. Later, in the 1920s and 1930s, she took to performing live stunts as well as speed runs and match races. In 1934, she crashed heavily into a tarmac grader after a stunt went wrong; she had driven through a wall of flaming boards at the Alabama State Fair, a stunt she had performed previously, and crashed heavily on the other side. She was seriously injured and died shortly afterwards.

Long after the Gordon Bennett Cup ban, another Championnat arose in France, which continued the all-star format of the Course des Artistes. The Championnat des Artistes was another sporting contest for showbusiness types and included motor racing. It was open to women. They often participated in the *concours d'elégance* events rather than the races, but some took to the tracks as well. The most famous of these was Hellé Nice, who would later race in Grands Prix in the 1930s and almost lose her life in a dramatic accident at the 1936 Sao Paulo Grand Prix, driving an Alfa Romeo.

Photographs from the 1924 Championnat, held at Parc des Princes, show music-hall star Mistinguett at the wheel, as well as women identified as 'Rahna', Gaby Montbreuse and Marthe Ferrare. Hellé Nice, a nightclub dancer and acrobat of some notoriety, won the ladies' race in 1929, probably driving an Omega.

At the same time as her breakthrough win in the celebrity championship, Hellé Nice was taking steps into more mainstream competition. The Journée Féminine de l'Automobile was organised by *Le Journal* newspaper for the first time in 1927. It too mainly consisted of concours-type events, but each year, there was at least one race and one speed trial. The event had a carnival atmosphere and was positioned squarely as entertainment, with sideshows, dancing and celebrity appearances.

There was a lot of crossover between entries into the Journée and the Championnat des Artistes. The first winner of the Coupe du Journal racing championship was Colette Salomon, driving a Salmson. Colette was a dancer and sometime film actress, and was photographed in full racing gear for *Vogue* that year.

Although the Journée attracted some of the 'serious' female racers of the time, including Violette Morris, a champion in multiple sports and a proven race winner, and Charlotte Versigny, who drove in the Monte Carlo Rally and Grands Prix in 1927, many of its regulars came from the showbusiness world: Mona Païva, a dancer; the aforementioned Rahna; and Lucienne Radisse, who was an actress and cellist, among others. These theatrical racers took part in the other women's events that sprang up in and around Paris in the late

1920s, including the Paris–St Raphaël women's rally, ladies' races at Montlhéry and the Paris–La Baule Rally.

Some were content to keep motor racing as a hobby, and to use it to publicise themselves, but others took it further. Hellé Nice, winner of the 150km Grand Prix Féminin in 1929 in her Omega, went on to race Bugattis and Alfa Romeos in Grands Prix, mostly in France, as well as rallying. Jannine Jennky, a former singer, is most famous for her win in the Coupe de Bourgogne in 1928, driving a Bugatti T35. One of her earliest forays into motorsport was the 1927 Journée, where she reached the final of the racing championship.

One of her rivals in the Bourgogne Grand Prix was 'Albertine' Derancourt, in an Amilcar. Albertine, real name Marie-Léonie, was not as skilled a racer as Jannine Jennky, but she appeared to enjoy taking part in the ladies' races and rallies around Paris. She rose to fame through her son, Albert, who learned to drive aged about 6, and formed part of a sideshow act with his mother.

Following formal prohibitions on female racing drivers in both Europe and the US between 1904 and 1909, women found ways of competing. In common with other sportswomen such as Annette Kellerman and later, Esther Williams and Sonja Henie, they effectively remarketed themselves as performers and found a way of competing that way. This is a motif that was commonest before the Second World War, but one we will encounter again and again.

.

Chapter 2

Society Ladies

Across the Channel in England, female racing drivers were somewhat slower to appear. The first glimmerings could be said to have happened in 1890, when Mary Ellis, then aged 10, became the first British woman or girl to ride in a motor car. Mary Ellis did go on to race both motorcycles and cars during the Edwardian period, alongside her cousin, Christabel, but this was far in the future.

In line with abiding national stereotypes, the British women pioneer motorists did not come from the world of the theatre. They were from the privileged upper classes, and the arenas in which they proved themselves were part of the aristocratic social sporting scene.

Britain's earliest female racing driver is often referred to as 'Miss Wemblyn', the winner of a race at the Ranelagh Club in 1900. A quick search of the genealogical databases shows that no-one by the name of 'Wemblyn' lived in the UK at that time. It would have been easy to dismiss Miss Wemblyn as apocryphal, especially as the details of her exploits are so vague.

'Miss Wemblyn' was in fact a Miss Weblyn, in all probability Theodora Jessie Weblyn, the daughter of a newspaper owner. The race that she won in 1900 was one of several that made up the Ranelagh Club's Automobile Gymkhana. The Ranelagh Club itself was a polo club, and the races took place on its fields. 'Gymkhana' is a term borrowed from equestrianism, and is originally from Hindi. Horseback gymkhanas consist of short, novelty races, such as weaving around markers, or dismounting and remounting halfway through, sometimes having donned an article of clothing or picked up an object. Light-hearted and social in nature, they are also useful in developing riding skills. Automotive gymkhanas were not very different. They were features of early motorsport almost everywhere; the Fête des Automobiles in Paris could be classed as a gymkhana, and there are reports of similar events even taking place in the US, which attracted a number of lady motorists, before motorsport became a more serious pursuit and was closed to women.

Four women took part in the UK's first all-female car race. This event was actually the first circuit race held at Ranelagh, and may have been the first to take place in the UK. It followed on from ladies' carriage driving competitions, which had been held from at least 1896 onwards. Earlier events took the form of trials, and were held on public roads. Theodora Weblyn drove a Daimler Parisian with 6hp. Second was Mary (Mrs Edward) Kennard in a De Dion voiturette. Miss M. Lloyd-Price was third and the final finisher in a 4hp Panhard. There was one non-finisher; Vera Butler's slightly larger, 6hp Panhard did not make it round the 1.5km course.

Theodora Weblyn, known as Theo, was in her mid-twenties in 1900. She and her sister, Katherine (Kate) were keen early motorists. Photographs from around the time of the Ranelagh race show them driving a different Daimler together, a 12hp, four-cylinder model capable of 26mph. This belonged to Montague Grahame-White.

Theo was from a comfortable wealthy background. Her father, Walter Weblyn, owned the *Illustrated Sporting and Dramatic News* newspaper. At the time of the Ranelagh race, she was living with her mother and sisters, after her parents' separation. Photographs show them travelling and enjoying sailing regattas near their home in Surrey.

It is unclear whether Theo entered any more races. An article in *The Star*, a New Zealand paper, in 1903, states that she drove the Lincoln to Nottingham stage of the 1,000 Mile Trial, although it does not give a year. The car was entered by Montague Grahame-White. In the same car, she is said to have undertaken a 140-mile solo trip, although again, the details of this are missing.

Her life suffered great upheaval when Kate died in 1901, at the young age of 29, and Theo married the following year. Her first marriage to Rupert Tattersall did not last long, and by 1911, she and her two daughters lived with their maid and nanny, being of 'private means'. She was married again in 1913, to Hubert Greenhill. In 1941, Theo, by then a widow of 65, was murdered during a robbery. The

'Man With The Monocle', a career criminal called Harold Trevor, entered her home posing as a prospective tenant for her flat, which she was letting. Theo saw him taking a cigarette case and attempted to call the police. Trevor hit her on the head with a glass bottle, then strangled her. He was caught due to his fingerprints on the broken glass, and hanged. None of the many newspaper reports covering the crime mentioned her past as a motor racing pioneer.

Vera Butler was another female motoring trailblazer in the UK, who left slightly more of a legacy. After her Ranelagh exploits, she set out on a motor tour with her father, Frank, and Charles Rolls, of Rolls-Royce fame. Unfortunately, her Renault caught fire, which ended her involvement with the tour. As a consolation, she took herself out ballooning instead. Her enthusiasm for ballooning was one of the motivations behind the setting-up of the Royal Aero Club, initially for balloonists. The same year, 1901, she drove her father across France, from Paris to Nice, over the Alps, in a Renault Type D. She had to contend with deep snowdrifts and very steep climbs, and made the journey quite comfortably, setting a women's distance record in the process. She may also have made another Alpine journey with another woman called Kitty Loftus, but details of this are extremely sketchy. 'Kitty Loftus' may well be a mis-spelling of Cissie Loftus, an actress of the time who was a keen motorist.

Vera retained her interest in motoring, and extolled the virtues of the 8hp Renault in a 1902 issue of *The Car* magazine. In 1903, she was involved in the running of 'hare and hounds' races between a balloon, and a pursuing group of motorists.

The same year, she married and became known as Mrs Vera Nicholl. She had previously been romantically linked with Charles Rolls, but this may well have been gossip. Vera's marriage appears to have ended her motoring career, although she had received a new Renault as a wedding present.

Mary Kennard, the second-place driver, was best known as a novelist, and was usually referred to as 'Mrs Edward Kennard'. She was another female early adopter of the motor car, who had been driving herself around for some time before she raced at Ranelagh. She was probably the eldest of the competitors, being 50 years old in 1900. One of her most celebrated motor-related achievements was not realised on the road or the track, but in the pages of one of her novels: *The Motor Maniac*, published in 1903, was the story of Mrs Jenks, a car enthusiast, her adventures in her car and with prospective suitors. It was a popular novel at the time, although it quickly fell out of favour.

As well as the De Dion, Mary reputedly owned a 15hp Darracq, a motor tricycle and a 40hp Napier.

The fourth driver, Miss Lloyd-Price, is a very mysterious figure. No other information about her readily comes to light, even a given name or a family connection. Her name does not appear on any further entry lists, although it is possible that she married, and competed again under another name.

Theo Weblyn and her rivals may have been the first women to race wheel-to-wheel, but they were not the first female competition drivers in the UK. Six months before the summer gymkhana, Louise Bazalgette drove her 3hp Benz 'Ideal' in the 1,000 Mile Trial. She was listed among the finishers, having driven around Britain, from London via Bath, through the Peak District and Yorkshire, into Scotland and back town to London.

In common with the other pioneer female British competition drivers, Louise Bazalgette had been an early and enthusiastic adopter of the motor car. The Bazalgette family, into which she had married, had a history of links to the Royal Family: an ancestor of Louise's husband was tailor to Prince George. This made Mrs Bazalgette a suitable subject for the newspaper society gossip pages, which detailed her motoring exploits. She was described as making the trip from London to Essex to call on friends, which would be a trivial journey nowadays, but was a much bigger deal in 1899, especially for a woman travelling alone. She also extolled the virtues of driving oneself into 'town' for a night at the theatre. Some sources have her as a participant in the first London–Brighton Run, held in 1896 to celebrate the raising of the speed limit from 4mph, and the removal of the requirement for a 'flag man' to walk in front of a moving car with a red warning flag.

Louise competed again in a few trials. She took part in the speed trials at Bexhill-on-Sea in 1903, where she came up against the much more famous Dorothy Levitt, whom we will meet in the next chapter.

Among the other crews on the 1,000 Mile Trial was Frank Butler's 6hp Panhard, built in 1896. His daughter, Vera, was acting as a passenger on the trial. Only a few months later, she was racing the Panhard herself at Ranelagh. Among the passengers in the other cars was Mary Kennard, who rode along in her husband's 8hp Napier. The car was entered by the Napier motor company, whose director, Selwyn Edge, was keen to exploit the publicity value of motorsports. Edward himself was a passenger, having employed a driver, Selwyn Edge himself, to tackle the trial. In a few years, Edge would become an influential, if contradictory figure in women's motorsports.

Fashionable lady motorists were a semi-regular feature of the 'social' pages. The purchase of a new car by a society matron, or a significant solo journey by a former debutante, were all fodder for the gossip writers. Motoring itself became rather fashionable among the upper classes, right up to the highest level; Queen Alexandra owned a Columbia electric Victoriette in 1901, in which she liked to drive herself around, accompanied by her secretary, Charlotte Knollys, in a 'compact and neat electric dogcart'. The queen and Miss Knollys normally stuck to pleasure drives in Sandringham's parks, rather than road journeys, but these were still reported approvingly. It is tempting to imagine that they challenged one another to races, out of sight of reporters and officials.

As well as gymkhanas, other social motorsporting events open to women included 'hare and hounds' chases across the countryside, sometimes following another motorist, but often tracking a hot-air balloon. A variation on this theme was the paper or confetti chase, where the drivers followed a trail of paper. The results of these outings, as well as write-ups of more general club motor tours, featured in the automotive press at the time.

Female motoring writers started to become more common, although their articles were usually on the subject of the vexing problem of what to wear in one's motor. Mary, Lady Jeune, was one such columnist, and her 1903 piece in *The Motor*, which exhorted its readers to give up on any idea of looking stylish when driving, in favour of practicality, was well received and can still be accessed now. Lady Jeune had taken an interest in women's sporting dress for some years. In 1895, she wrote a similar piece to her 1903 article, discussing cycling outfits. She was strongly against bloomers and breeches; several of her articles suggest that women should only take part in sports that allowed the wearing of skirts (or petticoats).

Similar articles appeared, many more positive towards practical motoring outfits for women. Some were written by 'Chauffeuse', who remained anonymous and is only assumed to be a genuine female, and Violet Jarrott. Violet, the Countess of Rosslyn, was the wife of Charles Jarrott, who competed in the great early continental races. She would have had access to a number of fast cars, and may have used them.

Both she and Lady Jeune were members of the Ladies' Automobile Club (LAC), and could well have taken part in its competitions. That said, the *Motoring Annual and Motorist's Yearbook* of 1904 states that Mary Jeune 'takes long tours on her car, but rarely drives herself'.

The Club was inaugurated in 1903, as women were not permitted as members of the Royal Automobile Club. Its first president was the Duchess of Sutherland, who led a victory parade of sorts around London. The duchess had been an early adopter of the motor car and was a skilled and experienced motorist, but preferred to engage a driver during the winter months.

The duchess, whose personal name was Millicent Leveson-Gower, was relentlessly active and constantly looking for new schemes to organise and causes to adopt. She was fully in favour of social reform. One of her earliest projects was a charity which provided training and work for young disabled men. Later, she earned the nickname 'Meddlesome Millie', a patronising rebuke to her social organising.

Millicent held court at the LAC's rooms at Claridge's, which were available for the use of all members – who paid a yearly subscription. The garage facilities at the hotel were also open to LAC members.

From the start, the LAC organised touring events as well as social opportunities, based in London. After 1904, it took over the running of the Ranelagh Gymkhana, which became an all-female affair. Eleven drivers contested the 1905 Gymkhana, which consisted of three races or tests of skill, and *concours d'elégance* competitions.

Results of these other events, held in 1906 and 1908 at least, are not available, although a few pictures of Edwardian ladies in cars attest to their existence. Lady Jeune, Violet Jarrott and possibly Vera Butler/Nicholl were likely to have been among the attendees, if not the competitors. Alongside them may have been Eleanor Edge, wife of Selwyn Edge, Lady Muriel Gore-Browne, one of the first women to race at Brooklands, in 1908, or Mrs George Thrupp, who won the Ladies' Race at the 1904 Ranelagh Gymkhana, by dint of being the only entrant who actually turned up. All of these women were members of the LAC, and most of them are listed as competition drivers in Dorothy Levitt's *The Woman and the Car*, from 1910.

Kate d'Esterre-Hughes was the club's long-serving secretary, who handled all membership enquiries. She was not directly involved with motorsport herself but was possibly one of the first female motorsport journalists. In 1906, she contributed an article titled 'The Race for the Herkomer Trophy' to the *Badminton Magazine of Sports and Pastimes*.

This chapter has a decidedly English bias so far, and it is true that most early motorsport activity was focused on England and Wales. Hillclimbs and speed trials were held in Scotland and Ireland, and a few women took part in them. A Mrs Mercredy contested the Glendhu hillclimb in Ireland in 1903 and 1904, driving a De Dion. She is listed as British, but it is not clear whether she was Northern Irish, or from the mainland. The same year, a 20-guinea cup was provided by a Mrs C. M. Lloyd, to be contested by the woman entrants of the Phoenix Park gymkhana. Mrs Lloyd may have been a member of the LAC, as someone of that name is listed in 1903 among its founder members.

The colonies were also the scene of some impromptu motorsport. In May 1905, the Ceylon Motor Club ran a non-stop trial from Kandy to Kegalle (in modern Sri Lanka). A Mrs Forsythe was the Class III winner, with a single stop made, caused by missing a gear.

The earliest Australian events which included women did not happen until 1915, when an all-female hillclimb was held at Station Hill, Tasmania. Dorice Rolph was the winner, in a Napier.

Motor racing in Canada was quite heavily influenced by that in the neighbouring US, plus the sort of fairground dirt tracks where women racers were restricted to plying their trade that existed there. Women were active participants right from the beginning, with Cora Smith listed as a winner of two races at the Toronto Exhibition Races in 1900. She was driving a Canada Cycle & Motor Co car, and may well have been a riding mechanic to her husband, William. This event was held on a half-mile dirt track.

Canadian motorsport was not all dirt tracks; road races became increasingly popular. The 1910 Oldsmobile Trophy ran from Winnipeg and back again, a route of some 140 miles. Jean Houghton started in her Knox, but was judged to have set off and arrived too late to be classified. Reliability runs and tours were also held.

Later, IMCA started operating in Canada, as well as a similar organisation run by Barney Oldfield. In the 1920s, some of the same women who did stunts and record runs in the US travelled to Canada, appearing at Calgary and Alberta. Elfrieda Mais was one, and later she had a rival in Marion Martins, who was probably the same person as Joan LaCosta.

As described in the previous chapter, women were explicitly barred from official motor competitions from 1909 onwards. However, this move was made precisely because there was a growing number of female competition drivers. The most famous of these was Joan Newton Cuneo, whose career straddled both the upper-class world of the long-distance tour and the more rough-and-ready fairground dirt track circuit. Having said this, Joan was staunchly upper-class, married to a wealthy businessman. She enjoyed motoring as part of the privileged lifestyle of a society matron.

The earliest recorded woman racing driver in the US looks to be the famed socialite Tessie Oelrichs, who raced an electric car at Aquidneck Trotter Park, Rhode Island, in 1900. She won one of the heats for electric cars, and was second in the final. Only a couple of weeks later, a ladies' race was held at Washington Park, a dirt oval in Chicago. Jeanette Lindstrom took on Miss M. E. Ryan, with Jeanette emerging as the victor. Little to no biographical data about these women exists, but at this early date, we can assume that they were from the monied classes, or were close to those who were.

As in England, less formal competitions were open to women. *The Automobile* in 1904 contains references to a women motorists' get-together at the St Louis World Fair, and the exploits of 'pretty little miss' Oriana Stevens, who won a 100-yard obstacle race in her Baker electric car in Cleveland. Oriana was only 12 at the time, and she defeated the vice-president of the Baker company. These reports sit alongside recaps of a more competitive ladies' race held in Chicago, between Neva Smith in a Pierce Arrow, and a Mrs Roenitz. Neva Smith was the winner.

Whereas the British publications carried stories of Queen Alexandra in her electric runaround, the US press and *The Automobile* featured the American equivalent of royal lady motorists. The same 1904 issue has a story about Alice Roosevelt, daughter of President Theodore Roosevelt, taking to motoring at the World Fair at St Louis.

Development in the UK was different. Shortly after the formation of the LAC and its boom years, the nature of motorsport in the UK began to change. High-speed trials and hillclimbs came to be its most prominent events, and the variety of available cars increased exponentially. Most of the women who participated in them were still from the monied classes, as were the men, but a subtle change was afoot. The society ladies, many of whom did retain their interest in motoring, made way for a new breed of female competition driver; one who was more concerned with speed than with socialising.

Having said that, when the Brooklands circuit finally opened its gates to women racers in 1908, it was the society ladies who made up the first grid for a ladies' race. The Ladies' Bracelet Handicap in July was Brooklands' organising club's sole concession to the existence of female drivers until 1920, although other clubs admitted women sooner.

It was a very small concession indeed, being a single-lap handicap for only seven drivers. These seven women were an interesting mix of curious aristocrats, ladies associated with Brooklands itself, and a couple of female enthusiasts. The winner was Muriel Thompson, driving an Austin 'Pobble'. The car belonged to her brother Oscar. Both of her brothers raced, and were involved in the setting-up of the BARC. Muriel would have been prohibited from helping them, since it was to be some time before the BARC allowed women as full members – and it was not keen on lady racers. The reasoning behind this was that the BARC was modelled on the Jockey Club, which did not admit ladies either.

The two favourites to win the race were Muriel, and Christabel Ellis, who drove the Arrol-Johnston 'Guarded Flame'. Christabel made a strong visual impression on the watching press, who were rather taken with her smallness and femininity. Much was made of her laid-back driving position, perched on a heavily padded seat, and the cord she used to tie down her long Edwardian skirts. She drove with a bouquet of sweet peas tied to the front grille of her car.

Despite her dainty and unlikely appearance, Christabel was a driver of some experience, who had previously driven a GWK friction-drive cyclecar in hillclimbs. She was the cousin of Mary Ellis, the first British female to ride in a car in 1890. The two later competed together in hillclimbs, aboard a sidecar combination.

Muriel Thompson made less of a splash, being a tall, no-nonsense sort of woman, and something of a familiar face, thanks to her family connections with the track and the BARC. A New Zealand paper compared her driving stance to that of an 'American jockey'. Despite the somewhat unflattering write-ups she received, Muriel was a fine driver, and a member of the LAC. She had won one of the races at the Ranelagh Gymkhana that year.

She would later go on to race 'Pobble' at Brooklands again, at non-BARC events. She was part of the winning Berkshire Motor Club team at the 1909 Inter-Club Team Trophy, and in 1911, and won the Declaration Handicap at the RAC Associated Motor Clubs meeting.

Both Christabel and Muriel would make names for themselves during the First World War. Muriel joined the First Aid Nursing Yeomanry (FANY) and saw service in France and Belgium. She worked in field hospitals and drove ambulances, working under fire. Her own Cadillac became a makeshift, high-speed ambulance. She was decorated by the Belgian military for her bravery, and remained in the Forces for some time after the end of the war.

Christabel became a commandant in the transport corps of the Women's Legion. She was in command of teams of female despatch riders, who played an important communication role. She too was decorated for her service, and remained in the military after the war.

The race itself started with Christabel leading, but her car's engine cut out near the start, and she was passed by Muriel and the second-place driver, Ethel Locke-King in her Itala 'Bambo'. Ethel was the wife of Hugh Locke-King, who owned Brooklands. Although he was its titular head, it was her money that allowed it to be built at all, and her project management skills that allowed the track to be finished as Hugh had become too ill to oversee things properly by 1906. Even with her considerable power and patronage, she was unable to sway the BARC in allowing women to race, although she was still at the helm when the rule was finally relaxed. She was actually the first woman to drive on the Brooklands circuit at all, having led the procession of cars at the track inauguration in 1907, driving her Itala. Sadly, she does not seem to have found any other opportunities to race.

Like Muriel and Christabel, Ethel distinguished herself during the War, managing twelve VAD hospitals and running one of them at Brooklands house.

Of the other entrants, one, Muriel Gore-Browne, was Ethel's sister-in-law, the wife of her brother Harold. She is listed as driving a Humber, but, for unknown reasons, did not make the start,. Muriel had no further involvement with motorsport, although during her life she survived two shipwrecks, one of those being the *Lusitania*.

Another driver listed as a non-starter was Ada Billing, driving a Mass (sometimes a Mors). She was another of the Bracelet racers for whom the race was a one-off, but she was involved with Brooklands for many years. Alongside her husband, Eardley, she ran the Blue Bird restaurant at the circuit, which was next to the airfield and existed for as long as Brooklands itself. Eardley was an aircraft engineer who built his own biplane, which was used as a training craft.

Nelly Ridge-Jones drove a Sunbeam to fifth place. The Bracelet Handicap seems to have been her only race. One of eight children, she was the daughter of a paediatric surgeon, Thomas Ridge-Jones, who was a Welshman based in London. The fact that her father, Thomas Jones, double-barrelled his surname with her mother's suggests that he 'married up', but this is conjecture. None of the other members of her family look to have been involved in motorsport, and it is rather a mystery as to what Nelly's connection was. She holds the distinction of being the first Welsh woman to race a car in the United Kingdom. She later served in the Red Cross in the First World War.

Fourth place, behind the unfortunate Christabel Ellis, was taken by a Mrs J. Roland Hewitt, in a De Dion. Mrs Hewitt is another obscure figure who does not appear in other Brooklands entry lists. She was Margaret Campbell Hewitt, born Margaret Campbell Muir in Scotland in 1883. At the time of the Bracelet race, she had a 3-year-old daughter, Irene. James Roland Hewitt, her husband, worked for Daimler and later became a director.

A postscript to the story of the first women's event at Brooklands is the match race that took place between Muriel Thompson and Christabel Ellis. It was part of the August Trophy meeting, and featured just the two of them, in the same cars as before. Despite a nine-second handicap, Christabel was again unable to overhaul Muriel, who was crowned the winner. This meeting was overshadowed by a fatal accident in the next race, the O'Gorman Trophy, in which neither woman was involved.

As the next chapter will show, the majority of the contestants for the Bracelet (the prize really was a bracelet), were not the leading female motorists of their day. Muriel Thompson and Christabel Ellis were obviously skilled drivers, but by 1908, there were many other worthy candidates for inclusion in the race: drivers with international experience and wins under their belts. Missing also were the

Continental drivers discussed in the last chapter; the likes of Camille du Gast would have jumped at the chance to race at Brooklands, away from the ACF and its regulations. The entry list for the Bracelet Handicap is clear evidence of the 'right crowd and no crowding' ethos that governed Brooklands, particularly in the early days. It could also be an illustration of the Brooklands authorities not taking women drivers seriously, or encouraging them from entering their events. Experience, speed and talent did not count for as much as connections.

This would remain the case until 1920, when the second official ladies' race at Brooklands was held, and for women in fast cars the floodgates opened.

Automotive gymkhanas faded in significance after about 1910, and a new breed of woman racer began to emerge, but the society lady retained a place in the British motorsport scene. The Women's Automobile and Sports Association (WASA), founded in 1929, was founded by two Ladies, Ermine Elibank and Iris Capell, as well as Gabrielle Borthwick. Irene Mountbatten, Marchioness of Carisbrooke, was its first president. The Association was intended to promote and support female motorists, and women in motorsport. Iris Capell and Irene Mountbatten were great examples of early twentieth-century 'do-gooding' society women – serial committee members and busy organisers. Iris would be instrumental in setting up the Women's Royal Voluntary Service during the Second World War, and had been a military nurse during the First World War. Irene Mountbatten had also been a nurse during the war.

WASA organised trials, often in the Cotswolds, and later fielded teams for the relay races at Brooklands. In 1934, the WASA team included Irene Schwedler, Margaret Allan and Doreen Evans, all driving MG Magnettes. They were third in the Light Car Club's Annual Relay. Margaret and Doreen at least were upper middle class rather than aristocratic; although WASA was led by Marchionesses and Ladies, it was open to women from a slightly wider range of backgrounds.

The French women's motor racing scene enjoyed some patronage and organisational assistance from the privileged classes, too. The

Paris–St Raphaël Rally, a women-only event that ran until the 1970s, was created by the Count de Chabot in 1929. The official starter for the first Rallye was Anne, the Duchess of Uzès, one of the first women in France to receive a driver's licence in 1899, and the president of a women's motor club.

Another female aristocrat who was involved with British motor racing in the 1920s and 1930s was Dorothy Paget, a diplomat's daughter. She had a go at competition driving herself, entering a hillclimb at Shelsley Walsh in a Mercedes in 1930, and doing some laps at Brooklands, but she is most famous as the patron of the works Bentley team, funding the 1929 victorious Le Mans stable. She was only 24 at the time. Sir Tim Birkin, himself a Bentley racer, gave her some racing tuition at Brooklands and was very impressed with her driving. However, she soon lost interest in motor racing and concentrated on horse racing instead. Dorothy was highly eccentric and apparently hated men, which may have explained her reluctance to continue in motorsport. She owned several racehorses and was a compulsive gambler, who placed most of her bets at night and slept all day. Her reputed 100-a-day nicotine habit was further evidence of her tendency towards addiction. She was known for her appalling temper and lack of manners, although she was impartial in her rudeness and attacked everyone.

The idea of the society lady as racing driver even survived one of the silliest stunts to be pulled at Brooklands, the 1931 Society Ladies' Private Handicap. The unlikely instigator of this prank was Barbara Cartland, who would later find fame as a pink-clad romantic novelist, but who was then a racy author and glider enthusiast. Ten MGs were borrowed for the 'handicap', which was little more than a filmed session of the ten drivers and their riding mechanics being silly on the famous banking. Princess Imeretinsky was named the winner, as she was the highest-ranked socially. Her riding mechanic was Lady de Clifford. The other drivers were Cartland herself, Paddie Naismith (an actress), the Hon Joan Chetwynd, Kathleen Meyrick, Hilda Banks, Clare Dean, Elizabeth Makins and a Mrs Wardrop. Some of the ladies had male riding mechanics, who were not named, although visible on the film.

The footage shot included scenes of cars weaving in and out alarmingly, with Princess Imeretinsky's car skidding over the finish line. The princess, born Avril Mullens, is shown on film claiming that she gained 'infinite satisfaction' from her win. For added realism, 'pit stops' were recorded.

Some sources claim that Paddie Naismith crossed the line first. Paddie, as well as being an actress, had worked as a chauffeur and was a member of WASA. She would later race at Brooklands on her own account. Joan Chetwynd was also a bona fide racer. It was she who lifted the lid on the staged nature of the Private Handicap, after a small outcry over the poor driving standards shown in the film. She claimed that she had agreed to take part in a film about women in sport but had been as shocked as the next man by the risky and ridiculous moves in which she had been encouraged to participate. Her verdict, in a letter to *The Motor*, was this:

'I have never seen a more shattering exhibition of driving in my life and count myself lucky to have come out of it unscathed.'

There may have been an element of face-saving in Joan's tirade. She was in the midst of making a name for herself as a competent race and rally driver and would not have wanted her reputation to be damaged by association with such a stunt.

Joan went on to race at Le Mans in 1931, driving an MG with H. H. Sisted. They did not finish.

Barbara Cartland went on to endow the Brooklands clubhouse with its 'Ladies' Reading Room', but played no further active part in motorsport, either real or staged.

Between the wars, there were pockets of upper-class female motorsport activity on the Continent as well.

One of the most fashionable venues for this was the Klausen hillclimb in the Swiss Alps, a 21.5km-long course up the Klausen pass. It was first run in 1922 and by 1924 was attracting drivers of the calibre of Rudolf Caracciola, who won the 1500cc class in his Mercedes.

Seventh in the same class was Princess Hohenlohe, driving a Bugatti. Her time was around twelve minutes slower than Caracciola's although she was not the last finisher.

She raced the Bugatti again on the pass in 1925, finishing fourth in class this time. She was one of four women who took part that year, the others being Kate (or Kathe) Rantzau, Maria Lepori and a Frau Howald.

Kathe Rantzau was the daughter of an aristocratic Austrian diplomat and achieved considerable success as an opera singer from 1917 onwards. She competed occasionally in other hillclimbs, including the Semmering climb in 1927, until her death in 1936, aged 51.

In 1923, she was tenth overall in a *Damenrennen* held in Vienna, Austria, entered by forty-nine women. Her car was an Austro-Daimler. The winner was Olga Fruhwald in a six-cylinder Graf & Stift. A film survives of the rally and among these forty-nine drivers were titled ladies, and one doctor.

The foremost of the genuine female racing nobility were the two Countess Einsiedels, Margot and Beatrix (Bea). Bea raced as 'Bea Gilka-Botzöw' following her marriage to Carl-Albrecht Gilka-Botzöw. She was born a Countess of the Einsiedel family. She mostly competed in hillclimbs, driving first an Austro-Daimler, then a Bugatti.

Margot, born Margot von Gans in France in 1899 and married into the Einsiedel family in 1921. Her husband was Adolkar Haubold Siegfried Freiherr von Einsiedel.

After having her two children, she took up motor racing in 1927, driving a Steyr. She performed well in both hillclimbs and circuit races, and participated in the Klausen climb, holding its ladies' record between 1927 and 1932.

In 1928, she had her biggest result; a twelfth place in the Targa Florio, driving a Bugatti T37. She was sixth in the Voiturette class. She raced in Germany, Switzerland and Italy until about 1932.

Margot's small victory was overshadowed by the stellar performance of Elisabeth Junek in a similar car. Elisabeth, one of the most famous and respected of the pre-war female drivers, led a lap of the Sicilian classic that year, fending off the likes of Tazio Nuvolari and Luigi Fagioli. Car trouble dropped her to fifth by the end, but a legend had already been created.

Elisabeth was from very different stock to Margot and the titled ladies. She had worked in a bank when she left school and had met Cenek Junek, a wealthy banker. The two went on to race together all around Europe, until July of 1928 when Cenek was killed in an accident at the Nürburgring.

Despite her different upbringing, Elisabeth had had no trouble fitting in at Klausen. In 1926, she was second in the 2000cc class, driving a Bugatti. She was one of four women who raced that year, including the German Franziska Lüning in her Fiat.

Ernestine 'Ernes' Merck, who made her Klausen debut in 1927, was the daughter of a minor nobleman and officer in the German army, but she also married into the motoring world. Her husband Wilhelm Merck raced.

Her first race was said to have been in 1922. By the time of her Klausen outing in 1927, she was driving powerful Mercedes cars with some skill. That year, she was third in class in a 6765 Mercedes and second in class in a bigger 8108cc model.

She was most famous as the model behind the 'Frau im Rot', who appeared in adverts for Mercedes. The Frau was a stylised Ernes, dressed in a red race suit and matching leather helmet.

Fame, however, did not make Ernes happy. She committed suicide in 1928, after the birth of her son.

A perusal of the entry lists of rallies between the wars will often bring up a minor royal: British-born Princess Shelagh of Liechtenstein competed alongside her husband Prince Ferdinand in the 1931 Alpine Rally in a pair of Austro-Daimlers; Princess Ferdinanda 'Dorina' Colonna of Padua contested the 1930 Mille Miglia in an Alfa Romeo 6C.

Of course, there is nothing in being high-born or well-married that gives one an innate desire to go fast. The society ladies of this chapter had the money to acquire fast cars and the copious leisure time needed to master driving and to travel to events. They overcame potential familial objections and, in many cases, were encouraged in their exploits by their husbands, who often raced themselves.

Familial objections may have kept the major royal ladies of Europe out of motor racing, for fear of accidents and controversy. Queen Alexandra had to content herself with spectating and leisure drives in the park, while the unlikely to ever reign Shelagh of Liechtenstein was free to amuse herself in competition. In more recent times, this has been true of the Monegasque princely family. Its strict rules of male progeniture possibly gave Princess Caroline more freedom to enter the 1985 Paris–Dakar Rally, as navigator to her husband Stefano Casiraghi. Her nieces, Pauline Ducruet and Jazmin Grimaldi, enjoyed the same privilege during the all-female Rallye Aicha des Gazelles in 2018.

Chapter 3

Career Women

Brighton Speed Trials, Madeira Drive, 19–22 July 1905

The first Brighton Speed Trials were held in 1905. Seaside speed trials were not a Brighton innovation; Blackpool and Southport had held their own for a couple of seasons previously, and Bexhill on Sea was another that had hosted trials in recent years.

The full course was about a mile long, but some of the races were run over a flying kilometre towards the end of the circuit. Cars raced against each other in twos and threes, with each class running heats and a final to decide the overall winner.

Taking a rather progressive stance, the first Brighton Speed Trials featured a dedicated race for lady drivers. This was for touring cars, which were production models. The race was supported by the LAC, and the drivers came from its membership.

Heat 1
1. Mrs Herbert Lloyd (Daimler 30hp)
2. Christabel Browne (Cupelle 10hp)

Heat 2
1. Maud Manville (Daimler 35hp)
2. Mrs Nevill Copland (Talbot 12–14hp)

Walkover
Mrs Guy Hardy (Panhard 10hp)
Mrs Benett-Stanford (Dixi 13–17hp)

Final
1. Mrs Herbert Lloyd
2. Maud Manville

Both women are said to have driven 'exceedingly well'. Mrs Lloyd made good use of her eighteen-second handicap, and defeated Maud Manville by ten seconds. Her prize was a fan, presented by the local railway company.

Women drivers were not restricted to the ladies' race, by any means. Only five years had elapsed since the first ladies' race at Ranelagh, but already, a new type of motoring woman was making her appearance. She may have begun life in the same way as the earlier 'society' lady drivers, who competed as recreation, but the driver at Brighton in 1905 was likely to be one of the first wave of female motoring professionals. With the motor car still being a relatively new invention, women took their chances at finding an opening within this new world.

Mrs Lloyd and Maud Manville both appeared in the other classes appropriate to their machines. Other women taking part in the Touring classes included Eleanor Madeley in a 6.5hp Cadillac, Victoria Godwin in her Ariel, and Muriel Hind in a Gnome.

The winner of the Ladies' Handicap, Mrs. Lloyd, was possibly called Elizabeth, and married to a senior army officer. She was fond of seaside events, and raced at Blackpool in 1905. In 1906, she proved an adept hillclimber, winning her class at the Longleat climb, and finishing fifth overall, from ten, in the Henry Edmunds Hillclimb in Sussex. It is mentioned in more than one article that she invented 'various novelties' to do with motoring, although what these were, we do not know.

Sadly, next to no information survives about Miss Browne, Mrs Copland, Mrs Hardy and Mrs Benett-Sandford. The last of these was part of a well-known Brighton family. Mrs Copland was a member of the LAC; in 1907, she is listed as a participant in its gymkhana at Ranelagh, although her car and the events in which she took part are not included.

Maud Manville was married to Edward Manville, the head of Daimler in Britain, and always used their cars. At Brighton, she not only performed well in the ladies' touring car contest, but won a race for 35hp Daimlers, against two male drivers.

Maud was a member of the Daimler team for the 1905 Herkomer Trial in Germany, a touring event consisting of speed trials, hillclimbs and regularity sections, designed to test reliability. She and her teammates performed extremely well on the hillclimbs but were let down by tyre problems in the longer sections. Maud herself drove particularly well on the high-speed sections, and won the Forsteinreider Park sprint outright, ahead of her husband. The preceding hillclimb, which the Daimler drivers had only practised with difficulty, gave her a fifth place. She was not among the overall winners, having suffered too many punctures on the reliability section, but was presented with a laurel wreath at the end of the event, in recognition of her being the first lady finisher the Trial had seen.

Maud entered the Herkomer Trial once more in 1906, and was eleventh in the final classification. She was part of a fourteen-car Daimler team, and was competing without her husband this time. As it had performed so well before, she used the same car as in 1905, and was the only finisher to do so. The Trial that year was considered much tougher than previous events, and Prinz Heinrich of Prussia, a fellow competitor and the originator of the Prinz Heinrich Trial, ordered a silver vase to be presented to her.

She spoke about her experiences in Germany in an address to the LAC, in March 1906. In it, she describes how she and Edward entered the trial for fun, having already decided on Germany and Austria for their summer holiday in 1905. She told of the terrible weather they encountered, the difficulty of practising for the hillclimb among so many other drivers doing the same, and of the royal reception she received, which included a toast being raised to her by Ludwig of Bavaria.

Maud was one of the earliest British women drivers to compete internationally, and for a works team to boot. She gave her talks in the hope of convincing more women to take up motorsport, not only for their own gratification but also in order to 'improve' the sport. In 1907, she was one of the judges at a show of new motoring clothing and accessories for women, alongside other members of the LAC. Unfortunately, her good work was cut short when she died in 1909, aged 37.

Brighton was Muriel Hind's first major appearance at the wheel of a racing car. She was 24, and had been riding a motorcycle for three years. Later in 1905, she would become the first woman to race motorcycles in the UK, when she entered the Albert Brown Trophy in October. She did not win, but received a certificate for her efforts.

As well as motorcycles, she used a three-wheeled Singer 'Tricar' in a number of hillclimbs and trials in 1906. In this vehicle, she won a gold medal in the London–Edinburgh 24-Hour run, and a bronze in the Land's End–John O'Groats Trial. She carried on in trials until about 1912. In 1910, she rode for the Rex marque in the Scottish Six Day Trial, with Beatrice Langston and Mabel Hardee.

Alongside her racing activities, Muriel was one of the first women to work in the motorcycle industry. She carried out road tests on new models aimed at women, and even had a hand in the design of a 1907 Rex motorcycle, the Blue Devil. After her competition career ended, she worked as a motorcycle journalist and promoted the motorcycle as an ideal vehicle for women.

Eleanor Madeley was unplaced in the Scratch Race for cars costing less than £200, carrying two passengers. She was driving her own car, but she does not seem to have taken part in any more races or trials. The Cadillac appears in a hillclimb at Frome later in 1905, but its driver is listed as J. Madeley, who was probably her father. Genealogical research shows that she was 27 in 1905, and travelled extensively, having been born in American Samoa, and spent time in New York as a teenager. Her father, James, was a civil engineer who was instrumental in building railways in Brazil. Her brother, another James, was also a civil engineer, so it is unsurprising that Eleanor became familiar with mechanical matters. She does not appear to have been a member of the LAC.

Victoria Godwin drove an Ariel Simplex, and was second in the race for cars costing £700 to £800. Like Muriel Hind, she was working publicly in the motor industry. Victoria was employed by the Ariel motor company, best known now as a manufacturer of motorcycles. She was apparently trained in building cars as well as driving them. According to a 1905 article in *The Motor Way* magazine, she only began racing in 1905. Although speaking from her 'pretty office' at the Ariel factory, she spoke of her training in car maintenance, and her willingness to teach this to other women. She also worked as a driving instructor, taking on both male and female pupils. She extols the virtue of motoring as a hobby for women: 'it tones up the system and produces self-reliance.'

Victoria continued to be a motoring personality until at least 1907. She undertook many record runs in Ariel cars, including a record-breaking trip from Land's End to John O'Groats, which took her five days, and an overland journey from Paris to St Petersburg. A 1907 article in *The Day*, a US newspaper, gives her record time for driving 2 miles as one minute and forty-three seconds, and stresses that she only ever uses stock touring cars, not racing models. A year earlier, a rather beautiful posed photograph of her, in motoring hat and veil, graced the front cover of *Bystander* magazine. Her public face may have been glamorous and gracious, but Victoria was one of a growing number of female motor professionals who had seized on the new technology and were challenging the assumption that women were naturally unsuited to handling technology.

Female drivers were not restricted to the Touring class, either. The big events at the Trials were the contests in the Racing Car class, for drivers in powerful, stripped-down specials. Claudia Lasell entered a 90hp Benz, and Dorothy Levitt an 80hp Napier.

Racing Car trials happened on all four days of the event. The first two days' contests were run over a mile from a standing start, and the subsequent two, a kilometre, from a flying start. On the third day, drivers competed for the *Daily Mail* 100-Guinea Challenge Cup. This was for racing cars weighing less than 1,000kg, from a flying start. The *Autocar* Challenge Cup was on offer for the fourth day of racing. This was an all-comers' racing car trial.

It is unclear which days Claudia Lasell raced. She was probably the only American woman racing at Brighton, and worked as an actress. She originally came from Boston. Her motorsport career appears to have been very short, possibly only a single season. She also raced in the Blackpool speed trials, but her results have been lost. Later, in 1913, she created a small scandal by hosting boxing matches in the ballroom at her parties. Therefore, she was not only one of the earliest American female racing drivers but the earliest female boxing promoter as well!

Claudia was a lady racer of the oldest type, a theatrical adventuress who enjoyed speed and spectacle. There was room for both kinds in the growing British motorsport scene.

Dorothy Levitt entered both the *Daily Mail* and *Autocar* Cups, and was fourth in both. She then caused a medium-sized stir by winning the Racing Car Sweepstake Handicap, defeating first Moore-Brabazon, then Ralph Gore. This was another all-comers event, which could be entered on the day by paying a £5 stake.

Of all the lady racers of the Edwardian period, Dorothy Levitt is the most remembered and celebrated. It is impossible to research this period in British motorsport history without running into her. She was a racer of the most modern variety, representing the Napier marque in trials in the UK and beyond.

Dorothy's introduction to motorsport came, in all probability, from Selwyn Edge, an Australian–English director of the Napier motor company, who also distributed De Dion and Minerva cars in the UK. She worked for Napier as a typist and secretary from about 1902, and caught the eye of Edge, who seems to have been instrumental in teaching her to drive. At different times, Dorothy herself claimed that she had learned to drive whilst still at home 'in the West Country', before catching the eye of a motor company executive at a country fair, or that Edge had taken her under his wing after she ran away from an unwanted arranged marriage. He then arranged for a six-month apprenticeship in motor engineering in Paris for her. This then became a career progression from Parisian factory cleaner, to machinist, then chauffeur.

Other sources, chiefly S. C. H. Davis's *Atalanta*, tell of a Napier apprentice called Leslie Callingham being grudgingly roped into teaching her to drive by Edge. Callingham was unimpressed and spoke mockingly of her perfume and 'tangles of bracelets'. Leslie Callingham later raced at Brooklands, and would have known Davis.

This contradictory picture of her start in motorsport is typical of what we read about her. It is possible that there are elements of truth in all of these accounts, but either Dorothy or the writer has edited her story in order to appeal to the likely audience. This media manipulation is sometimes considered a modern invention, but it has a much longer history than we might think.

Dorothy has become something of a legend, and it is hard to discern the facts from the exaggerations and possibly, lies, in her history.

Genealogical research brings up questions from the start. Her birth name was in fact Elizabeth Levi, and she was born in 1882, in London. Her family anglicised their Jewish name to Levitt or Levit, which was not an uncommon thing to do in the early twentieth century. After 1900, Dorothy appears on official documents as Dorothy Elizabeth. Next to nothing is known about her childhood or schooling. She lived in London, and must have had some sort of education, for she later made a living through writing.

The main evidence we have for her achievements and activities is her book, *The Woman and the Car*, published in 1909. This begins with a rather fanciful character sketch by a C. Byng Hall, which waxes lyrical about her virtues and her West Country, rural upbringing. Extracts from Dorothy's diary are then repeated, detailing her timeline in motorsport. The book itself is a 'chatty little handbook' for women wishing to own and run their own car, including chapters on road etiquette, maintenance, and of course, what to wear when driving. Her tone throughout is light and confident, with the distinct overtone of a cheerful, well-meaning bully.

Female motoring writers were beginning to proliferate at this time. Just a year before *The Woman and the Car*, an American writer and artist, Hilda Ward, published *The Girl and the Motor*, which was full of the same sort of chummy advice for novice female motorists. Unlike Dorothy, Hilda never did any competition driving. Vera Butler's writing was not specifically aimed at women, but is relevant nevertheless. Lady columnists in motoring magazines in the US and Australia appeared at about the same time. Eliza Davis Aria's *Woman and the Motor Car* treated the subject light-heartedly in 1906 but still remained a book written from experience.

According to her diary, Dorothy began competing in 1903, in a Gladiator. This was another make promoted by Napier in the UK. Her first success in the car was a class win in the Southport Speed Trials, held on the beach near Liverpool.

The following year, 1904, was a rather quiet one for Dorothy. She did not appear in any competitions until September, when she took part in the Hereford 1,000-Mile Trial. The reason for her absence is not entirely clear, although some contemporary newspaper articles say that she was ill for part of the year and went to Madeira to recuperate.

At Hereford, she became the first female 'works' driver, as she was representing De Dion in a factory-prepared car. This was not a racing model, but an 8hp touring car. Running the car solo, apart from an official observer, she almost won a gold medal but was let down by mechanical problems on the last day of the event. The following month, she was back in a Napier for the Southport Speed Trials.

Her heroics at Brighton in 1905 have already been recounted. This year, she drove both Napier and De Dion machinery, in trials and sprints. She won a manufacturer's award for De Dion in the Scottish Trial. At the Blackpool Speed Trials, she drove her most powerful car yet: a Napier with 100hp. Her results are not forthcoming.

Many sources talk of a match race between Dorothy and Camille du Gast at Brighton. However, the official write-ups do not mention such a thing. Camille was still very famous, and it was hardly likely to go unnoticed. It is also impossible to consider Dorothy or Selwyn Edge not using this as publicity. There is a small possibility that a private match race of some sort did happen, but it is more likely to have started as confusion between the results of car and boat races happening at the time. Camille was still very active in her speedboat in 1905. Dorothy also raced boats on occasion, and set one ladies' water speed record.

Later in the year, following her success at Brighton, Dorothy was invited by the French Mors company to drive their car in the Tourist Trophy, a road race on the Isle of Man. She was eager to take her starting place but could not. The official reason given was that she had withdrawn due to ill health, but it was generally known that Selwyn Edge had vetoed her drive for a rival firm. What effect this had on the relationship between Edge and Dorothy is not known, but she did not accept any more guest drives during her career. The Mors drive is not mentioned in *The Woman and the Car*.

Disappointments aside, 1906 was a busy year. Driving a 50hp Napier, she set speed records at Blackpool and Shelsley Walsh. In the Shelsley climb, she was sixth overall, twelve seconds off the winning time, and more than three minutes faster than June Larkins the previous year. Her Ladies' record stood until 1913. At this meeting, Dorothy also undertook a challenge against Freddie Coleman, in a petrol vs steam drive-off. Coleman's White steam car proved faster on the day, but the publicity was all very welcome.

At Aston Clinton, she was third in a hillclimb, and set a Women's Land Speed Record of 90mph, driving the Napier. This brought on the title 'The Fastest Girl in the World', which accompanied Dorothy's newspaper appearances.

June Larkins (sometimes referred to as Jane; usually as 'Miss Larkins') could perhaps be considered Dorothy's opposite number at the Wolseley company. As well as competing in yacht trials, she campaigned a four-wheeled Wolseley in 1905. It was a 6hp petrol model, and in it, she set the first Ladies' Fastest Time of the Day at Shelsley Walsh hillclimb. The car belonged to an A. A. Remington. That year, she attended at least two motor gymkhanas, and was second in a 'Coach House Race' at a gymkhana in July, in aid of Moseley Childrens' Hospital. That summer, she won a 'Towing Race' at a gymkhana at the Officers' Grounds, with Lieutenant C. Good as her partner. She and a Commander Mitchell were second in a 'Ribbon Race', where the two cars were joined by a ribbon as they drove around a slalom course. If the ribbon broke, they were eliminated.

June Larkins bears a similarity to Dorothy Levitt in that some mystery surrounds her. She was sometimes referred to as the niece of Mansfield Smith-Cumming, a naval officer and the first head of the British Secret Service. He was an early director of Wolseley and raced its cars on occasion. Digging around in his family tree turns up nobody called June. His sister-in-law, Georgiana Valiant, was married to a John Burton Larkins. They had a daughter, also called Georgiana, in 1878. Georgiana was in all likelihood June. She married Conway Rowley-Hill in 1910 in South Africa, where other members of her family settled.

It is somewhat surprising that June did not appear in the Brighton Speed Trials, although her time at Shelsley Walsh was not really competitive. A record was set in 2016 for running on foot up the Shelsley climb, which is about the same as June's 1905 time by car.

June's activities were not limited to competitions. She was employed by Wolseley to help its female customers learn to drive, and to run their own cars. In this way, she was following a tradition started by Vera Butler in 1903, taken up by Muriel Hind, and possibly continued or emulated by Dorothy. When the war began in 1914, there were several ladies' driving schools in London alone, some of which converted to training ambulance drivers.

In 1907, Dorothy's career went international. As part of the winning Napier team, she won her class at the Gaillon hillclimb in France. Slightly further afield, she took part in her first Herkomer Trial in Germany, and was either thirteenth or fourteenth, and the first female finisher. Her car was a Napier.

At home, the biggest news on the automobile front was the opening of the Brooklands circuit in Weybridge. Naturally, Edge wanted to get Napier and Dorothy in on the act, but the Brooklands authorities were rather hostile to women drivers, and did not accept Dorothy's entry. Photographs, however, exist of her, seated on a stripped-down Napier racer, with the Brooklands banking distinct in the background. It is possible that the pictures were merely posed, but it is another possibility that she was somehow involved with a 24-hour speed record attempt undertaken by Edge himself. During the run, he was accompanied by four other Napier drivers in two cars, but none of them was Dorothy. The picture is curious in that it shows Dorothy in a long skirt and woollen jumper, with no hat, rather than one of her usual motoring outfits of duster coat and veiled hat. If she was acting as one of Edge's support drivers, she may, for once, have not wanted to attract attention to herself, and dressed accordingly, although this was rather out of character.

In the media of the time, Dorothy's duties for Napier included working as a society ladies' driving instructor. In her 1906 *Deseret Evening News* interview, she claims to have taught 'a host of people from the queen and royal princesses down through duchesses and countesses to plain, everyday American visitors'.

This piece of information has become accepted as fact, and at least part of it is untrue. The queen at the time was Queen Alexandra, who was interested in motoring herself. However, as described in the previous chapter, Alexandra had learned to drive by 1901 at the latest, before Dorothy ever claimed to have got behind the wheel.

Of course, this could have been a mistake, or an exaggeration by the writer, but given the date, could it perhaps be an attempt to deflect attention from June Larkins and her work? The Dorothy publicity engine liked to portray her as a trailblazer, the first woman to achieve any number of motoring milestones. June had beaten her fair and square to become the first woman to drive up the Shelsley Walsh climb, and another works-endorsed woman driving expert would dilute the impact of Dorothy for Napier.

We do not know why Edge picked Dorothy. It has been hinted that the two were lovers; this is not unlikely. However, no proof exists either for or against, so it is a futile discussion.

Edge could well have chosen his wife, Eleanor, as Napier's poster girl. Eleanor Edge was certainly an expert motorist, and a founder member of the LAC. She had been a competitive cyclist, alongside her husband, in the 1890s. She may have been intending to race at the Brighton Speed Trials, for there are references in the write-up to a young man who was acting as Mrs Edge's mechanic.

Again, genealogical records give some sort of answer. In the 1901 census, Selwyn and Eleanor Edge were listed as living in separate households. It appears that they were no longer a couple, although they remained married until Eleanor's death in 1918. Interestingly, Dorothy mentions Eleanor in *The Woman and the Car*, in her chapter on the leading lady motorists of her day. Muriel Hind gets a mention too, as a woman who 'prefers the motor bicycle'. Victoria Godwin, another possible direct rival, is disregarded. Maud Manville was no longer competing in 1909, and had possibly already died, so she was safe to include also.

Dorothy Levitt, in *The Woman and the Car*, praises the LAC, and gives directions on how to obtain membership, as well as the benefits on offer. However, in all of the available membership lists for the LAC, Dorothy's name never appears.

The Club hosted an annual gymkhana at the Ranelagh Club, the successor to the original 1900 gymkhana that featured the first ladies' race. Again, Dorothy does not appear, or if she did, she kept very quiet about it, which was not in her nature at all, and not what Selwyn Edge wanted from her.

There are a few possible reasons for her non-membership of the Club. One is that she perhaps did not wish to join, although she speaks of it and its members in glowing terms in her book. Despite positioning herself as a role model and guide for women motorists, she seemed somewhat indifferent to racing against them, or appearing at women's motoring events, such as those organised by the LAC. When a ladies' race was finally held at Brooklands in 1908, she was not one of the starters. At various times, she challenged female racers in different countries to battle her for the title of 'Fastest Woman on Earth', but these calls never seemed to lead to anything. Her 1906 interview in the *Deseret Evening News* was one such appeal. A match race with Joan Newton Cuneo, America's most famous lady motorist, was talked about, but never occurred.

Whether this is down to Dorothy being a 'man's woman' who did not really like the company of her own sex, or something more calculating, is hard to tell. The legend that Dorothy and Selwyn Edge created did depend for much of its effect on her being the first, fastest or only woman to be doing something, and this would be diluted if she was one of many in a group of women, one of whom might defeat her at any time. If she did not win against male drivers, she still had the cachet of being the only, or fastest, woman in the contest, often by dint of having the best car at her disposal. Edge's promotion of Dorothy as a lone Amazon on four wheels is inaccurate, as she was one of a number of female sporting motorists who were carving out a niche for themselves in the automotive industry.

Another reason for her non-membership of the Club was her background. There were no official rules preventing Jewish women from joining, but prejudice would have existed, as evidenced by her father's renaming his family to sound more English. Among the titled ladies of the LAC, there was also a distinct danger of Dorothy's elaborately constructed public persona coming unravelled. The likes of Lady Wimborne and the Countess of Kinnoull would probably be familiar with the hunts with which she had claimed to have ridden, the shoots attended and the dignitaries she claimed to have taught to drive. In short, they were in a position to find her out.

The role of Edge in all of this is unclear. What would happen after 1908 seems to suggest that he was the one pulling the strings, and in 1906, he did prevent Dorothy from racing the Mors, and promoting a non-Napier car. There was little public acknowledgement of any kind of relationship between Dorothy and Edge, but as the head of Napier in the UK, he was clearly behind her promotional and sporting role within the company.

Whatever this relationship was, it came to an abrupt, but quiet, end in 1909. Following the 1908 season, Dorothy did not race any more Napier cars, or any cars at all. *The Woman and the Car* was published in 1909, and in it, she talked of how many miles a week she drove. However, this was in the course of travelling, and she does not talk about competition driving at all. One striking fact about the book, mentioned earlier, is that Selwyn Edge and Napier are not mentioned at all.

Without the support of Edge, Dorothy's motorsport options were curtailed. During 1909, after the publication of her book, she announced that her new challenge would be learning to fly an aeroplane. An Australian paper ran a small story in which she was said to have asked the Wright brothers to take her on as a pupil. In 1910, according to the *Bryan Democrat*, an American paper, she travelled to France and attempted to master a monoplane, but she found it too difficult and opted for a biplane, which she, 'as a woman', found easier to learn. The same article also alluded to her having invented an aeroplane, but no more details were provided. Given the nature of the publication – local and overseas – this was probably another exaggeration.

That year, she joined the Aero Club of Great Britain, the club founded just a few years earlier by Vera Butler and her companions. In March, she was booked to speak at the Criterion Restaurant on the subject of learning to fly, but it is unclear whether the event ever happened. It is no less clear whether she ever qualified as a pilot.

Dorothy remained somewhat in the public eye until 1912, making a small living writing motoring articles for women in the newspapers. After that, she simply vanishes from view.

Some of the other pioneering lady motor professionals had fairly short careers, sometimes affected by the war, or by financial problems. Muriel Hind was one of the exceptions. The war effort, ironically, meant that many more women learned to drive and to handle motors, and this led to another flowering of female automotive endeavour after 1915. Gabrielle Borthwick opened her Ladies' Automobile Workshop that year, and soon other women were offering training courses in engineering and driving in the UK. Perhaps Dorothy had become tired of media attention by now and was quietly working at one of these garages, or as a driver for hire at one of a host of female-friendly motor businesses.

Dorothy Elizabeth Levitt died on 17 May 1922, aged 39. She was found dead in her bed at her flat in Marylebone. The cause of death was found to be 'morphine poisoning, while suffering from heart disease and an attack of measles'. She was single. Her small, but not insignificant, estate of £224 was left to her sister. What became of her cups and trophies, her car and her motoring memorabilia, no-one knows.

There is some suggestion that Dorothy was involved with the Suffragette movement in some way. Again, we have no evidence for or against this. Unlike some other early female racers, such as Christabel Ellis or Muriel Thompson, she has no service record for the First World War.

Her elaborately constructed persona could be dismissed as the creation of a fantasist, but there was too much method in her madness for that. Media manipulation that successful was a surprisingly modern skill for an Edwardian woman to possess, and I think we should hail her for that. Had she been alive now, she would have found a job in the PR department of any of the car companies, without a doubt.

Chapter 4

Bad Girls

Bol d'Or, Fontainebleu, France, 1927

1. Violette Morris (BNC)
2. Lefevre (BNC)
3. Treunet (Sima-Violet)

We should be celebrating the fact that a French woman was winning races outright as early as 1927, against male opposition. This French woman driver should be something of a heroine, an admirable figure.

This chapter takes on the uncomfortable fact that some of the women who have achieved success and acclaim in motorsport have held some objectionable views and sometimes acted on them in deplorable ways. I have always found it difficult to write objectively about these drivers in the past, so have decided to tackle the subject in-depth and head on.

Motorsport itself, particularly at the highest levels, has always had an ambivalent relationship with the prevailing morals and political climate of its time. Hence, we see special pleading for the continuation of cigarette advertising, races being staged in countries undergoing political unrest or in places with a poor human rights record. Witness Grands Prix being held in Azerbaijan and Bahrain during civil unrest and in South Africa under apartheid.

Individuals working within motorsport have always held a variety of political views, including those that we now find unacceptable. This was particularly true of the inter-war period, when the full extent of the horrors of the Third Reich was unknown and fascism had a small but significant following in the UK. Fascism was never mainstream, but organisations like the Anglo-German Alliance tried to foster ties with Nazi Germany, and the British Union of Fascists

(BUF) was very visible. Apart from some heavily protested BUF marches, British fascism was largely not of the goose-stepping, window-smashing, murderous variety. It was more subtle, and often expressed as a desire to work with Hitler rather than start a costly and dangerous war. Some of its proponents convinced themselves that these views constituted a peace movement. This is not to downplay the antisemitism that was rife within its ranks.

Fay Taylour is probably best known today for her membership of the BUF, led by Oswald Mosley, and her internment in Holloway Prison during the Second World War. However, it is also true that she was a very capable competitor on both two and four wheels.

Finding the beginning of Fay's motorsport career is very difficult. Fay herself was a tireless self-publicist and re-inventor of her public persona, rather in the mould of Dorothy Levitt thirty years before. We do know that she was born in Northern Ireland, and that her early motorsport experiences were in the late 1920s in the new and growing discipline of motorcycle speedway. At different times, she described her racing adventures in Australia, New Zealand and Germany. Research into travel documents by Richard Armstrong tends to contradict her descriptions of lengthy and triumphant tours abroad, suggesting that her trips were often quite brief, or sometimes not at all consistent with her claims. In 1931, she talks of having travelled to India and won a road race between Calcutta and Ranchi, driving a Chevrolet. This story is proving very hard to verify, although she certainly did travel to India. Later, Fay was somewhat vague about what she actually raced there, allowing some to believe that it was a motorcycle race that she won.

The start of the 1930s roughly coincided with her transition to four-wheeled competition. Throughout her career, she would claim that she never possessed her own racing cars, depending on the goodwill of others for opportunities to race.

In another notable story, about-turn Fay also described the 1931 Brooklands Ladies' Handicap as her first ever car race, disregarding the Calcutta event. She may have meant 'first circuit race'. The handicappers were not convinced by her pleas of inexperience, and gave her a small five-second handicap, which she used to her advantage, winning the race from Elsie 'Bill' Wisdom, who was on scratch, and Lotte 'Irene' Schwedler, who had a considerable handicap. Fay's car was a Talbot, a car she would use again in 1931 and 1932.

After the BARC relaxed its prohibition on men and women racing against one another at Brooklands, Fay wanted to compete against the men but had to wait until 1938 to do so – at Brooklands anyway. She continued to appear in the semi-regular ladies' races held there, in a Riley, a Salmson and an Alfa Romeo. At the 1934 autumn meeting, she drove the Alfa in a Ladies' Mountain Handicap and was second behind Doreen Evans in her MG. However, after the race was over, she continued to tear around the track for another three laps. Her result stood, but she was fined £3 and prevented from taking any further part in the meeting.

Fay stood apart somewhat from the other ladies of the Brooklands' 'set' such as Kay Petre and Elsie Wisdom. She raced against them but never teamed up with them for relay races or at Le Mans, and she was rarely photographed alongside them. Her Irishness could have been a factor, but the Canadian-born Petre and Australian Joan Richmond never had any such trouble over their origins. Her frequent laments of not owning her own car were also nothing particularly unusual: Paddie Naismith used her lover's car exclusively and Victoria Worsley was another driver with limited disposable income who normally borrowed or shared her cars. Ingrained snobbery about motorcyclists was possibly a stronger reason for Fay's outsider status, particularly as Fay had come up through the speedway ranks and speedway was a new and somewhat disreputable discipline. She was often vocal about the discrimination she faced as a woman, which the more established Brooklands ladies tended not to do, and this may have alienated her further.

She might not have got the chance to brave the Brooklands banking against the men for some time but she did take them on in hillclimbs and trials, including the Scottish Six Days' Trial in 1933, for which she drove a Ford V8 and won a silver medal. Then, of course, there was the Leinster Grand Prix.

'Grand Prix' was a slight misnomer for the Leinster race as it was not an international event by any stretch of the imagination. It was a handicap race run over a circuit of approximately 13 miles. Fay, driving an Adler Trumpf provided by the Leinster Automobile Club, was given a generous handicap of a whole lap, plus two minutes, which she exploited mercilessly. Her only real opponents were Adrian Conan Doyle in a Mercedes and Austin Dobson in an Alfa, who started a lap behind but was catching her by the end. All Fay needed to do was to keep going and keep out of trouble, which she managed easily, and the victory was hers. Unfortunately, a printers' strike in Ireland meant that the news of her victory was not widely broadcast. This meant that it did not make much of an impact on the UK motoring press but also that Fay was free to manipulate the details in ways that showed her in the best light. What was really an amateur handicap became an international Grand Prix in her stories.

The summer of 1935 could have had Fay tackling some top-level international competition and also working alongside some of the established Brooklands ladies. She was on George Eyston's shortlist for his three-car, six-woman MG team, which would later be nicknamed 'The Dancing Daughters'. Doreen Evans, Margaret Allan and Joan Richmond were the lead drivers.

Fay's participation at Le Mans was precluded by a short spell in prison in June 1935. She refused to pay a £1 speeding fine, opting for a court appearance and a night in the cells of Holloway. A journalist covering the case had paid the fine on her behalf, but she insisted on taking her punishment and all the publicity that went with it. The prison governor even gave her the cab fare home the next morning.

For a while, she concentrated on rallying and racing midget cars on dirt tracks, with varying degrees of success and seriousness. Her midget outings were often match races against established dirt-track drivers and were rather reminiscent of the fairground races in the US, featuring the likes of Elfrieda Mais and Joan LaCosta. Throughout her career in midgets, she encountered other female racers, whom she always seemed particularly keen to beat. She was most put out when an inexperienced woman called Edna Wells roundly defeated her in Australia in 1952. Edna, who went on to do some long-circuit racing against a young Jack Brabham in 1953, had never driven a midget car before.

A few other Brooklands ladies dabbled in midget racing, such as Patricia 'Dot' Oxenden, who drove in exhibition races in the UK, but Fay's affinity with dirt tracks and ramshackle midget cars was probably another reason she did not fit in well with the British motorsport set. The Brooklands ladies were not averse to dirt and tough conditions, as many of them were successful rally drivers and even mechanics, but the midget-racing scene was the preserve of a different class of person.

Fay made her return to more mainstream motorsport in 1938 and this time she was competing against men. She drove an Alfa in the heats of the British Trophy at Brooklands in August but does not appear to have finished. At the Jubilee meeting she drove a Bugatti, but was unplaced. She was similarly unplaced at the Show Time meeting in October.

At this point, she was not yet a member of Oswald Mosley's BUF. At the end of 1938, she travelled to South Africa in order to race a Riley in the South African and Grosvenor Grands Prix. She did not get to enter these events and she ended up doing some midget racing and acting as a sales agent for Freddie Dixon, the car's owner. Onboard ship, she almost certainly came into contact with Oswald Pirow, a German-born South African politician, who had recently met Hitler, Mussolini and other key Nazi and Fascist figures. Her MI5 file, as studied by Richard Armstrong, describes her time in South Africa as lasting about six months, during which time she raced midgets against local drivers and did some 'full-size' racing, possibly in a Ford V8 or a Bentley.

After leaving South Africa, she went on to Germany, where she attempted to broker herself a drive in an Auto Union, an endeavour that led to nothing. She met with some political figures and made a radio broadcast on the German South Africa service.

In October of that year, she was announced as a new member of the BUF in its own magazine. In 1940, she was formally arrested and interned in Holloway prison as a Nazi sympathiser and a possible spy.

Fay was not the only woman who had been arrested. The most famous of the BUF ladies was Diana Mitford, who married Mosley. It is unclear whether Diana and Fay ever met. It is almost certain, however, that Fay met Enid Riddell, another racing driver. Enid, often incorrectly named as 'Joan', raced at Le Mans in 1937, finishing seventeenth in an MG Midget owned by George Eyston. Her co-driver was Dorothy Stanley-Turner. Enid competed throughout the 1930s, usually on the continent, and was an accomplished rally and hillclimb driver.

Enid and Fay were both members of the Right Club, another Far Right organisation, founded in 1939. The club was strongly associated with the actions of Anna Wolkoff and Tyler Kent, who were convicted of spying for Germany. Many years later, in 1973, Wolkoff died in a car accident. The driver, who was not seriously hurt, was Enid Riddell. Reports suggest that both were still involved in 'antisemitic activities' at the time. Enid may also have been involved in more petty crime; she was said to have had something to do with whiskey smuggling. This was the suggestion of April Ashley, the transsexual model, in her autobiography. Enid ran a nightclub called the Rascasse in Malaga, and was a proprietress in the mould of Kate Meyrick ten years previously. She died in 1980.

Both the BUF and the Right Club had their representatives at Brooklands, apart from Fay and Enid. Anecdotal evidence describes a considerable number of BUF badges visible on the cars parked outside the circuit. Pilot and aircraft designer A. V. Roe, was a member of both. Malcolm Campbell, despite being nominally a member of the Conservative party, was strongly linked to the BUF. Lord de Clifford, who sat in the House of Lords, was another member of the BUF. Lady de Clifford, the former Dorothy Meyrick, was a Brooklands hanger-on whose chief association with the track was her part in Barbara Cartland's 'Society Ladies' Private Handicap' stunt in 1931. She got into her own scrapes when she married Lord de Clifford; he was only 19 at the time and his parents had not given permission. Her personal politics are unknown and she does not appear to have been interned. Dorothy was the daughter of Kate Meyrick, a notorious early twentieth-century nightclub proprietor who spent several periods in Holloway Prison. However, Kate died in 1933, and does not figure in this part of history.

Unbelievably, Fay Taylour and Enid Riddell were both able to return to motorsport after their release from jail. Fay was ordered to return to Ireland, where she kept a low profile for some time, before returning to the UK in the late 1940s to race in a number of cars. Initially, these were midget cars again, but she bargained her way into the fledgling Formula Three series and famously raced against Stirling Moss. She was able to travel reasonably freely and raced a Effyhe single-seater in Sweden in 1953. She had not lost her talent for self-promotion; the year before, a single trip to Skarpnäck circuit in Sweden became a 'European tour' in her interviews. Even her Stirling Moss claim was something of an exaggeration; both entered a Formula Three race at Castle Combe, but they were placed in different heats. Moss won his, while Fay did not finish hers and did not qualify for the final – which was won by Moss. She also appears to have boasted of racing against Peter Collins, who had his final Formula Three race in 1951, at a time when Fay was in the US.

Enid acted as a rally co-driver to Betty Haig, the great-niece of Field Marshal Haig. Betty apparently had no problems with this arrangement, and in her writing of the time acknowledged that Enid had 'not been able to race much' during the war. She never talked about her own personal politics, but she does not appear to have been antisemitic. Another friend and co-driver of Betty's was the Jewish-born Anglo-German rally driver, Pamela Moy. Pamela's family was an old English Jewish banking dynasty; she married into the deposed German aristocracy.

Fay received similar treatment from the press, who simply stopped mentioning what she did during the war. She was free to travel the world, returning to South Africa at least once and doing some racing there. She attempted to get in with the nascent NASCAR crowd in the early 1950s, but this did not amount to anything much. In 1951, she took part in some match races at Morristown in New Jersey against Fred Pfisterer; the sprints appeared on a NASCAR bill and were promoted by Joe Sorrano but were not stock car races. Fay used a Jaguar, and Pfisterer an Austin-Healey. Her stock car outings were limited to jalopy races, sometimes 'powderpuff derbies' against other women drivers.

Her files and her personal correspondence show that she had not repented politically, and still remained a staunch antisemite. However, as she got older, her politics became more and more confused. At different times, she admired both Fidel Castro and John F. Kennedy and took an interest in Ho Chi Minh's Vietnam.

Fay's motive for her political fanaticism is hard to define. She was a person of extremes generally, who enjoyed unconventional activities and liked to push boundaries as hard as she could. Motor racing was the prime example of this. She also appeared to crave drama in her life and was a compulsive attention seeker who liked to manipulate the press. Evidence for this comes from her behaviour around her 1935 speeding trial and 'imprisonment', which involved much waving to photographers at the gates of Holloway. That, combined with her outsider status in UK motorsport of the time and the apparent lack of much going on in her personal life, left a space for extremism, the sense of belonging and action that it brought. There is no obvious conflict she had with Jewish people that could have led to her antisemitism – for example, it was almost certainly not Jewish promoters that barred her from entering speedway events – so we can only assume that she adopted it as part and parcel of Far-Right ideology. She died in 1983, having been very ill for some time.

The role of German and Austrian motorsport ladies during the war is not well documented. Some disappear to South Africa, like Margot Einsiedel, and some merely disappear from public life altogether. Most of the Klausen hillclimb set falls into the latter category, with one major exception.

'Princess Hohenlohe' was not technically a princess, being divorced from Prince Friedrich-Franz of Hohenlohe-Waldenburg-Schillingsfurst since 1920. She was born Stephany Richter in Hungary in 1891 and may have been living in London at the time of her Klausen debut in 1924. Motor racing played only a small part in her life. Fascism was more important to her.

Princess Hohenlohe acted as a go-between for Lord Harmsworth, the proprietor of the *Daily Mail*, and Hitler. Her actions helped to broker contact between the Fuhrer and members of the British establishment, which was then far more receptive to Far Right ideology than now. Like Fay Taylour, she would be interned in the

UK for part of the war before being allowed to remain at liberty afterwards. It is possible that she knew Riddell and perhaps Taylour.

Across the channel in France, another female racing star was drawn to the side of fascism, and it did not end well for her. We return to Violette Morris, whose win in 1927 opened this chapter.

Violette Morris was born in 1893, as Emilie Paule Violette Morris. She learned to drive during the First World War, during which she worked as a nurse and ambulance driver on the French battlefields, then as a motorcycle courier. She was a natural sportswoman who practised many sports to the highest level: shot put, discus, football, boxing and swimming were just some of them. In 1913, she was fifth in a swimming race, competing against men. She set a new national record for the shot put in 1917. In 1921, she entered the throwing events in the Women's World Games and set more records. Photographs show that her physique was suited to strength events; she was reasonably tall and very broad, with a muscular, although markedly feminine, shape.

She married Cyprien Gouraud in 1914, and they remained, nominally at least, a couple until 1923. After this, Violette mostly dated other women, and was open about the fact. Near the end of the war, after her discharge from the Red Cross following illness and the death of her parents, she began to adopt an increasingly masculine appearance. She is almost always pictured in a suit, worn with a shirt and tie and men's shoes. When challenged, she claimed that she dressed that way for practicality. As the proprietor of a motor accessory shop, she was only dressing as others in her position did, although they were usually male. In a 1930 court case, Violette claimed to have adopted trousers as her favoured mode of dress while she was working as a despatch rider in the Somme valley.

Her suits were normally accessorised with a cigarette in the corner of her mouth. She reportedly smoked about sixty per day, despite her athletic lifestyle.

A small number of writers has tried to 'reclaim' Violette as a transgender person, but she never directly claimed to be male herself. She used her obviously female given name and the female title,

'Madame', as well as entering ladies' races towards the end of her career. In 1929, she did undergo a bilateral mastectomy, but her own take on this was that it made it easier to fit into a small racing car cockpit. She also claimed that other sportswomen had had similar procedures. Early pictures do show that she had very large breasts, which would have easily interfered with any number of activities. It is not clear exactly what the operation was, and whether it would now be referred to as a 'breast reduction', rather than a mastectomy per se.

Her motor racing career started in 1922. The first major race she entered was the Bol d'Or, a 24-hour race held close to Saint-Germain on a sandy dirt track. Violette drove a Benjamin cyclecar, a rather flimsy vehicle with a 750cc engine. She was thirteenth overall. Photographs of her exist from this year at a Cyclecar Grand Prix, held at Le Mans, and at the weigh-in for the Circuit des Routes Pavées.

Driving the same car, she was seventh in the 1923 Bol d'Or. She is said to have raced in that year's Paris–Nice race and won. Again, pictures show her at the weigh-in.

Violette never raced full-time and competed simultaneously in athletics, boxing and motor racing, as well as managing a women's football team. She returned to the Bol d'Or again in 1927 and won, driving a BNC this time. This particular event was a favourite of hers and she was third in 1928, and tenth in 1930. That time, she was driving a 'VM' Special, custom-built for her. Other major races she entered included the 1927 Coppa Florio in Saint-Brieuc. She was thirteenth, in the BNC.

Towards the end of the 1920s, her interest in motor racing began to wane. She had kept up a decent racing career alongside a demanding schedule of athletic field events, swimming and football. She played for both the Olympique and Femina women's teams and acted as a team manager. However, accusations that she had been supplying her players with performance-enhancing drugs were made, leading to her being banned from organised women's football. She also stood accused of propositioning younger players for sex. Gradually, she was forced out of the French sporting scene, ostensibly for wearing men's sportswear in public. This was made official in a 1930 court case brought against her by the French sporting authorities. She was barred from athletics, football and most other sports, with motor racing being an exception.

It is generally believed that the authorities were not happy for her to represent her country as an openly same-sex attracted woman who eschewed femininity. It was considered rather modern for women to experiment with masculinity in the earlier part of the 1920s, but this became less respectable towards the end of the decade. After the court case, Violette gave an interview to a provincial newspaper journalist in which she attacked the women of the sports committees. She claimed that some other sportswomen were lesbians or cheating on their partners and railed against the hypocrisy she saw.

Kept out of sports, Violette became part of the Paris demi-monde. She was frequently photographed out with her lovers, always dressed in menswear. In 1926, she launched a career as a cabaret singer. Little information about her voice, or the style of music she performed, has survived, although she is occasionally described as a 'lyrical' singer.

Another denizen of the Parisian performing underground was Hellé-Nice, another racing driver who had worked as an exotic dancer in nightclubs. This world and the motor racing world overlapped to a surprising degree, particularly among women drivers. The ladies' races and celebrity events that were a feature of 1930s Paris would often feature the likes of Mistinguett and Mlle Ranha, a dancer. Ranha certainly raced occasionally. Music-hall performer and Moulin Rouge promoter Mistinguett normally limited herself to *concours d'elégance*.

It is unclear how well the two women knew each other, but they were certainly rivals on the track, at the beginning of Hellé-Nice's career. In 1929, the two faced each other in the Grand Prix Féminin, with Hellé-Nice in an Omega Six and Violette in a Donnet. Violette had already won two speed trials in two different cars; although the favourite to win she could not hold off Hellé-Nice.

The Grand Prix and speed trials were part of the Journée Féminine de l'Automobile, an all-female motorsport event held by the newspaper, *Le Journal*. Some serious racing drivers, such as Violette, did enter, but there was an equal number of actresses and vaudeville performers trying their luck. The event was promoted by *Le Journal*, and written up fulsomely in its pages. Both Violette and Hellé-Nice were flamboyant and notorious and the contrast between blonde, feminine Hellé-Nice and Violette, dark-haired and -eyed and *en travesti*, was made for drama. An extra *frisson* was provided by the whiff of sexual scandal that surrounded both; Hellé-Nice was known for her near-naked dance performances, and Violette was open about her same-sex relationships.

Incidentally, lesbianism among women racing drivers was not a new thing. Hélène van Zuylen, one of France's earliest female racing drivers, spent much of her life in a relationship with another woman. Across the Channel at Brooklands, Daisy Addis Price's lesbian status was an open secret, although it was only confirmed when she died in the 1940s, leaving her fortune to her 'lifelong lady companion'. At least two other Brooklands ladies, from slightly later on than 1929, appear to have been dating one another and one of these women left everything in her will to another unrelated spinster when she died. None of the others were linked to fascism or any political extremism in any way.

Violette lost interest in the motor racing scene after 1930 and carried on with her other business, showbusiness and sporting activities. She still had an income from her inheritance from her parents, with which she supported herself. Scandal still followed her; in 1937, she was arrested and charged with manslaughter for shooting an intruder in her home, a houseboat on the Seine. However, it was ruled as self-defence, as the man had allegedly threatened to throw Violette overboard, and she escaped punishment.

Her route into Nazism is really not clear. Among the guests entertained by her and her partner, Yvonne de Bray, on the houseboat, were a few Fascist sympathisers, such as Jean Cocteau. However, at other times, Violette was pictured with Josephine Baker, who was not only black, but would become a decorated heroine of the Resistance.

It is generally believed that she was recruited as a spy by the Nazis in 1936. Raymond Ruffin, who has written about Violette at length, claims that this happened after a meeting at the 1936 Berlin Olympics. Other sources dispute this and put her recruitment later. She would pass on information about Resistance activities and French defences.

Later, she co-ordinated counter-sabotage against Special Operations Executive (SOE) operatives set on disrupting the occupation. Between 1942 and 1944 she was a member of the French arm of the Gestapo and was apparently employed as a torturer. The SOE, in London, ordered her execution. She was apprehended driving a Citroen goods vehicle, stopped and shot at point-blank range in 1944. Her body was removed and dumped in an undisclosed location.

The precise nature of Violette's collaboration is debated. Raymond Ruffin's version of events, which paints her as a spy engaged in actions against the SOE's sabotage operations and obtaining at least some of her information through torture, is a widely discussed story. Ruffin's argument is based on a witness testimony from a Resistance member who was tortured by someone called 'Maurice' who closely resembled Violette Morris.

Another historian, Marie-Josèphe Bonnet, refutes some of these claims and maintains that Violette's collaboration took the form of black-market trading of construction materials and acting as a chauffeur. She also positions Violette's recruitment much later, during the war itself. An interesting point she makes is that there are no images of her at the 1936 Games, despite the fact that it was heavily photographed, and filmed by Leni Riefenstahl. Violette was quite famous, and would have been photographed if she were present.

Her views have been espoused by those who wish to position Violette as a figure in transgender history, although Violette herself never made any such claim. Even if she did, it would still be no reason to play down her wartime activities.

The truth may well lie somewhere in the middle, as it usually does.

The question of motive is usually answered by referring to Violette's rejection by the French sporting authorities, and her outsider status in French public life, which caused her to disidentify with France and all it stood for. There may well have been an element of self-protection there, too – the Nazis often persecuted lesbians and gender non-conforming women – a sort of 'kill or be killed'.

There are some similarities in the personalities of Fay Taylour and Violette. Both of them, in their way, enjoyed shocking people. But, whereas Fay went out of her way to do so, Violette's methods were more passive-aggressive. She just did things (like punching football referees or being caught by her husband having sex with another couple) and refused to repent or explain.

Raymond Ruffin claims that Violette was raped as a teenager by a boy who pretended to teach her boxing. Her early love life, with both men and women, had a strong exploitative element to it; she was 'groomed' (in modern terms) by an older woman, who sometimes passed her on to her own male partners for sex.

Ruffin also makes references to Violette having experienced something traumatic during her First World War service. Apparently, she herself referred to it in conversations with friends, but it is not specified what actually happened. This seems to be linked to a disillusionment with the French military and government, which she did voice on occasion. Shortly after her 1930 participation ban, her auto spares business fell victim to the Great Depression. This fuelled her anger considerably. Jewish financiers were convenient scapegoats for a complex process that began with the First World War.

A final mystery about women drivers and the Nazis exists. After the war, in 1949, Louis Chiron publicly accused Hellé-Nice of having been a collaborator. Some sources have him allege she was a Gestapo agent.

No hard evidence has ever been put forward for this. There are no references to Hellé-Nice in the available Gestapo files, although if she had been involved in covert operations this might not be a surprise. The exact nature of her collaboration was never specified any further than 'Gestapo'.

The only faintly damning factor is that she herself was unable to give a convincing account of what she did during the war, or even where she was. The records for the Second World War in Monaco have remained classified; she did live in or near Monte Carlo, and these files may give us some evidence in future.

Hellé-Nice did share some personality traits with both Fay and Violette. She loved drama and she too enjoyed shocking people. In the early part of her career as a dancer, she was sidelined from more mainstream entertainment shows and made her living as a more 'erotic' performer. According to Miranda Seymour's readings of her diaries, she really did admire music-hall stars such as Mistinguett, and would have wanted to follow in their footsteps. Violette Morris moved among this milieu too, down to racing in the women's automotive carnivals popular with both female drivers and intrepid actresses at the time. Romantic disappointment is also suggested as a strong factor in Hellé Nice's life by Miranda Seymour.

However, these factors alone do not a potential Nazi make. As suggested at the start of this chapter, we must also remember that some people will hold repellent views and even act on them, and there is not always a clear reason for that.

Chapter 5

Brooklands Speed Queens

2 July 1932, Guys Gala, Brooklands

Duchess of York's Race for Lady Drivers
1. Eileen Ellison (Bugatti)
2. Kay Petre (Wolseley Hornet)
3. Lotte 'Irene' Schwedler (Alvis)

Also ran
Elsie Wisdom (Invicta)
Fay Taylour (Talbot)
Kitty Brunell (Rover)
Miss H. M. Buckley (Alvis)
Sheila Tolhurst (Riley)
Lady Dorothy de Clifford (MG)
Miss G. Spencer (Frazer Nash)
Geraldine Hedges (Talbot)
Paddie Naismith (Salmson)
Mrs R. A. Cookson (Aston Martin)
Rita Don (Wolseley Hornet)
Joan Chetwynd (MG)
Victoria Worsley (Alvis)

When considering the lady drivers who graced Brooklands over the thirty-two years of its existence, it is hard to know which race to choose to illustrate the topic. At first, I wanted to use a mixed race because men and women did race together at least some of the time. However, the entry list for the Duchess of York's Race read like the closest thing to a Who's Who of the Brooklands Speed Queens.

The Guys Gala was not a regular Brooklands meeting. It was a benefit event for Guys Hospital in London, combining motor racing, celebrity and entertainment. As well as the usual scratch and handicap races, there were novelty events like a 'hazard race', track parades and passenger rides. Two races were organised for medical students of Guys itself. The mastermind behind it was Billie Bristow, one of the few women of the time to run her own promotions and publicity agency.

Celebrity guests included actresses Betty Stockfeld and Heather Angel, who had recently starred together in Carmine Gallone's film *City of Song*. They were pictured riding in cars with guests. Billie Bristow worked extensively in the film industry and it would have been easy for her to recruit any number of film personalities to tempt press attention. A year later, she would use Brooklands as the backdrop for the George King film *Matinee Idol*, which she co-wrote as well as publicised.

A 'Young People's Committee' promoted the event at other social and sporting occasions, selling programmes and souvenirs. The committee comprised debutantes and other young ladies, the most notable of whom was Margaret Whigham, later to achieve fame for her scandalous divorce from Ian, the Duke of Argyll. Her fellow debutante and programme seller Priscilla Weigall would marry legendary racer Lord Howe's son, Lord Curzon, two years later.

This was very much a Society event. The guests of honour were the Duke and Duchess of York, who would become the king and queen in 1936. The duchess, later known as the Queen Mother, put her name to a race for lady drivers. There were two dedicated ladies' events at the Gala: the Duchess of York's and the Women's Automobile and Sports Association's one-lap Handicap. Women also entered some races alongside men.

Another difficulty with deciding where to start with the Brooklands ladies is the question of when they were allowed to race there at all. The BARC, the track's governing club, did not allow women to compete alongside men at all until 1932, and even then, not on the faster Mountain circuit. This restriction was lifted in 1933. It is commonly said that no women raced at Brooklands at all after

66

the Ladies' Bracelet Handicap of 1908 until a date sometime in the 1920s. This is not actually true. While the BARC was not keen on women racing drivers, other motor clubs that used the track did not have these rules. From as early as 1909, women were racing against men, just not in BARC races. The BARC itself allowed ladies-only events from 1920. These were held a few times a year. Several of the Guys Gala race entrants were Brooklands regulars. Most had at least some experience.

The winner, Eileen Ellison, was actually rather a peripheral figure on the Brooklands scene. After 1934, she rarely raced in the UK, preferring France and South Africa. In 1935, she was seventh in the Albi Grand Prix, driving a Bugatti T37. Staying in France, she was also third in the Voiturette class of the Lorraine Grand Prix. Her South African Grand Prix appearance was in 1936, but she did not finish.

She was probably a better hillclimb driver than she was a true racer, but she managed some good results nevertheless, including a second place in the Cobham Junior Short Handicap in 1933 in the Bugatti. She entered some other Brooklands ladies' races but did not win.

Eileen often shared cars with Thomas Cholmondeley Tapper. She started out as a car owner rather than driver, with Cholmondeley Tapper at the wheel.

The women of Brooklands were rivals but they were also colleagues and teammates and often friends. Attempting to create profiles of each in turn without cross-referencing with another is impossible. For example, a year later, in 1934, the top three drivers in the Guys Gala race were all in action together in the Light Car Club's annual relay race. Eileen, Kay Petre and Sheila Tolhurst drove for the Singer team. Lotte Schwedler (whose name has become confused as 'Irene' somewhere) was part of the MG team of three Magnettes alongside Margaret Allen and Doreen Evans. The winners of the Ladies' Prize in this particular event were to be entered into the Le Mans 24 Hours the following year. Both teams were racing hard, but skulduggery was afoot. A Singer crew member found some papers in a garage which explained the pit signals that the MG team would use, giving the Singer crew an advantage and allowing them to anticipate all of their rivals' moves. Furthermore, the Singer team became aware of a loophole in the race rules; the Ladies' Prize was only to be awarded to a team finishing outside the top three. Thus, the Singer drivers hung back to enable them to win the prize. They were fifth overall, while the MG team was third.

Kay Petre was always a strong candidate for this sort of scheme. She was extremely charming, and popular with drivers, officials and media alike. Sammy Davis describes her in *Atalanta* as 'a dark-haired, very attractive, and very well-dressed little person' with 'a general air of amusing vitality' and earlier, as 'a gallant little person'.

Although she had learned to drive at 16 in her native Canada, Kay, born Kathleen Coad Defries, was a relative late-comer to the motor racing scene. At the age of 29, the Guys Gala was one of her first races. Just a month earlier, she had finished third in the Novices' Handicap in her own Wolseley Hornet, a birthday present from her British husband, Henry. She soon moved on to a Bugatti, which she claimed was her favourite car. She won the Walton Fourth Scratch Sprint in it in 1934, then the Merrow Senior Short Handicap.

She was clearly a talented driver, and motorsport writers of the time commented on her fast starts. However, she maintained a carefully humble image: that of a rather dizzy, lucky woman who survived on her nerves and wits and barely knew one end of her car from the other. Dennis May called her 'as mechanically minded as a Yeti'. She was too small to crank-start a car herself and needed assistance whenever this was necessary. Even after her retirement, when asked about her driving technique, she would claim that it was entirely due to her feeling for the noise and vibration of the car as it revved rather than any knowledge of how it actually worked.

If this was a bit disingenuous, as even Sammy Davis thought it was, it was an effective ploy for getting people on-side, and it at least meant that she was free of the crashing arrogance which often afflicts racing drivers. Even a personality as august and traditional as Malcolm Campbell was not immune to Kay's charm, and he helped her with car preparation and technique for her speed record runs.

Kay really wanted the Outer Circuit Record, describing it as a 'Petre Prime Target' in 1934. However, she did not have access to the biggest, fastest machinery needed to attack such a record. Instead, she started a series of battles for the Women's Outer Circuit Record. Her first rival was Elsie Wisdom, always known as 'Bill' since childhood, and another of her colleagues in the Guys Gala race. Bill drove the Parry-Thomas 'Flatiron' in their contest, an extremely temperamental and hard-handling car. It had been bought for her by her husband, Tommy Wisdom, a motoring journalist and racer who was most associated with the Frazer Nash marque.

Kay took the record in her Bugatti. Bill did not keep the Flatiron for very long as she found it very difficult and unpleasant to drive.

Bill Wisdom had learned to drive at an early age and had always taken an interest in cars, but she owed her competition career to Tommy. Her first race was a Ladies' Handicap at the 1930 BARC March meeting at Brooklands. She drove a Frazer Nash to victory over Jill Scott, who was in a Bugatti. Tommy had entered her without telling her. She was terrified to begin with, but her chief feeling towards Tommy by the end was annoyance that he had made the decision without her.

If this gives an impression of Bill as a reluctant racer keeping up with her husband, that is not the true picture. She was one of the best female drivers in the country in the 1930s and at times, could be in there with the best drivers, full stop. She is most famous for her win in the 1932 1,000-Miles Race, run over two days as the replacement for the Double Twelve which had been retired due to noise concerns.

Bill shared a Riley with Joan Richmond, an Australian driver who had arrived in Europe the previous year. They made the most of their opportunity and won comfortably, having led for long sections of the race. The duo averaged 84.41mph. Although this was not the fastest outright speed, they led their class and made the most of their handicap to come home in front.

Joan did not appear at the Guys Gala, which is quite surprising. The 1,000 Miles, held in June, was her Brooklands debut, so perhaps she was still under the radar when the Gala was organised. Joan was often photographed with the other Brooklands ladies and teamed up with both Bill Wisdom and Kay Petre for rallies.

Lotte Schwedler, third-place finisher behind Kay at the Gala and rival to her in the Light Car Club (LCC) Relay, also stood apart slightly from the other women. She was Ilse Charlotte Schwedler, a German national, who had originally come to England to work as a nanny. According to a family friend who knew her when he was a child, she was always Lotte, Charlotte or Carlotta. Her nationality did not seem to be much of a problem for her racing colleagues. She was a member of WASA who first appears in the finishing list for their 1930 Land's End Trial.

She often drove an Alvis belonging to Gerald Dunham and she would be instrumental in his daughter Hazel's later racing career, in the 1950s. Brooklands may have closed its gates for good in 1939, but the influence of its women's network continued for some time afterwards.

The Alvis gave Lotte her best result: a win in the 1933 Lightning Short Handicap.

Returning to Kay and her quest for the Ladies' Record brings us to one of the most famous events involving women at the track. In 1935, Gwenda Stewart, who lived in France and raced at Montlhéry, stepped up as Kay's challenger. She brought over a Miller-engined Derby, known as the Derby-Miller and built by Gwenda's third husband. Kay, ever-cheerful and sporting and without arrogance, offered to show Gwenda around the circuit and familiarise herself with its features. Gwenda was a very quick learner, and already had some experience of the banking.

Kay and Gwenda's battle was the last-ever match race held at Brooklands. The stake was 50 sovereigns. Gwenda drove the Derby-Miller, Kay an ex-John Cobb Delage. She had spent the past few months learning how to handle this beast of a car, with its 10.5l engine. It was by now more suited to record-breaking than to racing, but she got some good results out of it, the best of these being a third place in the Whitsun Senior Short Handicap.

Kay had the upper hand for the first runs, but Gwenda pipped her to the record on their last run.

It is not surprising that Gwenda did not appear at the Gala. She always said that she preferred record-breaking to racing, as it required less skill. She had previously set some outright records for a three-wheeler at Montlhéry, driving a Morgan.

Gwenda may have been the official fastest lady but she was never taken into the hearts of the Brooklands fans as Kay Petre and Bill Wisdom were. The likes of Sammy Davis had almost as much breathless admiration for Bill as they did for Kay. In *Atalanta*, Davis describes her as 'tall, slim, dark-haired with one exciting white lock … most amusing green eyes'. A soulful portrait of her in helmet and dark overalls, looking rather like Joan Crawford, is one of the abiding images of women racing drivers of the era. Another is Kay, photographed from above, sitting in the Delage. Her petite frame (she was somewhere between 4ft 10in and 5ft 1in, depending on whom you believe) makes a stark contrast to the huge, open car. She was one of the first drivers to make use of a custom-moulded racing seat in order to see over the dashboard. The seat, which she sometimes called 'The Petre Patent Pew for Petite Persons', was made using a cast of Kay, by sitting her in a bucket of plaster. She also employed wooden blocks on her pedals, for better reach.

I have sat in the Delage myself. At 5ft 2in I could use the pedals quite easily. Even allowing for a different seat, Kay must have been considerably shorter.

Brooklands had usually had a 'darling' of some description. In the 1930s, it was Kay and Bill. At the beginning, it was another very tiny and feminine driver, Christabel Ellis. In between, in the 1920s, Violette Cordery captured hearts and imaginations as she broke a long series of speed and endurance records in an Invicta. She also drove in the semi-regular ladies' races with her sister Evelyn. Lance Macklin, who ran the Invicta company, exploited Violette's driving talent and winsome good looks to promote his racing cars.

A little later, The Hon. Mrs Victor Bruce was the most famous woman to race in the UK. Again, she was better known as a record-breaker rather than a racer, although she was quite capable running wheel-to-wheel. In 1930, she and her husband drove their Alvis Silver Eagle to thirteenth place in the Junior Car Club's (JCC) Double Twelve. To the wider public, she was a daredevil pilot who had flown across all continents of the world. Her adventures were chronicled in the newspapers, sponsored by Ovaltine. Mary Bruce was born Mary Petre, and was a cousin to Kay's husband. It has been suggested that she was an inspiration to Kay in taking up motorsport.

Another of the Guys Gala racers, Kitty Brunell, had been a sweetheart of the British motorsport scene for the past few seasons. Kitty's biggest achievement was probably winning the RAC Rally in 1933, driving a four-seater AC Ace. In 1929, she entered the Monte Carlo Rally in a Talbot Six, aged 17. She was twentieth overall and third in the ladies' standings. She did at least two more Montes, but the 1929 event was probably her best one.

Kitty's popularity was probably down to her father, Bill Brunell, who was a photographer. There are many charming pictures of her in existence, thanks to him: from 1927, when she was a 15-year-old mechanic on another rally car, to her last events in 1933.

Paddie Naismith too was a much-photographed and popular figure. Away from the racetrack, she was an actress and an image of her was one of the first colour television pictures transmitted by John Logie Baird. Like Kay, she was unafraid of a little controversy. The supercharged Salmson in which she raced between 1931 and 1934 belonged to her lover, Derwent Hall-Caine, a former actor and Labour MP. Later in 1932, Paddie would win another ladies' handicap from Fay Taylour in a Talbot. Her best overall result was probably a third place in the First Long Handicap at the July BARC Meeting.

Fay Taylour has been covered in detail in Chapter 4. As mentioned there, she stood apart somewhat from the rest of the Brooklands' set, although she did take part in several ladies' events and won two. Both she and Paddie Naismith got into trouble with the stewards at the same meeting. Paddie was stripped of a third place in the 1934 First Kingston Junior Long Handicap because she had repeatedly violated the track limits at the Fork bend. She was excluded from the meeting and fined £2. Following the later Ladies' Handicap, Fay decided to ignore the flag for the end of the race and take three more laps in her Alfa Romeo. She too was excluded and fined £3. Paddie drifted away from motor racing after 1934, but Fay's wrist slap did nothing to discourage her.

As we have seen, gamesmanship was as prevalent among women drivers as it was among their male counterparts. Rita Don was outwardly a very respectable Brooklands' denizen; she was on the ladies' committee for the gala meeting alongside the Marchioness of Cambridge, Lady Iris Capell of WASA and Morna Rawlins (Vaughan), the surgeon-turned-rally driver who was also a senior WASA figure. Rita was also the sister of Kaye Don, a long-standing racer with many wins to his name.

Her conduct during the Gala was without suspicion, but her victory in the 1933 Ladies' Mountain Handicap came under scrutiny. She was aided by Freddie Dixon, another Brooklands regular who was supposed to be her riding mechanic. Some rumours suggest that he was controlling the car's throttle with a cable in his hand. More often, he is said to have had one of Rita's hatpins with him in the car and jabbed her with it when he wanted her to go faster. Rita, although inexperienced, won the race from Kay Petre in her Bugatti and Psyche Altham in her MG Magnette. Kay, always magnanimous, never complained. That was not her style. She was not averse to garnering a little advantage herself, as the LCC Relay story shows.

Relationships between groups of women are usually characterised as fickle and bitchy, but this does not seem to be true of the Brooklands ladies. They cannot all have been particular friends with one another, but most of them seemed happy to compete with and against one another. WASA provided one outlet for female solidarity, entering teams into relay races such as the Team Relay Handicap in June, just before the Gala. Margaret Allan joined forces with Lotte Schwedler and Geraldine Hedges. Margaret is another unaccountable absentee from the Gala. She was a fine driver and won the Junior Long Handicap at the 1933 Inter-Club Meeting driving a tricky Bentley known as 'Old Mother Gun'. Her opponents included Kay Petre and Paddie Naismith. She won three more Brooklands handicaps between then and 1935.

Bill Wisdom was also a member of WASA. In a 1934 interview she was asked by Mrs Sam Sloan what her 'favourite thrill' in a car was. She replied that overtaking was her favourite, but that she got a lot out of hillclimbs and that she had enjoyed a WASA trial to Westward Ho! Joan Chetwynd and Victoria Worsley were also WASA members.

Geraldine Hedges, who drove a Talbot in the Gala, usually shared her car with Patricia McOstrich. Patricia did not race in the Duchess of York race, but she was an entrant in the WASA Handicap in the same car. The car nominally belonged to Geraldine and one or another of the two women would race it at a time. They are normally described as 'good friends' or 'close friends' and may have been in a romantic relationship. Neither married, and both left their fortunes to an unrelated spinster when they died. As we saw in the last chapter, this was not as unusual as we might think. The same was true of Daisy Addis-Price who was one of the regulars in the ladies' races of the 1920s.

Both Geraldine Hedges and Patricia McOstrich won races at Brooklands: Geraldine in the Talbot, and Patricia in a Frazer Nash in 1937. Geraldine also drove a Frazer Nash in 1936, when she was part of a three-car, all-female, all Frazer Nash team for the LCC Relay. Her teammates were Kay Petre and Lady Makins, who shared her car with Kay and needed her help during a breakdown. They were eighth overall.

Patricia ran her own garage, Speedy Transport & Garage. She contributed to a careers guide for girls, writing about opportunities in the motor industry. Interestingly, she did not recommend motorsport to her readers as a career, unless they had 'plenty of money' and did not expect to earn a living from it.

Lady Makins was almost certainly Dorothy Makins, wife of a baronet, Sir Paul Makins. Her only other motorsport experience seems to have been the phoney 'Society Ladies' Private Handicap' the year before. Although it was reviled at the time, some of the 'Society Ladies' did try some legitimate motor racing. Three were in action at the Gala: Joan Chetwynd, Dorothy de Clifford and Paddie Naismith. The Brooklands sisterhood seems to have been rather forgiving to those who had got involved in silly escapades. As we have seen in Chapter 2, society ladies were natural committee women, and their organisational clout would have been very useful at the circuit.

Rallies offered another opportunity for teamwork. Joan Richmond had begun her European career in rallying as part of a three-woman Riley team with Kathleen Howell and Jean Robertson. They entered the 1932 Monte Carlo Rally but chose Melbourne, Australia as their starting point and drove overland to Monaco. All three made it, and Joan was seventeenth overall. Jean was nineteenth. Kathleen and Jean had come from another scene of female teamwork around motoring, Alice Anderson's Motor Service garage. Alice Anderson ran an all-female repair garage and car-and-driver hire firm. Both Kathleen and Jean and possibly Joan too had studied car maintenance with Alice, who trained female mechanics and drivers.

Later in the year at the RAC Rally, Joan and Jean teamed up again, this time starting from the more sensible point of Leamington Spa. The following season, Joan and Kay Petre rallied together on the Monte and the RAC Rally in a Riley. The Monte also had Bill Wisdom and Morna Vaughan competing together in a Standard. Some trans-national pairings happened, including Kay Petre and the French racer Anne-Cécile Rose-Itier. They drove an Austin Grasshopper. Kay considered Anne to be one of her favourite teammates, although her pacenotes were often reduced to 'Kay Stop' or 'Stoppez!' Their partnership was rekindled after the Second World War.

All-female teams in the major Brooklands races were quite rare, but in the continental classics they were common at the time. Women drivers were a feature of Le Mans throughout the 1930s. The first ones were Frenchwomen, Odette Siko and Marguerite Mareuse, who were seventh in the 1930 race driving a Bugatti T40.

At the Sarthe circuit, 1935 was the year of the lady driver. In that year's 24 Hours, ten female drivers took part. Six of these were from the Anglo-Australian MG team run by George Eyston. They were later dubbed 'The Dancing Daughters', probably after something from a radio programme. At the time, they were referred to as 'George's Young Ladies'.

Joan Richmond and Eveline Gordon-Simpson shared one MG Midget PA. They finished in twenty-fourth place and were the first home of the Young Ladies. Doreen Evans and Barbara Skinner were not long after them in twenty-fifth and Colleen Eaton and Margaret Allan were twenty-sixth.

With the exception of Colleen Eaton and Barbara Skinner, a hillclimb specialist who drove a Morris Minor, the Young Ladies were all Brooklands regulars and it is quite surprising that none of them raced at the Gala. Colleen was Australian and does not appear to have done much in the way of circuit racing apart from Le Mans.

Doreen Evans could have been excused for her absence from the Guys Gala as she was only 16 years old at the time and not yet able to drive. Having said that, she did learn as soon as she could, and she was racing an MG single-seater from the age of 17. By 1934, she was taking part in the aforementioned LCC Relay and was one of the thwarted MG team who finished third. She was from a family of racers and along with her two brothers, Kenneth and Dennis, campaigned a number of MGs throughout the 1930s. To begin with she entered a lot of trials, including several organised by WASA. She won a Ladies' Mountain Handicap at Brooklands in October 1934, the same race from which Fay Taylour was excluded. In 1935, she won the Second New Haw Short Handicap in a Q-Type, defeating Kay Petre and five men. That year, she was seventh in the JCC's International Trophy, driving solo in an R-Type this time. At the same event in 1936 she had a lucky escape in the R-Type. She jumped out of the burning car, which then rolled down the banking towards where she was running away. Miraculously, she was unhurt.

None of the other women of 1935 finished, but then again, many all-male teams did not make it either. Kay Petre and Elsie Wisdom drove a Riley together, the two Brooklands golden girls as teammates for once. Gwenda Stewart, Kay's conqueror in the speed record runs, shared a Derby with Charlesworth. She tended to prefer male co-drivers, although pictures and articles show that she was happy to socialise with other motorsporting women.

Gwenda shared the Derby-Miller with Pat Driscoll for the 1935 Brooklands Racing Drivers' Club (BRDC) 500 Miles although they did not finish. She drove a Duesenberg in the 1936 500-Mile race with George Duller and they were seventh.

Anne-Cécile Rose-Itier also had a male teammate in Robert Jacob. Anne was the highest-placed woman that year, having steered her Fiat Balilla to eighteenth place. She would compete at Le Mans on four occasions, the last being in 1938 when she was twelfth in an MG Midget with Pierre Bonneau.

Of course, the Brooklands ladies often formed teams with their male counterparts. There was no prohibition on this. Bill Wisdom usually rallied alongside Tommy, her husband. Victoria Worsley, who was in action at the Gala, was a member of WASA and certainly not the sort of woman who did not rate other women. However, her best drives tended to come in the company of male teammates. Her career was quite short, lasting between 1928 and 1932, and the Gala was one of her final events. The best result of her career was probably a seventh place in the 1931 Double Twelve, sharing an Austin Seven with Latham Boote. Adrian Conan Doyle, brother of Arthur, was another teammate of Victoria's in the 1932 LCC Relay but they did not finish. Victoria was driving a 'Worsley-Harris Special'. Stories abound of the pitlane parties that surrounded Victoria's teams, with gramophones playing and picnics.

Victoria was another female racer who built up something of a persona for herself. She always cast herself as a bit of a chancer and claimed that she could not afford to own a racing car of her own, so she always borrowed or shared them. For employment, she acted as a chauffeur to her father. That her father was a baronet and that her niece Katharine would become the Duchess of Kent suggests that there was some disingenuity at play here, although she could have been referring to ready cash rather than wealth. Victoria's career ended with her marriage to Roland King-Farlow, a timekeeper at Brooklands.

Both Margaret Allan and Doreen Evans' careers declined very sharply after their marriages. The latter moved to America, and though she continued to love speed and adrenalin, she never competed again. During the war, she drove her father up Pike's Peak for fun. She also loved to ski, and fly aeroplanes.

We might expect this to be a common motif in the motor racing world of the 1930s but it is not usually the case. Both Bill Wisdom and Kay Petre took up the sport after they were married, in Bill's case, encouraged by her husband. Joan Chetwynd shared her passion for fast cars with her husband, and Gwenda Stewart shared hers with all three of her husbands. Another entrant in the WASA race at the Gala was Dorothy Barnato, who was married to Bentley Boy Woolf

Barnato at the time. The fact that her racing career did not seem to continue was perhaps down to her divorce the following year.

The most famous mixed team of the time was probably the Austin works squad of 1937. Kay Petre drove the little side-valve car while Bert Hadley and Charles Goodacre used the more conventional Austin Sevens. Both Hadley and Goodacre were young, younger than Kay, and it always looks as if the three of them enjoyed racing together. Kay and Bert Hadley first teamed up for the Empire Trophy at Donington, which was never Kay's favourite circuit. Hadley was twelfth but Kay did not finish. At the same track in June, all three retired from the Nuffield Trophy. An oil pipe on Kay's car had fractured, spraying her with hot fluid.

They raced at Brooklands Crystal Palace as well as Donington, and took part in hillclimbs at Shelsley Walsh. Their most successful venture together was a win in the 1937 JCC Relay, all three driving Austin Sevens.

In September, Kay's time with Austin came to an abrupt end. She was practising for the BRDC 500 at Brooklands when Reg Parnell's MG slid down the banking and clipped her Austin, sending it into a violent roll and throwing Kay on to the concrete. She was seriously injured and in a coma for some time. The accident made the front page of the *Daily Sketch*.

Kay did recover, although she needed corrective surgery on her face. This was the beginning of the end of her career. Interestingly, she was visited in hospital by none other than Bernd Rosemeyer, who left his British Grand Prix winner's garland for her. Kay had befriended him in South Africa earlier in the year when she went over for the Grand Prix season there. A 1500cc Riley was sent over for her to race, but it was down on power. A new engine Kay had been promised had not been fitted. In true Kay style, she raced anyway. She did not manage to finish the South African or Rand Grands Prix, but she was sixth in the Grosvenor Grand Prix.

The exact details of her meeting with Rosemeyer are not quite clear, but the two became friends. Inevitably, rumours of an affair started. These were denied by Elly Beinhorn, Bernd Rosemeyer's wife. She always defended Kay when asked about this. In a 2003 interview, when she was 95, she remembered Kay as 'so sweet, a real personality' and 'a good driver, above average. She didn't dare to start any flirt with Bernd because she immediately understood she was going nowhere.' If this sounds somewhat defensive, she also said that she and Kay were friends.

Kay and Elly were the only two women ever to drive the Auto Union C, a 6-litre, V16 monster. Kay said at the time that she did not drive it very far and she did not go anywhere near as fast as the car was capable of going.

After her rehabilitation from her 1937 crash, she never raced at Brooklands again, although she did do some hillclimbs and took part in a ladies' race at Crystal Palace against Anne Itier and Bill Wisdom, among others. By this time, Bernd Rosemeyer had died during a speed record attempt in Germany.

Kay's attempt to get back to a semblance of normality took another blow when she was involved in another accident at Brooklands, this time as a spectator. A car slid off the track and she was caught in the carnage, suffering more facial injuries.

At the same time, she was petitioning for Reg Parnell to have his racing licence restored. He was blamed for her 1937 crash and banned from racing. Kay never held him responsible and took her accident as a predictable risk of her trade. Parnell got back to the track fairly quickly; he also resumed his career after the war and was an early British Formula One driver.

Unbelievably, her life hit another setback in 1939. She was following the Monte Carlo Rally as a motoring writer for the *Daily Sketch* and driving a fellow writer, Reggie Empson, to the start. Her car collided with a lorry and Empson was killed. Kay endured more head and facial injuries. She then had to go through a manslaughter trial. Although she was not found guilty, she was ordered to pay £4,000 in costs to Empson's widow, Stella. Photographs of Kay in old age always show her with a lacquered mask of makeup, which may have been to cover scars.

The last couple of years of Brooklands' existence were without its Anglo-Canadian superstar, but another lady driver came through and replaced her somewhat. Dorothy Stanley-Turner had the same winning way with men and a very Kay-like cheek and charm. Sammy Davis said of her, 'there has … never been anybody better at getting her own way by looking delightfully helpless plus a masterly control of very bright blue eyes.'

Dorothy was the last woman driver to win at the circuit before its closure in 1939. She drove an MG Q-Type to victory in that year's First August Mountain Handicap. This was her second overall win after a victory in the 1937 Second Easter Road Handicap.

She did not start her career until 1937 so was not in the running for the Duchess of York's race, but she was very much part of the female network based around Brooklands. Joan Chetwynd taught her to drive and when she was unable to take part in the 1938 Le Mans 24 Hours, Bill Wisdom stepped in to take her place in the MG PB she had prepared. She did at least one Monte Carlo Rally with Morna Vaughan of WASA.

Her first Le Mans appearance was in another PB owned by George Eyston, of 'Young Ladies' fame, in 1937. She shared the car with Enid Riddell, whom we met in the previous chapter. They were sixteenth overall. This race produced one of the best examples of Dorothy's powers of persuasion: when the car's fuel cap failed, she improvised a repair using an orange as a replacement cap. Somehow, the watching officials were convinced by her that this did not contravene any rules, and that she should be allowed to proceed.

She was not quite as lucky in the Nuffield Trophy that preceded Le Mans, and it was probably a good thing. A stone had flown up from the track surface into her MG and hit her in the eye. She received prompt first aid and suffered no permanent damage, but as soon as she was patched up, she was trying to get back in her car. An official wisely prevented her from doing so.

The war put an end to racing at Brooklands. The track was sold and used as a military airfield. After the war ended in 1945, the track was never reopened.

The Brooklands ladies, like the socially conscious society ladies who preceded them, contributed a lot to the war effort. Dorothy Stanley-Turney joined the WAAF. Joan Chetwynd also embarked on a military career, becoming an officer in the WAAC. Gwenda

Stewart became a skilled lathe operator in a munitions factory. Even Kay Petre, who was still recovering from her head injuries and working as a journalist, volunteered her services to the Ministry of Food. She wrote articles on cooking with rations and on a budget. In typical Kay style, she had gone into journalism claiming to be incapable of writing, spelling correctly or typing, but proved quite a success.

Some were not able to assist with the war effort. Lotte Schwedler spent the war interned as a 'hostile alien' due to her German passport. She spent some time on the Isle of Man, effectively a prisoner.

A few of the Brooklands ladies returned to circuit racing after the war. New tracks were gradually built, often on the sites of former airfields, like Silverstone. However, actual motor racing was slow to get started again and opportunities were much more limited than before. For a start, there were no new cars. The country was still very much in austerity mode and motorsport was a low priority.

The social climate had also changed. Women were shunted out of industry to make way for returning men. The national mood was one of longing for the comfort of home and reassuring social order, encouraged and emphasised by advertising. In a way, it harked back to a time before the First World War, almost. Even fashion started referencing the Victorian period, as if the more streamlined, modern silhouettes of the 1920s and 1930s were a temporary aberration borne of necessity. Women as racing drivers no longer looked quite as forward-thinking or glamorous.

This was not the end for women in motorsport, by any means. Largely without access to competitive racing cars, or a place to compete, they turned to rallying, which could be done on open roads and in production vehicles. Bill Wisdom was one of the first to venture out again. In 1948 she entered the Monte Carlo Rally with Betty Haig and Barbara Marshall, in a Morris Minor. She went on to rally with Sheila van Damm at the start of her career, and with Tommy once more. This lasted until they had another big crash on the 1953 Alpine Rally, after which she scaled back her competition calendar. However, she was still active as late as 1955, when she was sixty-eighth on the Monte in an Austin.

The female motorsport network grew some more branches. Bill's daughter, Ann, became navigator to Pat Moss, winning two rallies outright with her. Both Sheila van Damm and Nancy Mitchell, who would win European Ladies' Championships within the next decade, benefited from Bill's expertise.

Lotte Schwedler also emerged unscathed from the war. She was released from internment and became a British citizen in 1947. Her name became Charlotte Sadler. Between 1950 and 1953, she rallied a Hillman Minx around Europe, sometimes assisted by Hazel Dunham, Gerry Dunham's daughter. The Tulip Rally in the Netherlands became a particular favourite of hers. She finally hung up her helmet for good in 1959.

The closest thing to the Brooklands ladies' set after the war was probably the British contingent in the European Rally Championship. Anne Hall, a successful driver in her own right, spent two years as navigator to Sheila van Damm in a Sunbeam. Lola Grounds and Mary Handley-Page were two other female drivers who switched seats with ease in the 1950s. Francoise Wilton Clarke, French-born, sat beside Lola, Mary and Sheila at different times.

The closeness of some of the women is shown in photos from a party hosted by Lorna Doone Snow in 1962. Lorna was a sometime rally driver herself, content to cash in on her society connections and party-girl lifestyle but sometimes quite effective in a Jaguar. She brought together a group of women who had driven in the Monte Carlo Rally. In the newspaper report of her get-together, she claimed that she had invited a group of elite rally drivers and made them undergo matching hairstyles. Lorna's victims included Mary Handley-Page, Sheila van Damm and Francoise Clarke. Pat Moss and her navigator, Ann Wisdom were also there, with Pat's brother Stirling Moss as a token male guest (it is not clear whether or not he had a makeover). It is worth mentioning that the Moss siblings had Aileen Craufurd Moss as their mother; she had raced and rallied a Marendaz at Brooklands in the 1920s.

Another guest of honour was a 59-year-old Kay Petre. She had since retired from her job as colour consultant for BMC, where she had overseen the interior designs for the Mini. Her multiple head injuries had caught up with her and she had been suffering with headaches and memory problems. I believe that her last outing in a car on a track had been the previous year; she drove some demonstration laps in a side-valve Austin at Oulton Park. Margaret Jennings, the former Margaret Allan, had joined her on track.

Kay maintained an interest in motorsport for some time afterwards. She became friends with hillclimber Joy Rainey and often watched her race. However, towards the end of her life, she became less and less willing to talk about it. She devoted a lot of time to playing bridge and enjoyed an active social life in London, despite being a widow. She died in 1993.

Bill Wisdom died suddenly in 1972. She was 68. Eileen Ellison did not live to enjoy her old age either, dying of liver cancer in 1967 aged 57. She too was a widow, having lost her husband Brian during the war.

Before her death, Eileen emigrated to South Africa, where she married Owen Fargus. They travelled a lot and entertained widely. Eileen developed a love of open-water swimming; she brushed off concerns about man-eating sharks in the South African waters by claiming that they did not eat women.

Travel and the sea featured prominently in Gwenda Stewart's later life, also. She settled down, if that is the right word, to a globe-trotting lifestyle aboard a boat, with her third husband, Douglas Hawkes. They spent a lot of time in the Greek Islands. She died aged 96, in 1990.

Chapter 6

Good Old Gals

10 July 1949, Daytona Beach

NASCAR Strictly Stock Series, Round 2
1. Red Byron (Oldsmobile)
2. Tim Flock (Oldsmobile)
3. Frank Mundy (Oldsmobile)
4. Joe Littlejohn (Oldsmobile)
5. Bill Blair (Lincoln)
6. Frank Christian (Oldsmobile)
7. Bill Snowden (Mercury)
8. Gober Sosebee (Oldsmobile)
9. Jimmy Thompson (Chrysler)
10. Jack Etheridge (Mercury)
11. Ethel Mobley (Cadillac)
12. Herb Thomas (Ford)
13. Slick Smith (Buick)
14. Marshall Teague (Hudson)
15. Billy Carden (Ford)
16. Howard Elder
17. Woodie Wilson (Mercury)
18. Sara Christian (Ford)
19. Fonty Flock (Hudson)
20. Louise Smith (Ford)
21. Buckshot Morris (Ford)
22. Buck Baker (Kaiser)
23. Bob Flock (Ford)
24. Sam Marshall (Hudson)
25. Curtis Turner (Buick)
26. Fred Johnson (Ford)

27. Benny Georgeson (Buick)
28. Glenn Dunnaway (Lincoln)

Motorsport in the US, in the first two-thirds of the twentieth century, was not normally a welcoming space for women. As we have seen before, women drivers were banned from most formal competitions in 1909, and if they wanted to compete at all they had to go abroad, or join up with one of the promoters of dirt-track and fairground racing, who would probably give them some track time for demo runs or speed trials, and perhaps let them race from time to time.

NASCAR today retains a defiantly macho, distinctively Southern, and quite traditional image, so it is a surprise that female drivers have been part of it from the very beginning. Some of its early protagonists, particularly Richard Petty, have said disparaging things about female racers, and its most visible female presences are trackside beauty queens, and drivers' consorts.

Perhaps if we look at NASCAR in its historical context, the presence of three ladies on its second-ever starting grid makes more sense. North American Stock Car racing was the brainchild of Bill France, a racer himself and a promoter. His background was the dirt and board tracks of the racecourses and fairgrounds. When he created Strictly Stock in 1949, it was intended as a reputable governing body for oval racing, where professional drivers would get the chance to compete away from unscrupulous fairground promoters, who often ran off with their money.

NASCAR and Strictly Stock were also run independently of the AAA, which was America's leading sanctioning authority for motorsport. Crucially, it was the AAA who barred women from its competitions in 1909. Dirt oval racing, from which NASCAR evolved, was the traditional territory of the female racer. The likes of Alex Sloan and Omar Tofts understood the publicity value of women in fast cars, and Bill France was wise to it, too.

The second Strictly Stock event at Daytona was not the first time women had graced the NASCAR ovals. The first round, held at Charlotte, had Sara Christian taking to the track. She was driving a 1947 Ford, one of the oldest cars in the field, and was classified fourteenth. She completed just under 150 laps of the 200-lap race due to her car overheating. Some sources claim that she handed the car over to Bob Flock after thirty-eight laps, but she is usually credited as its driver.

Sara came into motorsport through her husband, Frank, a racer and successful team owner between 1949 and 1955. She was 31 in 1949, and had two children. Frank and Sara lived in Atlanta, Georgia, which was Sara's home state. As well as being a team owner and having numerous other legitimate business interests, Frank was involved in the illegal trade in alcohol. 'Moonshiners' driving loads of prohibited liquor across the US were part of the lore of early NASCAR.

Sara's 1949 Charlotte start was the beginning of a series of firsts for her: she was the first woman to start a NASCAR race, then became one of the first women to race against another woman in a NASCAR race. During the same race, Frank drove one of his team's cars, making it the first time that a husband and wife had competed against each other.

In September 1949, she finished sixth at Langhorne Motor Speedway, making her the first woman to finish in the top ten of a NASCAR event. She followed this up with a fifth place at Heidelberg. She was thirteenth in the first championship.

Relatively little seems to be known about Sara as a person. She is described in some contemporary newspaper reports as a 'housewife', although it is likely that she assisted Frank in at least some of his business activities. Later, these included a farm and a motel.

Her first race is said to have been in 1948, at the newly constructed New Atlanta Speedway, which Frank had a hand in creating with Bob Flock and Charlie Mobley. One of its opening events was to be a ladies' race, between Sara, her sister Mildred Williams and Ethel Flock Mobley, who was Bob Flock's sister and Charlie Mobley's wife. Sara won, and ignited her interest in the sport. Sara and the others may have competed in other ladies' races, but actual results are very hard to come by.

Mildred Williams never progressed to anything like Strictly Stock, but Ethel Flock Mobley did. It was almost inevitable, given how both her and her husband's families were involved with the

Above: 1970 World Cup Rally, Bron Burrell, Tina Kerridge and Tish Ozanne.

Right: Anita Taylor's official picture for the 1967 12 Hours of Sebring programme.

Above: Bron Burrell, Tina Kerridge and Tish Ozanne with Puff the Magic Wagon at the start of the 1970 World Cup Rally.

Below: The 'Carmen Curls' all-female racing team, with drivers Gabriel Konig and Micki Vandervell, raced in the 1971 Formula F100 championship with a glamorous crew of lap timers and pit signallers. They were sponsored by Carmen hair products and their team uniforms included the 'latest fashion wig' from Carmen.

Janet Guthrie, appearing as a Ring Free Motor Maid in the programme for the 1967 12 Hours of Sebring.

Lea Lemoine on her Clement – De Dion tricycle, winner of the first-known race for women in Paris in 1897.

Lella Lombardi, the only woman to score points in a Formula One championship race.

Above: Liane Engeman poses on a Mini before the 1967 Sebring 12 Hours.

Below: On-track action at the 1900 Ranelagh Gymkhana, scene of the first-ever women's circuit race in the UK.

Above and below: Rivals Helle Nice and Violette Morris took opposing approaches to life and style.

Who was Who in the Motor Gala—at Brooklands.

Miss Betty Stockfield at the wheel of a 1900 Benz.

Mrs. George Duller with the award-winning Rolls-Royce.

Miss Sheila Macdonald adjusting Miss Paddy Naismith's crash helmet.

Miss Ellison, winner of the Duchess of York's race receiving the trophy from H.R.H.

Miss Katherine Horlick & Miss Betty McGowan.

Mrs. Peter Gold & Miss Sylvia Tolhurst

A GALA afternoon with a good racing programme and a Concours d'Élégance was organised by the Junior Car Club at Brooklands in aid of Guy's Hospital. The Duke and Duchess of York were present to watch the racing, and her Royal Highness presented the prizes. The Duchess's race for women-drivers was won by Miss Ellison with her Bugatti. A bevy of Society girls sold programmes. This attractive company included Miss Katherine Horlick, Miss Diana Coventry, daughter of the Hon. Mrs. Charles Coventry, and Miss Jean Longsden, daughter of Mrs. Washington Singer.

Lady Weigall (in wheel chair), Mr. Frank Freeman and programme-sellers, Miss Diana Coventry, Miss Betty McGowan, Miss Peggy Gordon Moore, Miss Jean Longsden

Competitors in the Concours d'Élégance: Miss Heather Angel, Miss Renée Gadd, Miss Molly Lamont, Miss Betty Stockfield.

PHOTOGRAPHS BY PLANET, BARRATTS, S. AND G., ALFIERI, AND L.N.A.

The Daily Sketch details some of the female contributions to the Brooklands Guys Gala in 1932.

The frontispiece of Dorothy Levitt's 1909 book, The Woman and the Car.

sport. Ethel's brothers, Tim, Bob and Fonty, were stalwarts of the early stock car racing scene. There had been nine Flock children altogether; the youngest was Charles, who died in infancy. Tim was the youngest surviving child. Ethel's elder sister, Reo, died in 1936, of tuberculosis. Reo had been a pilot and wingwalker since her teenage years. The eldest Flock was Carl, who raced speedboats and took over his father's bootlegging business after his death in 1928. Lee, their father, was meant to have named Ethel after the fuel he put in his taxi (her name is occasionally spelt 'Ethyl'), just as he had named Reo after a make of American car.

None of the other Flocks was involved in motorsport, although Ruby Flock, wife of Bob, owned a car which she entered for other drivers occasionally.

In keeping with the family nature of NASCAR, which continues to this day with the Earnhardt and Petty dynasties, Ethel and Sara Christian may have been related to one another. Sara's maiden name was Williams, as was that of 'Big Mama' Maudie Flock, Ethel's mother. They were both from bootlegging families, and the elder Flock brothers were said to have been employed by an uncle known as 'Peachtree' Williams, as drivers, until Peachtree's murder. Both families also hailed from, or lived in, Atlanta. (The Flocks originated from Alabama, but lived and raced in Georgia.)

Ethel Flock Mobley enjoyed a longer racing career than Sara Christian, who retired in 1950 after one more Strictly Stock race. She only ever competed in two top-level NASCAR races, but she took part in over a hundred Modified stock car races from about 1939 onwards.

Her second Strictly Stock outing was at Langhorne Motor Speedway, again in Charlie's Cadillac. She retired early on, and was classified 44 out of 45 entries.

Ethel may not have been NASCAR's first female driver, but she could lay claim to a couple of firsts of her own: she was part of the first brother-sister entry in NASCAR, and the Daytona race was the only time that four siblings had competed directly against each other. She was very pleased to have beaten both Bob and Fonty this time.

Piecing together the rest of Ethel's racing career is quite difficult. Many reports talk of a 'driving competition' in Florida in June 1949, in which she took on fifty-seven men, and finished eighth. There was a circuit at Tampa, Speedway Park, which did host a meeting on 12 June 1949, although the results are lost. This track was a half-mile dirt oval. There was also Tampa Fields fairground track, although there is no record of a meeting there in June, and details about it are generally scarce. There were also no relevant meetings at Daytona in June, and Bill France would have jumped at the chance of using Ethel as a promotional tool, had she finished eighth there. Another alternative is that this 'driving competition' was some sort of rally or gymkhana event, rather than a race.

She did race at Macon in Georgia, becoming the first woman driver to compete against men at Central City Park Speedway in August. She was sixteenth.

It is unclear how many of her reported hundred Modified races were women's events, or 'powderpuff derbies'. In 1950, she was definitely third in an 'Amateur Sportsman' race at Orange Speedway, competing against Sara Christian. That year, she raced at Langhorne again, while her brothers tackled the Grand National race, although her finishing position and her class have been lost.

Ethel continued to race after the birth of her first daughter, Darlene, but when Darlene's younger sister came along in 1952, Charlie became less supportive of his wife's racing activities and she retired. Darlene has written about her mother, with whom she had a good relationship. The two were photographed several times at different circuits.

The NASCAR woman with the most longevity was Daytona's twentieth-place finisher, Louise Smith. As well as enjoying the longest career of any of the early female drivers, she has inspired more stories than any of the others, some of which may even be true.

Estimates for her first year of competition range from 1946 to 1949. One story that is often repeated is this one: Louise was invited to race at Greenville-Pickens by Bill France, who had heard of her reputation as a fast road driver who could outrun any police officer. She was duly provided with a racing car, given the instruction to drive fast and not stop unless she saw a red flag. She finished third in her first event (some versions have her winning it), and, not recognising the chequered flag, continued to charge around the track, until an official finally stopped her by waving a red flag. Prior to this experience, she had apparently never seen a race nor been near a track.

Other stories have been advanced of her smashing up her husband's car at Daytona during her first race. Louise herself spoke about her debut in the Columbia Record in 1965. She said that a car builder named Hickey Nickles offered her a drive in a women's race at Greenville, which she won despite the flag incident.

Noah, her husband, did not race himself, although he was in the automotive trade, running a junkyard. She did crash at Daytona in 1947, and apparently was driving a Ford in road trim. The story goes that she had told Noah she was going on holiday.

Louise's background of fast driving and evading the law was never fully explained. She always distanced herself from talk of her being a bootlegger but never offered much of an alternative view. The rumours about her continued, and if all accounts are to be believed, she was a bar brawler who took on all-comers, male and female, who could drink any of them under the table and beat any of them at cards. Not long before she died in 2006, she told historian Deb Williams that 'if you won a race, you had to fight. You might as well get out swinging a tire tool or something'. She was, according to her own legends, a true 'good ol' gal', in the style of the oldest of old-school stock car drivers.

Louise's early racing exploits were mostly at small dirt tracks in South Carolina, and the results are not forthcoming. After she had been spotted by Bill France, she did travel quite widely, and competed as far afield as Canada. She is said to have won thirty-eight races during her ten-year career, some of which came before her NASCAR debut. Most of these were in the Modified class, and a few were in midget racing.

The July 1949 Daytona race was her first official NASCAR event. She was 20, driving her own 1947 Ford. She took part in two more Strictly Stock races that year, at Occoneechee and Langhorne respectively, finishing twenty-seventh and sixteenth. Her Ford at Occoneechee was sponsored by her husband's firm, Smith Auto Parts.

She had another season in NASCAR in 1950, and entered five Grand National events. The first of these was the season opener at

Daytona. It ended shortly after it had begun, with a crash on the first lap that left Louise's Ford upside down. This dramatic accident may have got mixed up in the stories of her destroying Noah's car during her first race.

Her second race was at Langhorne, a track with which she had some familiarity. This time, it was the car itself that let her down; she was classified twenty-fifth after retiring just over half way with engine trouble. She was then nineteenth at Dayton, this time driving a Nash entered by the Leslie Motor Co. She crashed out again at Hamburg, then was nineteenth at Occoneechee. She was still in the Nash.

Her last top-level NASCAR races were in 1952, after a year's break. That year, she drove a self-entered Oldsmobile, which overheated during her first race, at Central City Speedway. Engine problems struck again at Langhorne, then she was ill for the Morristown race, and had to drop out very early on.

In addition to driving, Louise acted as a car entrant for J. O. Staton, who drove her Ford. His car was also struck by mechanical gremlins. Louise continued to enter her cars for other drivers, off and on, for many years, long after she herself retired in 1956.

Before she bowed out, there was still some room for her reputation as a crash-happy driver to grow. Her worst accident was probably at Hillsborough, when she flipped her car off the track and into a neighbouring wood, landing on the roof. She escaped serious injury and even posed for pictures with the written-off car afterwards. At other times, she was not quite so lucky. It was good fortune that stopped her from picking up any life-changing injuries, but she had her share of broken bones and hospital stays.

The end of Louise's career was as sudden as its beginning, and has the same aura of apocrypha about it. One night in 1956, she was meant to have been setting off for a race the following day, but she told her team that she wasn't coming, as she had been 'saved' that evening. Noah Smith, increasingly unsupportive of his wife's sporting activities, had enlisted the help of a local pastor in persuading her to give up motor racing. It is hard to believe that someone apparently as strong-willed as Louise would be swayed by the words of a common preacher. We can only guess what ultimata, threats and emotional blackmail may have taken place.

She did, as mentioned before, continue as a car entrant, on and off, until the 1970s, and she enjoyed watching stock cars into later life. However, for a long time after her withdrawal from the tracks, her main involvement with the sport was her patronage of the Miss Southern 500 beauty pageant for 'race queens'. This event began as part of the build-up for the 1955 Southern 500 at Darlington Speedway.

Bill France's initial experiment with women drivers did not fizzle out due to their lack of talent, but seemingly due to unsupportive partners and the pressures of home and family. Louise Smith retired to become a good Christian wife (although she was never a mother) and henceforth remained femininely in the background, letting others do the driving. Ethel Flock Mobley could not juggle a racing career, the demands of another child and the expectations of a husband. Sara Christian, probably the most naturally talented of the three, simply disappeared from the entry lists, although Frank Christian continued as a multi-car team owner until 1955.

NASCAR's three First Ladies were not the only ones to take to the track in the early days of the series. Ann Chester raced against Louise Smith and Sara Christian in 1950, driving a 1947 Plymouth in the Hamburg Grand National event. Like Smith, she crashed out, just before half distance. This was her second NASCAR race, the first having been at Vernon Fairgrounds raceway in New York. She was just in the classification in twenty-second place, following engine trouble.

Ann was from New York, a quite different background to the traditionally Southern women drivers before her. Another New Yorker who tried her hand at NASCAR that year was Ann Bunselmeyer, who raced a Packard at the Vernon track in October. She was sixteenth, in a Packard. The Vernon race was her only NASCAR appearance.

Another Ann, Ann Slaasted, made a single NASCAR start in 1950. She was driving a Lincoln, and finished twenty-second at Dayton. Ann hailed from the north of the country too, although she was a Midwesterner from Wisconsin, rather than a New Yorker.

These three drivers are all rather obscure, and had very brief careers. None of the three seems to have been married to other drivers, team owners or promoters, and it is likely that they had built up some racing experience on the dirt tracks of their home states.

Even more obscure is Dorothy Shull, who tried to qualify for the 1950 Southern 500, in an Oldsmobile. Louise Smith did not qualify that year either. Dorothy was born in 1925 and died in 1999, but other than that, little is known about her. A woman named Dorothy Baldwin raced against Sara Christian at a New York fairground in 1949, and this could be the same person, competing under a maiden name, although this is guesswork.

A few seasons later, in 1954, another two women made their NASCAR Grand National debuts. Both were from California. Marian Pagan, known as 'Mopsy', entered her local race at Oakland, driving a Plymouth. She had an unremarkable but clean race, and was eighteenth.

Marian was married to racer and car owner, Eddie Pagan. Her racing background was the women's stock car (jalopy) league in California. This was an active sporting association, which attempted to distance itself from 'powderpuff derbies' by adopting the epithet 'Lady Leadfoots' for its members.

Despite hailing from the same state and being active at the same time, FiFi Scott does not appear to have been one of the Lady Leadfoots. She first appears in the Pacific Late Model division, driving a Hudson at Sacramento. She did not finish, due to clutch problems. The following year, she entered the Hudson into two Grand National races, at Phoenix and Tucson in Arizona. She went out with a puncture at Phoenix, but was thirteenth at Tucson.

The female NASCAR pioneers were mostly married to other racers, and this was reflected in lower-level stock car competition. As mentioned before, 'powderpuff' races were initially staged between the wives and girlfriends of drivers competing at that meet. This pattern of female participation was as old as US motorsport itself: in 1901, a race meeting at Joliet, Illinois featured a Ladies' Race, contested by Mrs Tucker and Mrs Burdett. Both of these ladies were married to fellow racers in action at the event.

One of the biggest problems faced by female drivers who got into the sport through their husbands was the lack of seat time. In most cases, a couple would share a car, and this meant that only one partner could enter the feature races. This was usually the man, who was often the titular owner of the car. In a way, powderpuff races were counter-productive for the women who raced in them, if they wanted to progress in the sport. Only women with access to their own racing car were able to enter the 'real' championships, score points and accumulate prize money.

This is not to say that women's races were completely ignored as a training ground for future drivers; Sara Christian and Ethel Flock Mobley both caught the attention of Bill France whilst racing against other women. However, they were often not taken seriously, and their results not recorded. The standards of driving could be poor, but this was almost to be expected when the participants had fewer opportunities to race than their male counterparts. It does not take into account either some of the shocking driving that could be encountered among male drivers, at any track.

Some groups of female drivers supported one another in gaining access to their own cars, and organising their own championships. The aforementioned Lady Leadfoots was one of these groups. The lynchpin of the Leadfoots was Hila Paulson, also known as Hila Sweet. She competed in some lower-level NASCAR races in 1956 and 1957, but never a Grand National event. Hila was originally married to Ummie Paulson, a mechanic and car owner. One of her earliest motorsport successes was helping to launch Parnelli Jones on to the national scene, in 1953, along with Ummie. The pair later divorced.

Much of Hila's career was spent racing against other women. She is said to have won fifty-eight races in a row, and at some point, she was asked to enter the main-draw, 'men's' races rather than the powderpuff events. As early as 1955, she was racing against both men and women, and at San Bernardino that year, she even took on Parnelli Jones in a match race, and won.

Both of Hila's NASCAR starts were at Gardena Stadium in California, the home track of the Leadfoots. On both occasions, she used a Chevrolet belonging to Ummie Paulson. In 1956, she parked up after twenty-one laps, and in 1957, she crashed out on the twelfth lap. Both of these races were part of the West Coast Late Model Division series.

Alongside Hila and Mopsy Pagan, other members of the Lady Leadfoots included Hila's sister, Edna Bates, and Mary Jo Erikson, who was married to another racer, Rip Erikson. There were, of course, many more of them than this, and Leadfoots came and went over the years. Hila Paulson Sweet at least tried some other racing disciplines during her career, and raced a Jaguar sportscar in a Ladies' Sports Car Club of America (SCCA) race at Ascot in 1959.

Women appeared at all levels of stock car competition, encouraged by the lower cost of entry and possibility of sharing a car with a partner or family member. Every local speedway seems to have had its own female star, although most of these only seem to be remembered as names now. Even the Colored Speedway Association, formed to allow black American drivers to race without prejudice, had at least a few.

After FiFi Scott disappeared from the scene, NASCAR itself became a firmly men-only enclave, with one or two exceptions. As at Indianapolis, women were banned from entering the pitlane. Even drivers' partners, who would become some of the most visible of the women of NASCAR, were excluded.

Between 1954 and 1957, a woman called Betty Skelton drove the pace car at Daytona for official NASCAR-sanctioned races. In 1957, this was a translucent gold Corvette that had been designed especially for her. Betty, a personal friend of Bill France, holds the honour of being the first woman to be granted a competition licence by the AAA in 1954, although she never did any competitive circuit racing. She did set a series of speed records, starting with a 105.88mph run at Daytona, in a Dodge stock car. Later, she would set new records at Bonneville, usually in a Corvette. Betty was an experienced aerobatic pilot, and in addition to her speed record attempts for General Motors, worked as an advertising executive for the company. As if this were not enough, she worked as a stunt performer for film and TV, and was part of a group of thirteen women who underwent assessments at

NASA, to determine whether women could be astronauts. Betty and the others performed well, but were never selected.

Proving that collective memories can be short when it comes to women's achievements in motorsport, a woman named Mary Skipper Allen was hailed as the first woman to enter a NASCAR race in 1964, despite that milestone having been passed fifteen years earlier. Mary, from Charlotte, attempted to qualify her 1962 Mercury for a race at Concord, but was five seconds off the qualifying time. The 'buxom redhead', whose story was reported extensively in the papers, did not try again.

It was not until 1965 that a woman would climb into a NASCAR stocker again, and even then, that was a one-off. Clemmons, South Carolina native Goldie Parsons raced Buck Baker's Oldsmobile in the 1965 Tidewater 300, finishing fourteenth. She was another driver who made her name in powderpuff derbies, winning a race at Cabarrus Twin City Speedway three months before her NASCAR debut. After Goldie parked up in 1965, NASCAR's top-level series would be all-male for another eleven years.

It is worth remembering that NASCAR was not the be-all and end-all of US stock car racing. Regional series of varying degrees of formality existed up and down the country and in Canada, far from the NASCAR heartlands of Georgia, the Carolinas and Florida. These championships for modified production cars were the most cost-effective forms of motorsport, as they did not require purpose-built racing chassis or lots of specialist parts. Keeping things regional meant that it was possible to get regular track time without expensive cross-country travel. Naturally, these factors made it easier for women racers to take part.

Women were active in stock car racing in Vermont, particularly at the Catamount stadium, and several female drivers from Canada crossed the border to compete there. Some of these drivers used stock cars as a stepping stone into road-course-based motorsport. One notable example of this was Monique Proulx, who raced Ministocks at Catamount, and went on to compete internationally in single-seater and sportscar races.

In 1976, a woman turned a NASCAR wheel in anger once more. Janet Guthrie made her debut at Charlotte, in May, driving Lynda

Ferreri's Chevrolet in the World 600. She finished the race in fifteenth place, twenty-one laps down but still in midfield.

Janet had already turned heads in 1976, when she attempted to qualify for the Indianapolis 500 in May, just before she took to the track at Charlotte. That month, she had also qualified for the Trenton Champ Car race, driving Rolla Vollstedt's car. She did not finish, but battled bravely during the race itself.

The press coverage that her qualification attempt earned impressed Charlotte's promoter, Humpy Wheeler, and its owner, Bruton Smith. They were looking for new ways to increase gate receipts and expand their audience, and were determined to get Janet Guthrie in a car at their track. Lynda Ferreri was a bank executive who had no experience of stock car racing whatsoever, but she knew the pair from her work with the local Chamber of Commerce and liked their idea, so agreed to come in as a car owner. The Chevrolet itself was bought by Smith, although he was keen to obscure that fact.

Janet's arrival at Charlotte polarised opinions. Richard Petty was not amused; he was quoted in the papers as saying 'She's no lady. If she was, she'd be at home. There's a lot of differences in being a lady and being a woman.' Hardly the words of a gentleman.

This is often thought to be NASCAR's default response to a female driver, but Janet's experiences at Charlotte showed that this was not always true. During her early qualifying sessions, she really struggled for pace in the car. Rival team owner Junior Johnson took an interest, and did not believe that Janet was really that slow. He got Cale Yarborough, his own driver, to test the Chevy, and he found it just as slow. Johnson then shared the set-up on his car with Janet's team, and they got her up to speed, and into the race. She qualified in twenty-seventh place.

The early women of NASCAR were all from similar backgrounds to their male rivals, but Janet Guthrie was not. She was from Iowa, and had a background in engineering. Her early motorsport experiences were in sportscars, before she switched her focus to single-seaters. She was highly educated and worked as a nuclear physicist when she was not racing. It was only due to a direct ban on female astronauts that she had not had a chance to get on to the space programme.

The likes of Petty were vocal about their mistrust of Janet, but Junior Johnson and Cale Yarborough obviously thought she deserved a chance, and were not threatened at all by her presence.

Janet made thirty-three NASCAR starts altogether, always driving Lynda Ferreri's car, and usually sponsored by Kelly Girl. He best year was 1977; she took part in nineteen out of thirty-three races, with a best finish of sixth, at Bristol. This was one of four top-ten finishes, the others being ninth places at Charlotte and Rockingham, and a tenth at Michigan.

That year, at the Firecracker 400 at Daytona, three women once more took their places on the grid. Janet Guthrie qualified twentieth then Lella Lombardi, the Italian ex-Formula One driver, in twenty-ninth and Christine Beckers, a versatile Belgian sportscar and rally driver, in thirty-seventh. Unfortunately, none of them finished: Guthrie went out early on with engine trouble, Christine Beckers' brakes failed, and Lella Lombardi crashed.

Before the race, the three drivers were invited on to the podium for a small presentation by the Grand Marshal, Lee Petty. Standing by was an older woman in a long formal dress, with huge hair and cat's-eye glasses. She was Louise Smith, now in her guise of raceway beauty pageant patron. According to people who met her in later life, Louise never lost her enthusiasm for NASCAR and stock car racing in general, and loved to spectate whenever she could.

Janet Guthrie raced on and off in the Winston Cup until 1980. She did not top her 1977 season, and the rest of them were much shorter. At the same time, she secured herself some more Indy rides, including three Indy 500 starts. In 1978, she finished ninth, after starting in fifteenth place. For many years, this was the highest finish for a woman at the Brickyard.

Janet's record was finally toppled in 2005, by Danica Patrick, who was fourth. In 2009, she would beat her own record with a third place. This came a year after her landmark win in the Motegi Indycar race. In 2014, driving for Newman-Haas Racing, Danica was sixth in a NASCAR Sprint Cup race at Atlanta, equalling Janet's best finish from 1977.

Between Janet and Danica, three other women have taken on NASCAR's top-level prize. Robin McCall competed in two races in 1982, when she was just 18 years old, making her the youngest female NASCAR driver, and one of its youngest, full stop. She drove Jim Stacy's Buick at Michigan twice, but could not finish either time.

Patty Moise had five starts between 1987 and 1989, also usually driving a Buick. Two of these races, in 1988, ended in finishes; the best of these was a twenty-sixth place at Daytona. Both Patty Moise and Robin McCall are chiefly remembered now for their marriages to other NASCAR personalities: Elton Sawyer and Wally Dallenbach respectively.

Shawna Robinson had some decent seasons in the second-tier Busch Series in the mid-1990s, starting once from pole at the 1994 Atlanta race, then finishing tenth at Watkins Glen later in the season. She also had a good run in the similar ARCA stock car series in 2000, driving Michael Kranefuss's Ford for a full season. She managed ten top-ten finishes, the best of these being a fourth, at Pocono. This was enough for sixth in the championship, and could have been enough to secure her a decent Winston Cup drive. Michael Kranefuss ran her for one race in 2001, at Michigan, and she made it to the end, in thirty-fourth. In 2002, she was set to do a whole season for Beth Ann Morgenthau's BAM Racing team, but money and politics intervened, and she only made seven starts. Three were converted to finishes, the best being twenty-fourth at Daytona. After that, she made some Busch Series and Craftsman Trucks appearances, but never made it back to the Cup.

Time will tell if any female driver will prove Richard Petty wrong.

Chapter 7

Death and the Maiden

Reims 12 Hours, 30 June 1956

On lap twenty-seven of the 1956 Reims 12-Hour race, a Porsche 550 ran slightly off the track on a tricky left-hand bend, both wheels on the driver's side leaving the circuit. The car was destabilised, slid and then went into a violent roll, leaving the circuit's perimeter entirely. The driver, on her first stint at the wheel, was thrown from her car and landed some distance away, her skull seriously fractured.

Annie Bousquet was taken to hospital but died en route. She was either 31, 33 or 35, depending on which information source is consulted.

Death is a sad but inevitable possibility in dangerous sports. Programmes given out at even the smallest British rally or club meeting carry the warning 'Motorsport is Dangerous'. As the great Kay Petre once said, 'if you race fast cars, you have to face up to the risk that one day you will cop it.' Annie Bousquet was not the only racing driver killed in an accident that year, but her death had many more repercussions than the others.

She was not even the first female driver to be killed in action. Nina Vitaglioni crashed her Stutz at Stockton Park in the US in 1918, taking part in an all-female race meeting promoted as 'The Speederettes'. Her riding mechanic and three spectators also lost their lives. In 1932, 21-year-old Renee Friederich crashed her Bugatti fatally on a hillclimb section of the Paris–St Raphaël Rally, another women-only event. A year earlier Aniela, the Baroness d'Elern, was racing in the Algerian Grand Prix when her Bugatti hit a telegraph pole whilst attempting an overtaking move. She did not survive. Closer to the date in question, Giuliana Pini and Margherita Pantaguzzi died in a crash on a road section of the 1954 Rallye Femminile Perla di Sanremo, an all-female rally. The same year, 20-year-old Luisa Rezzonico crashed her Lancia Aurelia during the Autogiro d'Italia, suffering fatal injuries. All of these incidents raised questions and caused considerable sadness in the motorsport world, but they happened during quite minor events, often women-only rallies that were not much covered by the press outside their own countries.

Safety concerns in all branches of motorsport were still quite a minor priority in the 1950s. Car design was only just beginning to incorporate such rudimentary features as siting the fuel tank away from the cockpit. Protective flame-retardant clothing was only just appearing, seat belts were not commonplace and even crash helmets were still very basic, more in common with those worn by polo players. Safety measures, such as they were, were mainly for the protection of spectators.

The year before Annie's death, the worst motorsport accident in history had occurred during the Le Mans 24 Hours. Pierre Levegh's Mercedes collided with Lance Macklin's Austin-Healey and took off, breaking up in the air and crashing into a spectator area at the side of the track before exploding. Levegh and eighty-three spectators were killed. A further spectator died after being hit by the Austin-Healey.

The carnage of the 1955 race led to a raft of very quick actions. Motor racing was suspended across much of Europe, pending improvements to the circuits. In America, the leading sanctioning body, the AAA, was dismantled. Motor racing remains illegal in Switzerland, apart from that involving electric vehicles. Mercedes pulled the plug on its works racing team, ostensibly to concentrate on road car production.

Mostly, racing resumed again fairly quickly, once increased spectator safety was assured at its venues.

Annie's accident and subsequent demise would have similar rash consequences, which lasted for somewhat longer.

According to different sources, Annie, née Schaffer, was born in Austria, in either 1921, 1923 or 1925, At the time of her death, she was a French national, having married a Frenchman, Pierre Bousquet. The couple seem to have met when Pierre was a prisoner of war in Austria, or on some sort of military duty there. They lived in France after their marriage.

Annie was apparently an only child, from a privileged background and sporty in her outlook. She loved adventure; even before she got in a racing car, she seems to have been something of a risk-taker. According to Jean-Francois Bouzanquet, Pierre taught her to drive, but she only got the idea of racing when she met Gigi Villoresi and Alberto Ascari in a bar in Sestriere, Italy. She had injured herself skiing, and was soon planning to start her own racing career. Her first event was the Sestriere Rally, with Alberto Ascari himself. Pierre also raced, although it is hard to work out where he fits in this story.

As with many women drivers, something of a legend built up around Annie, and as she was no longer around to correct or clarify, it became an accepted fact.

The year of her first competition was 1952. The results of that year's Sestriere Rally include neither Annie nor Ascari. It is possible that another rally, held in or around Sestriere, was her first event. Bouzanquet says that it was a female-only rally; it may have been the Perla di Sanremo women's event. If this assumption is correct, then Ascari did not accompany her. The Perla di Sanremo was for female crews only.

She does appear on the entry list for that year's Alpine Rally, driving a Renault 4CV, although she was unable to finish as the car's gearbox gave up during the first day, on the Col d'Izoard stage.

The French newspapers of the time do not mention much about Annie at all and her participation in any 1952 event is hard to confirm. She did enter the Tour de France that year, driving a Panhard X86 with a driver named Dubor. It was presumably Dubor's car. Their finishing position is not recorded.

The following year, she continued to race the 4CV and pushed herself on to the bigger stage. She finished on her first attempt at the Mille Miglia, albeit in 282nd place. She shared the 4CV with veteran French driver, Simone des Forest, who had raced alongside the likes of Hellé Nice in the 1930s. Driving solo, she earned her first big finish in a race when she came ninth in the Hyères 12 Hours. She also had her first accident, rolling on a corner at Agen and seriously injuring herself, necessitating a month in hospital. She was driving a DB Panhard and had reportedly been trying to keep up with another, more experienced driver at the time. This is sometimes alluded to as evidence of Annie's slightly over-zealous competitive streak and over-confidence, but it is hardly unusual behaviour for a racing driver.

Also in the Mille Miglia was Gilberte Thirion, sharing her Porsche 356 with Ingeborg Polensky, another Porsche racer, who was married to Helmut Polensky. Annie and Gilberte may have met during this event, for they were soon racing as a team, and were apparently good friends off the track.

For the 1954 season, they bought a Gordini T15S together, and embarked on an ambitious international season of competition. An early disappointment was their entry for the Sebring 12 Hours being rejected, probably due to their sex, but possibly for other bureaucratic reasons. The early part of their season progressed well, with Annie earning a sixth place in the Agadir Grand Prix in Morocco, and an eleventh in the Dakar 2 Hours, in Senegal. The European leg of their programme did not run quite as smoothly. Annie did not start the Nîmes Grand Prix, then the duo, driving together, were fifty-fifth in the Mille Miglia. Gilberte, driving the car with Olivier Gendebien, secured an entry in that year's Reims 12 Hours, as well as a solo drive in the Spa Grand Prix. In a different T15S, she drove for the Gordini team at Le Mans, although the car's ignition failed quite early on and Gilberte did not even get to drive.

In 1955, Gilberte continued to race the Gordini, which was still owned jointly, but Annie did not. The two drivers distanced themselves from one another and their friendship apparently cooled. The cause is given as jealousy, with both prone to envy when one was seen to have a better car or team than the other during an event. This may not have been the only factor; Gilberte's relationship with Olivier Gendebien gave her other opportunities and inspiration as well as another teammate.

At the end of 1954, Annie started racing a Porsche 550. She drove in the Tour de France with Marie-Claire Beaulieu, the former Marie-Claire Cibié of Cibié headlights fame. This particular car seems to have belonged to Marie-Claire, who competed in rallies and the Tour. The 550 appears to have been a good fit for Annie's driving style, and they were eighth overall. In a 356, Annie was then fifth in the Coupe d'Automne at Montlhéry.

It is here that we see things begin to unravel for Annie. On the surface of it, she was at a good point in her racing career, having begun to get to grips with a fast and difficult to drive car, achieving some results in the process. However, her first race of 1955, the Agadir Grand Prix, ended in a heavy crash and a hospital stay for Annie. She had broken her leg. The car was also badly damaged and had to be taken back to Zuffenhausen in Germany for repairs. It looks as if this particular 550 was beyond economical repair, for Annie at least, and she took delivery of another.

Her next race was the Bol d'Or in May. She was sharing Josef Jeser's 550 at the suggestion of Huschke von Hanstein, the Porsche competition manager. Jeser agreed to this as Hanstein had offered him further assistance for a Le Mans entry. Annie managed to start the race, which was a round-the-clock enduro, but lost her nerve when another driver had a leg amputated after an accident. Jeser drove solo for twenty hours and was second.

Later that month, still convinced that the 550 was the key to her racing success despite mounting evidence to the contrary, she drove in the 12 Hours of Hyères again with a Guatemala-based Czech racer called Jaroslav Juhan, who was a works Porsche driver. The brakes failed fairly late on and they did not finish.

In January 1956, Annie faced tragedy of a very personal kind when Pierre Bousquet died in a road traffic accident. His car skidded on black ice. Although the Bousquets may no longer have been a couple at the time, Pierre's death affected Annie deeply, as would be expected. She did not compete for several months.

Part-way through the year, Annie accepted a works drive with Triumph for the Mille Miglia, and drove a TR2. Driving solo, she was a respectable ninety-fifth, out of 182 finishers, and ninth in class.

This year she appears to have become close to Alejandro de Tomaso, and his wife, the American racer Isabelle Haskell. The circumstances of this are not very clear. She shared a Maserati 150S with Alejandro for June's Paris 1,000km, held at Montlhéry. The car was presumably the de Tomasos'. Annie and Alejandro started from twenty-eighth place, out of forty, but did not finish. For her next race, she arranged to use her new Porsche 550, which she would be sharing with Isabelle this time.

The next race was the Reims 12 Hours and we already know how that ended. A few different theories have been put forward for the cause of Annie's crash, but the most convincing one concerns the run-up to the race itself. Annie was in the habit of driving her new Porsches to and from the factory in Zuffenhausen near Stuttgart to collect them and to drop them off for repairs. She was having some work done on her light blue 550 just before the Reims race and had driven to Germany and back practically the day before. Observers estimated that she was extremely fatigued, and that she had probably not slept for forty-eight hours before embarking on another lengthy race on a tricky course. This caused her lapse in concentration and observation, and therefore her accident.

No other drivers were implicated in the accident and no other mysterious factors have been evoked, like the stories of children or other people on the track causing Jim Clark's fatal accident. Surprisingly, no-one has even tried to make spurious spiritual connections between Annie's crash and James Dean's death the previous year; both involved a Porsche 550, which in Dean's case has developed a malevolent life of its own, supposedly killing other owners. Annie's death, though attention-grabbing, was a racing accident.

Annie's over-confidence and desperate competitiveness are often alluded to in discussions of her death. She is frequently portrayed as someone pushing far beyond her skill level, in an attempt to seize glory for herself. This was meant to be especially true when she was racing against men. However, looking at the evidence, which is far from complete, the situation was more multi-faceted. Her loss of nerve at the Bol d'Or, for example, was not the behaviour of a glory-hunter out to prove herself against men. Such a woman would surely feign injury or battle on through, rather than admit that she was scared. The suggestion itself that she was out to prove herself against men is not fully played out by the evidence. Her partnership with Gilberte Thirion ended up becoming a rather fierce rivalry, if stories are true. No particular grudge matches against male drivers are particularly evident in her race results and none are discussed in accounts of Annie's racing life.

The effect on Annie of Jean's death is talked about a little. It obviously upset her deeply, and she was absent from the circuits for a good few months after it happened. Taken in conjunction with her Bol d'Or experiences it could explain a dip in form, or a new reticence, but by June, she seems to have been pushing as hard as ever. It could well have been that she became less concerned about her own well-being and therefore took such risks as not resting adequately before a twelve-hour race, and driving cars that she had had difficulty with before.

The relationship between Annie and Gilberte Thirion is not explored very much in articles about either of them. They were no longer racing together at the time of Annie's death and seem to have been far less close personally. However, Gilberte did state the Reims accident as one of the reasons for her retirement in 1957. She had been competing in the same class of the 12 Hours that year with Roger Loyer.

Annie's accident had repercussions far beyond the personal. As a result of the negative publicity it caused, the Automobile Club de l'Ouest (ACO), organising club of the Le Mans 24 Hours, informally banned women drivers from its sanctioned competitions. This was probably influenced by the greater negative press it received in 1955, after Levegh's accident and its terrible aftermath.

Women drivers were not banned from all French motorsport and many did continue to compete, but for the next fifteen years they were barred from the blue riband event of non-Formula One competition. Only one woman, Maria Teresa de Filippis, was active in Formula One at the time, so all of the others, as well as de Filippis, were denied a stage upon which to show their talents to the world.

It is hard to say how many drivers' careers were affected by this decision. Rosemary Smith, the Irish event-winning rally driver, certainly did have her entry turned down during the 1960s. She was named as one of the Rootes team three times, driving a Sunbeam, but did not get to compete. This was not due to lack of experience; she raced at Sebring and Daytona and in the British Saloon Car Championship

(BSCC). The main problem she had during a long sportscar race was boredom. One of her mechanics was once concerned to find what looked like paint shavings, sheared off from somewhere in the car. The cause of this 'damage' was Rosemary, keeping herself alert as she drove by picking off her nail polish.

There were some talented female sportscar drivers active during the 1960s. Among them were those on the driving roster of the Ring Free Oil 'Motor Maids' team, which competed at Sebring and Daytona between 1966 and 1971. Among their number were Donna Mae Mims, Judy Kondratieff, Janet Guthrie, Smokey Drolet, Rosemary Smith, Anita Taylor and Liane Engeman. Janet Guthrie would go on to race at Indianapolis, and certainly had the talent to get a powerful car through a long race. She also worked in the aerospace industry and on her own cars, giving her the advantage of mechanical sympathy and the ability to work effectively with mechanics. Smokey Drolet was less well-travelled, but was a talented racer nevertheless. Anita Taylor was fast and extremely well-connected in the motorsport world, being the sister of former Lotus driver Trevor Taylor and a member of the works Ford team. Liane Engeman was also a capable driver who was skilled at getting sponsors on board. Her performances at Sebring and Daytona for the Ring Free team were often hamstrung by cars barely out of showroom specification, but she had considerable talent in touring cars.

The US had a good number of female racers, active mostly in small sportscars since 1964. Judy Kondratieff was among their number. She later married Howden Ganley and was involved in Formula One as a timekeeper, initially with McLaren. She could maintain twenty lap charts at once, using one stopwatch. A career in administration, PR and even engineering followed. She did end up playing an active role at Le Mans as she acted as a consultant for more than one team during the Group C era, advising on timing and aspects of engineering.

Many of the US women drivers who started racing in the 1950s did not compete outside America. Sierra 'Smokey' Drolet was one of these, although she did race at Sebring and Daytona in the major races and once travelled to the Bahamas for Nassau Speed Week. Her career began in 1957 when she raced a Triumph TR2 locally, in

Florida. A growing number of women racers started organising their own events within the SCCA, and Smokey sometimes took part in these, winning one at Courtland in 1960, driving a TR3. However, she usually preferred to test herself in the open classes.

Suzy Dietrich was another one-time Ring Free Motor Maid, racing an ASA 411 in the 1967 Sebring 12 Hours with Donna Mae Mims. She too rarely competed outside America, and the furthest she went was Nassau, in 1956 and 1957. She was a versatile driver who often drove MGs and an Elva, as well as a Porsche 550 and 356.

Would Ring Free have sent their Motor Maids to Le Mans, had they thought that their entries would be accepted? It would have been interesting to see.

Isabelle Haskell was another possibility for a Le Mans seat, had the ban not happened. She was perhaps not as highly regarded as some of her contemporaries, but she had money and connections, which counted for almost as much as they do now. She could drive a car well and had finished in the top ten of endurance races at Sebring and Buenos Aires. In 1959, she was put forward as a driver for Alejandro's team, but her entry was turned down.

The ACO's ban on female drivers was finally lifted in 1971. The first beneficiary of this was Marie-Claude Beaumont, a multi-skilled race and rally driver who was then part of Henri Greder's GM team. She and Greder shared a Chevrolet Corvette in the 1971 race, but did not finish. This was the first of six Le Mans starts for Marie-Claude. Her best finish was in 1973, when she and Greder were twelfth and won their class, in a Corvette.

Marie-Claude's participation opened the floodgates for women to race at the Sarthe track again. By 1974, there were two all-female teams taking part, one of which (Christine Beckers, Marie Laurent and Yvette Fontaine in a Chevron B23) won their class. Three all-girl teams raced in 1975, bringing the total number of female drivers up to eight, a number unheard of since the 1930s.

The leading female team was the Porsche Carrera RS of Anny-Charlotte Verney, Corinne Tarnaud and Yvette Fontaine. They were eleventh. The 2-litre class was won by the Moynet-Simca of Marianne Hoepfner, Christine Dacremont and Michele Mouton. They were twenty-first overall. The Elf Switzerland Alpine-Renault A441C of Marie-Claude Beaumont and Lella Lombardi did not finish.

One of the most illustrious crop of girl racers ever seen was the class of 1975. Lella Lombardi was part-way through a second season in Formula One, battling heroically in an outdated March. Yvette Fontaine had already won the Belgian Touring Car Championship in 1969, driving a Ford Escort. Marie-Claude Beaumont was well into her sportscar career and was also quite a successful rally driver. On the rally side, Michele Mouton was starting to show the form that would later win her four World Championship rallies in the early 1980s. Anny-Charlotte Verney would race at Le Mans on ten occasions, usually in a Porsche, with a best result of sixth, in 1981, when she shared a Porsche 935 with Bob Garretson and Ralph Kent-Cooke.

Annie Bousquet had largely been forgotten by this time. The ban on female drivers blamed on her death was over, and this was a laying to rest of sorts. She was remembered in the name of a corner at Reims and in an annual motorsport prize for women in France.

Before the triumphant return of women racers to Le Mans, another woman was battling her way through top-level motorsport. Maria Teresa de Filippis, as mentioned above, would have stood a good chance of finishing Le Mans, but she never got the chance. She made up for it, however, by marking her place in the record books as the first woman to race in Formula One. She too had her career blighted by the shadow of death. Maria Teresa herself lived to be an old lady and died in 2016, aged 89, but her active racing career was ended by tragedy.

Maria Teresa was a racer of the old school; an Italian noblewoman (she had the title Contessa) with a taste for adventure. Her brothers both raced cars, and for much of her young life, Maria Teresa rode horses, winning several prizes for showjumping. She only became involved with motorsport for a bet in 1948, when her brothers made a wager with her that she would not be as successful in a car as she was on her horse. This was not a challenge to be taken lying down. Maria Teresa entered a hillclimb in her Fiat 500, hoping to finish at least. She walked away with a class win, a 'Driver of the Meeting' award, and whatever stakes her brothers had offered.

She quickly took to motor racing and bought her own sportscar, first a 750cc Urania. In 1949, her first full year of competition, she was sixth in the Stella Alpina in this car.

The Urania was soon replaced by a Giaur, another small sportscar. In 1951 she earned her first podium finish in this car in the Coppa Ascoli, then followed it up with fourth place in the Coppa Cidonio.

While racing the Giaur, she met Luigi Musso, soon to become a Grand Prix driver for Ferrari, in 1950, and had a close relationship until 1953. The pair were certainly lovers for at least some of that time. At some point, Maria Teresa claimed to be engaged to Luigi. They never married; by 1952, he was already married to another woman, although that did not stop him from consorting with Maria Teresa and probably others. She got over any disappointment quite quickly, and remained friends with Luigi after they parted company at the end of 1953.

Her love affairs were no distraction to Maria Teresa. During her time with Musso she posted some very good results, normally in an OSCA. She was second in the 1952 Circuito di Sassari in an OSCA 1100 and then repeated the performance in 1953, in an OSCA MT4. One of the best results of her career was achieved in this car: fourth place in the Pescara 12 Hours, a brutal road race. She was sharing the MT4 with a driver called Sgorbati. They won their class, steering Maria Teresa's 1100cc OSCA to a finish among the 2000cc and GT cars. Driving solo, she was fifth at Avellino.

Another year in the MT4 added to her tally of creditable performances, including a second place in the Napoli Grand Prix and a third place in the Circuito di Reggio Calabria.

For 1955, she bought the Maserati A6GCS that Luigi Musso had driven the year before. This year, she entered more long-distance road races, including the Mille Miglia, which she did not finish. She was third in the Messina 10 Hours with Musitelli and ninth in the Targa Florio. Non-championship Grands Prix continued to be a happy hunting ground for her; she was second at Pergusa and fifth at Bari. She entered the Catania-Etna hillclimb and won it outright.

As well as triumph, she suffered two serious accidents. The first was at Mugello, in her usual favourite haunt of Sicily. The race was broken up by a lengthy stop to retrieve the Maserati, still containing Maria Teresa, from a precarious position halfway over a cliff. Later, in Buenos Aires in 1956, one of her first overseas races ended in a collision with a telegraph pole. This time she was injured and she had to take some time out from competition to recover. This was a bit of a blow to her career, as she was now being invited to drive for the Maserati factory team and was racing outside Europe for the first time in her career. She was not the only woman driving a Maserati in international sportscar races – Isabelle Haskell was also active in South America at the same time, in a 150S – but she was the only one in a works car.

Maria Teresa was aware of the risks she was taking, but not prone to dwelling on her mishaps. Where her own safety was concerned, she had a useful talent for compartmentalising and moving on. Even Juan Manuel Fangio, who was an admirer of her driving, commented on her lack of fear.

Her next event was the Napoli Grand Prix in May, which gave her another second place. This was her best finish of the year in a season plagued with electrical and mechanical problems and minor accidents. That said, she was now involved with both the official Maserati team and Scuderia Centro Sud, who also fielded Grand Prix cars.

In 1958, she received delivery of a Maserati 250F and set her sights on Grand Prix racing. Her first event in the car was the non-championship Siracuse Grand Prix, in which she was a promising fifth. In May, she became the first woman to attempt to qualify for a World Championship Grand Prix. Racing as a private entry in the 250F, she did not make the qualifying cut, along with fourteen men, including Bernie Ecclestone in a Connaught. The 250F had been a world-beater in the hands of Fangio a few seasons previously but was now starting to look old-fashioned next to the Vanwalls and Climaxes that dominated this year.

Her first Grand Prix start was at Spa in Belgium a month later. She qualified the Maserati in nineteenth place and made the finish in tenth. She was the last classified finisher but had made it to the end in a race of high attrition.

Scuderia Centro Sud entered her car for the Portuguese Grand Prix at Boavista. She qualified in fifteenth place but went out on the sixth lap with engine trouble. As a private entry again, she qualified for her home Grand Prix at Monza and narrowly missed out on a classified finish, the 250F's engine failing again on the fifty-seventh lap.

Maria Teresa's year of triumph was marred by sadness. Luigi Musso, her friend, teammate and former boyfriend, was fatally injured during the French Grand Prix, held at Reims. His accident was similar to Annie Bousquet's: he was thrown from his Ferrari after it skidded into a ditch on the Muzione hairpin. He suffered catastrophic head injuries and died later that day in hospital.

Maria Teresa remained tight-lipped about her feelings for Musso at the time and concentrated on the rest of her season with her usual sangfroid. She had put her romantic feelings for him far behind her and embarked on another close friendship, of somewhat ambiguous nature, with Jean Behra who ran the Porsche Formula One team as well as racing himself. He got her a drive in a Formula Two-specification Porsche prepared by the works team for the Monte Carlo Grand Prix, but she could not qualify, one of eight who did not make the cut. Wolfgang von Trips, the other Porsche driver, crashed out.

Maria Teresa never got the chance to race the Porsche again. Jean Behra was killed during the support race for the German Grand Prix when his car went over the AVUS track's steep banking. She retired from the sport immediately. Having remained strong through the deaths of Luigi Musso, plus other drivers to whom she was not as close, and putting aside her concerns for her own safety, Behra's passing was the last straw. She turned her back on motorsport completely and did not even attend a race for many years.

Female racing drivers (usually discounting lesbian women) often have a moral and emotional dilemma less commonly faced by their male counterparts: facing the possible death or incapacitation of a husband or boyfriend. It is still quite common for women drivers to have partners who also race. As far back as 1928, Elisabeth Junek suddenly quit motor racing after the German Grand Prix, where her husband and teammate Cenek had been killed. Like Maria Teresa,

Elisabeth was known for her fearlessness and she is best known for her fifth place in the 1928 Targa Florio, a road race run on appalling roads over a very long distance. She led the race from Louis Chiron for the second lap. The original Nürburgring was the scene of some of her other triumphs, and she won her class there in a sportscar race in 1926, driving a Bugatti. Despite all her reserves of resolve and grit, she reacted to her bereavement by selling all her cars and leaving the motor racing scene completely.

Just a few years after Maria Teresa's retirement and Annie Bousquet's death, Jean Bloxam hung up her helmet in the UK, following the death of her husband, Roy. This was 1961 and she had quite an illustrious career behind her, starting in 1954. It was Roy who entered her into a ladies' race at Goodwood, in an Aston Martin DB2. She was third. In subsequent years, she would go on to win races in a series of Astons, including an ex-David Brown DB3S.

Roy was killed during a race at Goodwood, driving a Lister-Jaguar. Jean did not abandon the motor world entirely but she never raced again, having owed her start in the sport to Roy.

The tensions between a driver's role as a sportsperson and as a partner are always hard to manage, and some couples have to engineer novel solutions. Piero Taruffi promised his wife Isabella that the 1957 Mille Miglia would be his last race. Isabella, surprisingly, agreed to come along as his co-driver. They drove a Ferrari 315S, and won. The race itself was marred by tragedy; Alfonso de Portago lost control of his car and ploughed into a group of spectators, killing nine of them as well as himself and his co-driver Edmund Nelson. Piero Taruffi later became an outspoken critic of the primitive safety measures at race meetings.

He lived to see his daughter, Prisca, compete in rallies and sportscar races in Italy, under improved safety conditions.

Chapter 8

Saloon Girls

The Small Car Trophy, Crystal Palace, 3 June 1963

1. John Whitmore (Austin Mini Cooper S)
2. Paddy Hopkirk (Morris Mini Cooper S)
3. Christabel Carlisle (Morris Mini Cooper S)
4. John Rhodes (Austin Mini Cooper S)
5. John Fenning (Morris Mini Cooper S)
6. Edward Lewis (Morris Mini Cooper S)
7. Elizabeth Jones (Austin Mini Cooper)
8. Martin Davidson (Austin Mini Cooper)
9. Bill Borrowman (Austin Mini Cooper)
10. Anita Taylor (Ford Anglia Super)
11. Michaelle Burns-Grieg (Austin Mini Cooper)
12. John Ralph (Austin Mini Cooper)

The Small Car Trophy was a round of the British Saloon Racing Championship (BSRC), run as part of a double-header at the Crystal Palace circuit with the Norbury Trophy for larger cars.

The BSRC was the precursor of the British Touring Car Championship (BTCC). As of 2020, the 1963 Small Car Trophy was the only time that three women competed together in a top-line British saloon championship.

The modern BTCC is the preserve of touring car specialists, including some full-time professionals. It was a completely different story in the 1960s. In the Norbury Trophy alone there were three contemporary Grand Prix drivers: Graham Hill, Richie Ginther and Roy Salvadori (Hill was third in a MkII Jaguar). These were not one-off guest appearances either. The BSRC was a big deal, with decent prize purses, and taken very seriously by manufacturers and drivers alike.

Although she never set foot in a single-seater, let alone a Grand Prix car, Christabel Carlisle was a genuine professional racing driver. That year she was racing for Don Moore's team in a Moore-prepared Mini Cooper S. This car was used by works drivers John Whitmore and Paddy Hopkirk.

The Small Car Trophy was actually one of the last races Christabel ever entered. Driving an Austin-Healey Sprite at Silverstone in a support race for July's British Grand Prix, she came up against oversteer whilst trying to overtake on the outside. Her car ploughed into the pit wall, then bounced back across the track. She was knocked unconscious and had to be cut from the wreckage. A marshal who had been stationed by the pit wall was fatally injured. Concussion has wiped the memory of the crash from Christabel's brain – she claims to remember correcting a slide, then waking up in the St John Ambulance tent – but upon learning of the marshal's death, she questioned her ability and judgement and retired from motor racing.

Much later, she admitted that the fun of motorsport had started to wear off, mainly because of increasing commercial pressures, and that she had been thinking of moving on anyway. The sport's growing focus on money did not sit well with her, and she was not comfortable with the 'Emma Peel' image that the press tried to give her. Although undeniably pretty, she was quite conservative in her appearance, but still very feminine. Her tailored driving overalls featured covered buttons and Peter Pan collars and were often commented upon. One of these suits, based on a Chanel design, is now on display at the Silverstone Experience.

Christabel's career was very short; she only had her first race in 1960. That year, she first experienced motor racing as a spectator, attending Brands Hatch with friends. Unlike many, she was not instantly entranced by the noise and thrill and found spectating boring and uncomfortable. However, something must have been awoken in her; she would only go back to a circuit if she was racing herself.

Her interest in motorsport did not come completely out of the blue. She had intended to enter a few rallies for fun in her new Mini and her uncle Chris McLaren raced. Chris was her mother's youngest brother and was only five years older than her. They would later compete together in 1963, finishing eighth in the Nürburgring 6 Hours in a Mini.

Future teammate Paddy Hopkirk, described her as 'a polite wee thing, very posh'. Christabel's grandfather was a baron, and she had enjoyed the trappings of upper-class life. Her coming-out party in 1957 was covered by *Tatler*, as were her appearances at other debutante dances and weddings. Whitney Straight, who had raced at Brooklands, was among her family circle of friends. She lived in London and worked as a piano teacher.

Her first car was an 850cc Mini which she had received as a twenty-first birthday present from her parents in 1960. During her first test day, she caught the attention of BMC competitions manager Marcus Chambers, and so a career began. Jack Sears was testing a Healey at the same time and Chambers had him show her the ropes. She was not the quickest driver to begin with, but both men were impressed with her consistency and aptitude for learning. Unfortunately, her first race at Brands ended in a crash, as her car was understeering and she was unable to follow her lines.

Her first full season was 1961. After some club races, her first BSRC outing was the British Empire Trophy at Silverstone. As a private entrant, she was sixth in class. She wanted to enter the Grand Prix support race for saloons but the BRDC would not accept her entry, fearful of negative publicity. At the Oulton Park Gold Cup in the autumn, she got into her first big on-track battle, taking on the Don Moore Minis of John Whitmore and Vic Elford. Whitmore led the class, but Elford had to fight for second from Christabel. The last race of the season at Snetterton had Christabel duelling with Whitmore himself, making him fight for his class championship.

John Whitmore moved on to the works BMC team in 1962 and Christabel effectively took his place in the Don Moore Mini. The small-car class was a constant battle between the works drivers, John Whitmore and Love, and Christabel. She was third in the class in the first race at Snetterton, following some car trouble. In the St Mary's Trophy at Goodwood, she swept to her first class win after her two rivals both failed to finish. It was back to third place at Aintree, but she was close behind, having fought from sixteenth on the grid. The works boys got the upper hand again when she failed to finish at Silverstone and her misfortune continued at Crystal Palace, dropping out with clutch problems. The Aintree Grand Prix support race had her splitting Love and Whitmore in second. She was third, but with a decent eighth overall at Brands Hatch, then the clutch failed again in the season-ending Oulton Park Gold Cup. John Whitmore won the small-car title.

Before her accident and subsequent retirement, Christabel's 1963 BSRC was shaping up to be her best yet. She was eighth overall at the end of the year, despite missing the last four rounds. She started with a class second at Snetterton, taking advantage of Whitmore's non-finish. She was second again, behind Whitmore this time, at Oulton Park. This pattern continued at Goodwood where she was tenth overall. She did not finish at Aintree or Silverstone, the latter after an accident. She was then third overall at Crystal Palace, and third in class at Silverstone. This was her BSRC swansong. At the time, Colin Chapman had been eyeing her up as a potential Lotus driver in their Lotus Cortina. Christabel later said that she was unsure about driving bigger cars.

As well as the BSRC, Christabel raced small sports cars, including John Sprinzel's Austin-Healey Sprite, at home and at the Nürburgring. In 1961, she even raced against Hollywood legend Steve McQueen and was second overall, between winner Vic Elford and McQueen himself, all in Minis. She led the race for a time. At the end of 1962, she was fifth in a celebrity Morris 1100 race at Snetterton. The other 'celebrities' were Grand Prix drivers of the time, including Jim Clark and Jack Brabham.

Christabel's achievements would be enough to fill a whole book; she did in fact write one, titled *Mini Racing*. However, as we already know, she was far from the only woman competing in the BSRC and one of many active in British saloon racing at the time.

Women drivers had made occasional appearances in the BSRC before Christabel came along – in 1960, a Mrs C. Wagner drove a Mini at Snetterton – but Christabel was the first to be a real contender and complete a full season. By 1962, she had two rivals make their BSRC debuts: Elizabeth Jones and Anita Taylor.

Anita and Christabel had some things in common. They were young, from privileged backgrounds, ambitious and very feminine at the same time. Anita came from a motorsport family; her brother was Trevor Taylor, who drove in Grands Prix for Lotus as a teammate to Jim Clark. To begin with, Anita favoured Ford power over BMC. Her preferred racing car was a Ford Anglia. She made her BSRC debut in the 1961 Bowmaker Trophy at the Silverstone International meeting. She was seventh in class.

Her next BSRC outing was the Small Car Trophy. Her Anglia was the only non-Mini in the race, the heaviest car, and probably not the best. She was not among the frontrunners in her next three races. At the Oulton Park Gold Cup, she raced against her brother, who was in a Team Lotus Cortina. Earlier in the season, Trevor had been the entrant for the Anglia. The siblings often worked together and even ran their own team, Aurora Gears, named after a company owned by Trevor. Their car was a Mini which they used both together as a two-car team, and separately, in the 1964 BSRC. The car was not the most competitive, again, but Anita did manage a ninth place in that year's Small Car Trophy. The two ended up racing hard against each other in the Oulton Park Gold Cup with Anita coming out on top, in fifteenth place.

After another year spent scrapping for minor positions in a Mini, Anita returned to the Anglia. In 1966, she joined the Broadspeed team for the BSRC. Broadspeed was one of the leading racing teams of the time. At the Silverstone International Trophy, she was ninth overall and won the 1-litre class, having taken the lead on lap six. In the next race at Crystal Palace, she was sixth, just behind her Broadspeed teammate, John Fitzpatrick, and the rival Hillman Imp of Bill McGovern. Mechanical issues plagued the rest of her season, but she did have the satisfaction of beating Trevor again in the Guards Trophy at Brands Hatch. He was making a guest appearance for Broadspeed.

She was awarded a works contract with Ford in 1967. This included another season in the BSRC with Broadspeed, which started well at Brands Hatch with a class win. Her best overall result was seventh, at Oulton Park. Her main rivals that year were her teammate,

John Fitzpatrick, and Bernard Unett in an Alan Fraser Imp. She was normally able to challenge them effectively.

It was an exciting year for Anita in 1967, with travel to the US involved. She was chosen for the 'Ring Free Motor Maids' all-female team. She was twentieth in the Daytona 24 Hours with Smokey Drolet and Janet Guthrie. The team's Ford Mustang was probably mixed up with Anita's Ford contract. Later in the season, she and Smokey Drolet raced in the Sebring 12 Hours and just got to the finish in thirty-fifth. This time, the car was an Alpine-Renault A110.

Despite her status as a Ford works driver, she was not entered for any of the other major sportscar races, or even the European Touring Car Championship. She did get an entry into the Shell 4000 Cross-Canada Rally in a Lotus Cortina but did not finish after getting first lost, then stuck in wet ground.

With Ford, Anita found herself coming up against a similar set of problems to Christabel Carlisle three years earlier, although they expressed their frustrations differently. The increasing commercial focus of motor racing meant that Ford took the less risky option of using Anita's considerable beauty and popularity rather than her driving prowess as a promotional device. After all, the outcome of a race depends on many factors, whereas a promotional film can be controlled to give the desired effect. Anita spent time setting records for the fastest caravan towing speed and participated in economy runs to demonstrate the practicality of Ford's latest cars. She 'starred' in an advertising film and was photographed in and around Ford cars, increasingly in fashionable outfits rather than her driving overalls.

Anita was undoubtedly very beautiful and obviously enjoyed fashion, but she was also a quick and determined racing driver, and it was this side that she wanted to demonstrate as a works team member. Having grown up with three elder brothers, she had a thick skin when it came to sexist jibes and patronising comments, but she was still frustrated. Many years later, she appeared in a TV documentary about Ford, and commented that the company were using her as a model – 'and I was not a model'.

Her career lasted longer than Christabel's did but it came to an end at the close of the 1967 season. It was not just the disillusionment with her Ford works deal, but a marriage to an unsupportive husband that put paid to it. The marriage did not last long, but Anita did not resume racing. She remained on the scene due to her family and was close to Trevor until his death from cancer in 2010.

This image of the woman driver as a glamorous Amazon was quite a new one, or at least new to its then-audience. Pop culture was starting to celebrate 'strong women'; the first female cosmonaut flew in space in 1963, TV cop shows often featured high-kicking action-girl sidekicks and the music charts were full of youthful, confident female singers.

There are some similarities with the portrayals of the ladies of Brooklands who often posed for pictures in similar ways, sitting on the bonnet of their cars or perched sideways on the driving seat, and usually added some noticeable feminine accoutrements to their racewear.

Women had always been looked upon to provide some glamour at race meetings, but in the 1960s, they became more visible again, taking active roles. More so than drivers, women were seen as timekeepers, pit managers and spectators. The timekeepers and team officials were often the partners of male drivers. Some made a career of sorts out of it: Sally Stokes, who was Jim Clark's on-off girlfriend, even gave out fashion advice for women in the pits. She recommended trousers and a 'pretty mac'.

Some female drivers tried to exploit this new appetite for attractive, personable girls in fast small saloons. A third finisher in the 1963 Small Car Trophy was probably one of these. Michaelle Burns-Grieg was Scottish, and had been competing for a while in a number of motorsport disciplines, including hillclimbs. Her Mini Cooper sometimes ran as part of the Scottish Racing Drivers Club team. Between 1963 and 1965 she made several appearances in the BSCC, the best of these being her eleventh place in the 1963 Small Car Trophy. She was also fifteenth at Snetterton in 1965.

Michaelle was usually driving a privateer car in the small-engined class so would not be expected to challenge for overall wins, but she obviously did take her racing seriously to have ended up at this level.

Still, she is chiefly remembered now for the numberplate on her Mini, which read 'SEX1'. This, and a few rather attractive pictures of her posing in the car, seems to suggest someone who was more at home with using their feminine charms in an attempt to gain attention and sponsorship. Michaelle appears to retire after 1965. In 2012, a woman of the same name stepped down from the leader's post for the Conservative Party in the Scottish Borders. If this is the same person, there was certainly more to her than met the eye.

Elizabeth Jones, the seventh-place finisher in the 1963 Small Car Trophy, was rather a different proposition. She had learned to drive a racing car at about the same time as Christabel and Anita in 1960, but was already 30 years old. Initially, she gravitated towards single-seaters and was eighth in a Formula Junior race at Silverstone.

Her first BSCC race was in 1962, also at Silverstone, and she was fourth in class. She continued to be a fairly regular presence in the BSCC until the end of 1964. Her best race finish was a fifth place, earned in the 1964 Small Car Trophy.

She drove for both the Downton Engineering and Alexander Engineering teams during her time in the BSCC. Both of these companies made and sold aftermarket tuning kits for Minis, so saloon racing was a valuable promotional tool for them. The massive potential for modification that came with the Mini meant that a racing version was within reach to more prospective racers than before. Aftermarket kits such as those marketed by the firms above made it even easier. Women appear to have been a beneficiary of this development; the low price point of the original road-going Mini meant that it became a popular choice for women wanting their own car. A Mini Cooper, plus modifications, was still much cheaper to run than the Jaguar MkIIs and Ford Mustangs that it could race against, putting it within reach of a race-ready young woman funding her own sport. John Aley advertised a stripped-down, basic circuit Mini for as little as £400.

Perhaps due to Liz Jones's age, her married status (although she competed under her own family name) and possibly her more introverted personality, she was not used as a promotional model for her teams. Although her profile was lower, she still got her share of drives in the bigger European events, such as the Brands Hatch 6 Hours which she entered in 1962, 1963 and 1964, in an Alexander Engineering Mini each time. Her teammates were Pauline Mayman, Timo Mäkinen and American racer and journalist Denise McCluggage. Her best finish was eighteenth in 1963, with Mäkinen, but her most impressive drive was probably her first in 1962. Driving the Alexander Mini with Pauline Mayman, she failed to finish, but another simultaneous drive in a Ford Anglia with Alan Mann and Tony Hegbourne led to thirteenth and a second in class.

Pauline Mayman was primarily known as a rally driver and in 1963 was combining circuit racing with a works BMC rally drive in Europe. That year, she was sixth in the Alpine Rally, driving a Mini. The year before she had co-driven for Pat Moss, and helped her to a win in the Baden-Baden Rally. Pauline was a similar age to Liz, having been active since the late 1950s. After their respective retirements, they both bred and showed dogs competitively.

Briefly, Liz was a works BMC driver too, for the 1963 Tour de France, again with Pauline Mayman, but engine trouble put them out. Later, until 1965, Liz acted as a rally co-driver, sitting alongside Shelagh Aldersmith and Daphne Freeman. Her last major rally seems to have been Monte Carlo in 1965, where she took the wheel of a Mini herself with Patricia Ozanne as navigator.

Liz and Christabel had met on the track before in 1961. Christabel, in her first Mini, had won a ladies' race from Liz in an Austin-Healey. Shelley Marten in a Turner, was third. Pat Coundley, in her Lotus Elite, spun off. Ladies' races became quite popular in the early 1960s, receiving attention from national newspapers. One such race, the 'Fast Girls Trophy' at Brands Hatch in 1963, was won by Joey Freeman in an Aston Martin. Anita Taylor and Michaelle Burns-Grieg both crashed and dramatic pictures of Anita's furiously rolling Anglia accompanied the *Daily Express* article. Michaelle managed to rejoin the race and finish in second place. Sally Stokes, in a Mini, was third.

Like Christabel, Anita and Michaelle, Liz's racing career was quite short, although it seemed to fizzle out gently rather than coming to an abrupt end.

I have already compared the BSRC in the 1960s to Brooklands in the 1930s and it was not just in 1963 that this was so. Several more women tried their luck in Britain's top-level saloon racing series, with varying results. Just as in the 'golden days' of Brooklands, there were some distinct types of female racer. There was what we would now call the 'marquee name', the glamorous stars of the circuit, who were usually young, attractive and often in works cars. Both Kay Petre (Brooklands) and Anita Taylor fell into this category. In addition to their star quality, they had solid driving skills and were capable of winning. Another group was the hard-working amateurs, like Liz Jones or someone like Victoria Worsley at Brooklands.

Then there were the aristocrats like Christabel Carlisle, who competed with varying degrees of seriousness and competence. Gabriel Konig, an Irish racer, came out the year after Christabel, so fell into this category. She never raced in the BSRC but campaigned a Lotus Elan at Goodwood and the Nürburgring. In 1966, she won a race in a Hillman Imp, then in 1967, a Modsports class championship in an MG Midget.

Then there were the Racer Wives. These women got into motorsport primarily through their husbands, who were established competitors. Ruth Urquhart-Dykes was one in the 1920s, as was Jill Scott in the 1930s. In the 1960s, Jean Aley and Pat Coundley were active in the BSRC.

Jean Aley was married to John Aley, another British racer and car builder. They both used and worked with Minis; John ran a race preparation business building lower-cost racing Minis. Jean raced not only in the UK but in Germany, and took part in two runnings of the Nürburgring 500, then a round of the European Touring Car Championship (ETCC). Both times, she drove a Mini. In 1965, she shared with John but they did not finish. Earlier, in 1962, she teamed up with Daphne Freeman, a former secretary to Stirling Moss, who enjoyed some success as a circuit racer, but more as a rally driver. The car developed engine trouble so they did not finish. Jean and Daphne were driving for the Blez International team with John Aley in the team's sister car. At that year's Tourenwagen Grand Prix, Jean and John shared another Mini in almost showroom trim. Jean took the car into a class fifth, which was maintained by John.

In 1963, Jean shot to a brief height of fame for the wrong reasons: she had entered the Monte Carlo Rally with Shelagh Aldersmith in her Mini. They only got as far as the end of Jean's drive before the radiator blew up. John took the blame for not checking it properly.

Jean was in many ways an archetypal motorsport wife. In the 1960s that meant far more than waiting anxiously in pitlanes in fashionable clothes and team-branded ear defenders. It also meant more than making tea and washing overalls. Jean took an active part in supporting John's career and in the running of the team. She filled the traditional female role of lap-timing armed with a stopwatch, as did many motor-racing wives at all levels of the sport, right up to the likes of Helen Stewart and Nina Rindt. It was often also down to Jean to drive John's Mini to the circuits, with him following behind in a van with the rest of the team's equipment. He considered this quicker and easier than towing the car on a trailer. John credits Jean with contributing to much of his success.

Pat Coundley was the second wife of John Coundley and made her name as a racer in 1959 with a D-Type Jaguar. She was to race a number of Jaguar sportscars around the UK, often in sprints, between then and 1964, as well as entering a Ladies' Handicap at Brands Hatch in a Lotus Elite.

She made her BSRC debut in 1964, driving a Lotus Cortina. That year, her main focus was the BARC Spring Grove saloon championship, in which she managed three top-ten finishes: tenth at Oulton Park and two ninths at Goodwood. In the BSRC she raced at Goodwood, Oulton Park and Aintree, but could not make an impression.

She returned to speed trials and hillclimbs. In 1964, she won the Ladies' Prize at the Brighton Speed Trials, driving a D-Type. She had driven a Lotus 19 single-seater in another class. In May, she set the fastest time of the day at the Antwerp Speed Trials in the D-Type, achieving 161.278mph over the flying kilometre. This was the fastest speed ever recorded by a woman driver at the time, and made the front page of the *Daily Mirror*. A team in the US, with a jet car and Lee Breedlove as its driver, disputed this but they had not recorded their speed on a two-way run, so Pat's record stood.

Women drivers in touring cars in the 1960s are associated with Minis and Ford Anglias, small 'cute' cars, but they were capable of handling bigger machinery, too. Jacquie Bond-Smith drove a 7-litre Ford Galaxie in the European Touring Car Championship in 1965. She was thirteenth in the Snetterton 500km with a class win, having started from pole in Division 3.

In 1964 and 1965, she made some appearances in the BSRC, driving a Lotus Cortina. This was a private entry and she was not able to challenge for overall honours. Her best finish was a seventeenth place in the 1965 St Mary's Trophy at Goodwood.

Later that year, she raced a Lotus Elan, scoring one third place in a GT race at Silverstone. She is most famous for her membership of 'FLIRT', the First Ladies' International Racing Team. FLIRT was assisted by the Marcos factory, who provided them with a Mini Marcos in 1967. The team consisted of Jacquie, her sister, Joey Cook, and Jackie Smith, another saloon racer and motorsport artist.

The FLIRT Mini Marcos appeared at the Nürburgring 1,000km, driven by Jacquie and Joey. They did not finish. The same driver pairing was thirty-seventh in the Mugello Grand Prix in July. Driving solo, Jacquie was twenty-first in the Nürburgring 500km. The team had some other club races in the UK, in which Jackie Smith took part.

FLIRT's results were modest, but they were a small team, not particularly experienced, especially compared to some of their contemporaries in the World Championship for Makes. Again, the novelty value of their sex was a double-edged sword; the attention they garnered as a group of attractive young women in a racing car was enough to win them some support, but the publicity meant that they did not have the latitude to learn the ins and outs of the car that they probably needed. This is a theme that crops up repeatedly in the history of women's motorsport.

The phenomenon of (usually) young female drivers in saloon racing in the 1960s was not confined to the UK. From across the Irish Sea, rally driver Rosemary Smith travelled to compete in ETCC and BSRC races, in Rootes machinery. In 1963, she was ninth in the ETCC race at Zolder, driving a Sunbeam Rapier. The same year, she drove a Rapier for the Alan Fraser team at Brands Hatch in the Molyslip Trophy.

Female drivers from even further afield came to England to further their careers. Liane Engeman learned to drive a racing car in her native Netherlands but moved to the UK in 1965. Her first BSRC races in 1966 were almost a disaster; she crashed her Mini in her second race at Brands Hatch.

After trying a few different cars, including Formula Vee and small sports prototypes, she had another try at the BSRC in 1969. She was driving a Ford Anglia for D. J. Bond Racing. Her best finish was nineteenth at Brands Hatch, third in class. Her BSRC season seems to end after a collision with Les Nash at Crystal Palace, in another Anglia.

By 1969, the BSCC was pretty small fry for Liane, anyway. In 1968, she got her first taste of the ETCC, driving an Anglia for the Johnny Lion team. She was sixth at Zandvoort, fourth in class. That year, she had raced in the Sebring 12 Hours for the third time with Janet Guthrie and Donna Mae Mims. They were twenty-third and sixth in class in an Austin-Healey Sprite. The three women were part of the Ring Free Oil 'Motor Maids', who had earlier counted Anita Taylor amongst their number. In 1966 and 1967, Liane and Janet drove as a pair, in a Matra Djet and an AMC Javelin. They were twenty-third again in 1966, but did not finish in 1967, following a crash. A driver called Paul Hawkins threw a series of accusations at the Ring Free team, claiming that they had caused the accident and should not have even been there, but no action was taken against them by the authorities, who considered it a racing accident.

From now until 1973, Liane would compete on and off in the ETCC and in the Dutch touring car championship. She was very competitive in the Dutch series, with 1970 being her best year. She drove a Frami Racing Ford Escort and scored two class wins and two outright third places, although one of these was taken away from her when her car's ride height was found to be illegal.

She often drove Alfa Romeo cars as well as Ford Escorts and Capris. During her career, she moved very frequently between teams, which must have meant that she struggled to get any continuity in her racing, understand a car and put together a title challenge. Her team-hopping has been put down to fallings-out and personal differences, although this is an accusation often levelled at women who have simply had enough of a situation that is not running to their advantage. Like Anita Taylor, Liane was both blessed and cursed with model looks, which got her plenty of attention but made being taken seriously as a racer by teams and by the public rather more difficult than it needed to be. She was a strong competitor who could have gone much further than she did.

The Low Countries in general were another hub of female racing action. While Britain had Anita Taylor and the Netherlands had Liane Engeman, Belgium had Nicole Sol, a sprightly former model who was married to Tom Sol, another racer. Between 1966 and 1969, she was a strong contender in the Belgian touring car championship. In her first race, in 1966, she was fourth in a Lotus Cortina. Switching between the official Alfa Romeo team and the Ford of Belgium squad she notched up a couple of wins, including an outright win at the Marche hillclimb in an Alfa Romeo TZ and fourth overall in the 1967 Belgian Touring Car Championship. For another of Ford's model drivers, she was surprisingly effective and was soon taken very seriously.

The presence of two other superb female drivers at the time probably helped her case. The greatest of these was probably Yvette Fontaine, who won the Belgian Saloon Car championship outright in 1969. She was another Ford works driver, using both an Escort Twin-Cam and a Cortina. This was the first time a woman had won a national saloon title. She narrowly missed out on defending her crown in 1970, having to settle for a class championship as a consolation.

Her partnership with Ford lasted from 1968 to 1974 and took in circuit racing, hillclimbs and rallying. Towards the end of her involvement with the team, the global fuel crisis meant cutbacks to Ford's motorsport programme so she competed less frequently. In comparison to Anita Taylor and Liane Engeman, Yvette was treated as a bona fide racer, rather than a novelty act. She was supported for full seasons in the Belgian championship and offered many drives in the ETCC. Apart from a few photographs of her perched on the bonnet of her car, she was excused modelling duties.

Yvette had always been interested in motorsport and was a frequent visitor to Zolder as a child. Her first forays into competition driving were in rallies when she was 18. She drove a Mini in the Tour of Belgium, despite not even being comfortable with the 60kph average speed that the rally demanded, and went over the time limit. Circuit racing came a little more naturally to her and she caught the attention of the Alfa Romeo Benelux team in 1965, but she still had to learn and develop as a driver before she was up to championship pace. The support of the Alfa and Ford teams was important here, as there were times when they could have dropped her when her curiosity value decreased.

Yvette raced at Le Mans twice, in 1974 and 1975. Both times, she was part of all-female teams. In 1975, she drove an 'Ecurie Seiko Sato' Ford-engined Chevron B21 with Christine Beckers and Marie Laurent. They won the 2000cc class, and were seventeenth overall. She went better in 1975, when she was eleventh in Anny-Charlotte Verney's Porsche 911 Carrera RS. Corinne Tarnaud drove alongside Anny-Charlotte and Yvette. They were second in their class.

Christine Beckers, Yvette's teammate in 1974, was Belgium's other female leading light on its motorsport scene. Her circuit career began a little later in 1967, after rallying an NSU Prinz for a year. By 1968, she was an Alfa Romeo works driver, and in 1969, she won on the circuits, the hills and the special stages. In an Alfa GTAJ she won the Benelux Cup at Zandvoort, the Fastest Time of the Day (FTD) at the d'Houyet hillclimb, and the Ostend Rally.

Throughout her lengthy career, which lasted into the 1980s, she took part in the ETCC, four runnings of the Le Mans 24 Hours, the Monte Carlo Rally, the Spa 24 Hours, the Paris–Dakar Rally and even a NASCAR race. She was one of three female drivers in the 1977 Firecracker 500, alongside Lella Lombardi and Janet Guthrie.

Her best finish at Le Mans was another eleventh, which she achieved in 1977, driving for Vic Elford's Inaltera team with Lella Lombardi. Her best result on the Dakar was fifth in 1984, driving a Range Rover. It was her last competitive outing.

In Denmark, Mette Kruuse drove a Volvo P544 for her debut in the Danish Touring Car Championship in 1968. She was quite a consistent driver and earned a couple of fifth places. Later, in 1971, she became the latest of Ford's lady works drivers in a 1600cc Escort. She had a best finish of second at Djursland. That year she made a guest appearance in the BSRC, in the Escort but did not finish. She continued racing until 1974.

At the other end of Europe, Gloria Castresana Waid was a regular at the Jarama circuit, which opened in 1968. Usually she drove a Mini, but in 1968 she had an outing in a Hillman Imp that was usually raced by her husband: the 3-hour ETCC event held at the circuit. Sadly, she did not finish.

Gloria was also a very useful rally driver. In 1965, she was seventh in the Isla de Tenerife Rally in a Mini. Two years later, she acted as a co-driver to 'Miss Spain' in the all-female San Isidro Rally, in another Mini. They won the slalom section, and this became one of Gloria's most remembered moments.

Outside Europe, the girl-racer bug also bit. Anne Wong, a young Singaporean, had actually travelled to the UK to develop her motorsport skills, attending the racing school at Brands Hatch that was run by John Webb, who would shortly become the managing director of the circuit. Webb, with his wife Angela, took an interest in female drivers; among their later protégées was Divina Galica, who crossed over from skiing, and Ann Moore, a showjumper who competed for a season in 1971.

Anne Wong proved an able student. In 1970, she won the Macau Guia touring car race, in a Mini, from the back of the grid.

Women drivers continued to be a regular feature of UK saloon grids into the 1970s. As we will see, the Brands Hatch-based Shellsport operation was keen to use them as a promotional tool, bringing a series of mainly British drivers through the ranks via the Shellsport Escort Championship and women-only events such as the 1972 'Fast Girls Challenge', which ran at Brands Hatch using Ford Consuls. Gillian Fortescue-Thomas was the winner and went on to race in the Spa 24 Hours, among many other races.

The works teams in the big championships were harder nuts to crack, however. A Ford executive once told Jenny Birrell that he'd rather put Miss World in one of their BSCC cars and have her go off at the first corner than take a chance on a female career racer. Jenny did do two seasons in the championship in 1972 and 1973, driving a Chrysler Avenger that was not the most reliable.

Susan Tucker-Peake did race a Ford run by the Broadspeed team in 1970 and former dancer Wendy Markey was signed up by Mazda, backed by *Penthouse* magazine.

Through the 1980s, a few more tried their luck. Geunda Eadie won her 1980 Ford Fiesta drive in the 1979 Fabergé Ladies Fiesta Championship, but only did one season. Barbara Cowell made more of an impression.

After the decade turned again, the BTCC, as it now was, became increasingly professionalised and an almost male-only enclave.

Chapter 9

Rally Girls

As we have already seen, no matter how arduous and dangerous a motorsport situation, women have proved themselves capable of having a go, if not succeeding. The treacherous Sicilian dirt roads of the Targa Florio, the unprotected banking of Brooklands, Le Mans in the 1950s and Formula One in the deadly 1970s, female drivers have been there, in the mix.

In 1970, the *Mirror* newspaper decided to organise a long-distance rally, partly to celebrate the British motor industry, and to create some excitement in a rather dull world. The committee, from the RAC, elected to link the rally to that year's other big sporting spectacular, the World Cup, for which England were defending champions. The route of the rally would run from Wembley, the site of the 1966 World Cup Final, to Mexico City, where the 1970 final would be played. One hundred and six teams would be accepted to take the start, although not all would be in with a chance to complete the 16,000-mile route; the slowest cars to reach Lisbon would not be loaded on to the ship that would convey the competitors to South America.

The event was almost certainly inspired by the London–Sydney Marathon Rally held two years earlier. The distance between London and Sydney was greater, but this rally was 'only' 10,000 miles long, taking a more direct route. The Ladies' Prize had been won by an Anglo-Australian team of four, driving the unlikely choice of a Volvo 145S estate. Team leader, Elsie Gadd, an Australian surveyor and property developer, had no motorsport experience but did have considerable personal funds and a certain degree of toughness. Anthea Castell was also inexperienced but tough, having worked on a sheep station in the outback. The motorsport nous came from the British part of the team, Jenny Tudor-Owen and Sheila Kemp. Jenny in particular was an experienced race and rally driver, who normally drove an MGB.

None of the Gadd team entered the World Cup Rally, but two of the other female drivers who had taken part in the 1968 event did. Rosemary Smith, driving an Austin Maxi, was the favourite for the Coupe des Dames. She was a talented rally driver who had won the Tulip Rally outright in 1965. Jean Denton, who had tackled the Sydney event in an MGB, drove an Austin 1800. Although relatively new to rallying, she had proved herself on the circuits in an MGB, and also a Cooper single-seater. Jean was working for IPC Magazines at the time and used her contacts and marketing experience to put together a really good sponsorship package, with *Woman* magazine as the chief sponsor. Jean and her two teammates, Liz Crellin and Pat Wright, were featured in the magazine with their car, which was named 'The Beauty Box'.

The other all-female entry in the WCR was led by Tish Ozanne, a veteran rally driver who had served as Pat Moss's understudy at BMC in the 1960s, before buying up her works Mini and setting out on her own. She was a skilful driver, although her favoured surface was tarmac, and she preferred high-speed sections over navigational tests. Her co-drivers were Katrina (Tina) Kerridge and Bronwyn Burrell. Tina had built a reputation for herself, mainly in trials, but her career always had to play second fiddle to that of her husband, Paul Kerridge. She managed to beat him in her early trials, in a Hillman Imp, and also shone in overnight endurance trials. This was especially true when her weekends would sometimes be taken up by an overnight trial, then a production car trial the next day and would stand her in good stead for the World Cup Rally. It was to be her first taste of international competition, as Paul would not allow her to enter the bigger rallies, and he had the money and the cars. Even though she had proved herself to be a good driver, he preferred her to be at home with the children. She believes that her trial experience was one of the reasons Tish asked her to join the team. Their car for the World Cup Rally was an Austin Maxi, owned by Tish Ozanne herself. It was later christened 'Puff the Magic Wagon'.

Bronwyn Burrell is a British-based New Zealander. She had been taught the art of high-speed driving by Jim Clark, who impressed her greatly with his car control and smooth driving. He had been patiently showing her the lines around Brands Hatch in a Lotus Cortina when she asked him to 'really let it go' and take her round at top speed. Clark's answer was 'I just did,' and an observer's stopwatch showed that he had unofficially broken a class lap record.

Her first single-seater race ended in a crash and a neck injury, which put paid to her hopes in that direction but did not put her off motorsport completely. She had driven a number of rallies, including the RAC Rally. Often, her cars were borrowed, and usually from men, who declined to let her use their cars again when she beat them. At that time, rallies had a strong endurance element, and Bronwyn had once competed in the RAC Rally with a sick navigator, meaning that she drove for five solid days and several nights, with just one night's sleep.

Neither of these two teams were officially supported by British Leyland (BL), although they did enjoy some help from them for part of the rally. The BL drivers travelled and socialised together, as well as helping one another out. Among the other drivers was Prince Michael of Kent, in another Maxi, who was representing his Hussar regiment with two other military men. Five works BL cars were entered, four Triumph 2.5s and an Austin Maxi. Drivers included Paddy Hopkirk, Brian Culcheth and Andrew Cowan.

Footballer Jimmy Greaves drove a Ford Escort with Tony Fall. The Football Association acted as one of the sponsors for the BL team, and *Shoot* football magazine sponsored Roger Clark's Ford Escort. However, the rally was far from being a completely football-themed event. Many novel sponsorship deals were put together.

Two other female teams took part. Claudine Trautmann, a multiple French ladies' rally champion, drove a Citroen DS21 with Colette Perrier. She was a highly experienced rally driver who was completely comfortable with the DS, having driven one extensively in stage rallies. The second was actually a mixed team, led by Lavinia Roberts, an American. Her car was a Ford Mustang and she had two co-drivers in David Jones and Lieutenant Arthur Hazelrigg, both also

American. Lavinia appears to have entered at least one other rally, the 1971 Southern Cross event in Australia, but she is the most obscure of the World Cup rally women. This is partly because she dropped out very early on. Even the other competitors interviewed do not really remember meeting her.

Unusually, female navigators were almost entirely absent from the World Cup Rally. Of all the active competition roles within motorsport, this one is still the most commonly filled by women. Often, male drivers' wives co-drove for their husbands, as is still fairly common in club rallies today. By the time the World Cup rolled around, female professional co-drivers also existed. A surprising omission from the event was Valerie Domleo, a British competitor who came into navigation through her skill with maps and bearings, a product of her fascination with maths. She won two rallies outright during a long career: the 1960 Morecambe Rally (with Anne Hall) and the 1965 Tulip Rally (with Rosemary Smith). Away from motorsport, Valerie was a physicist who worked in the motor industry.

Given the date of the rally, there are a couple of other notable female absentees. Pat Moss-Carlsson was the grande dame of rallying in the 1960s, notching up outright wins in Sestriere, Baden-Baden, the Acropolis and the gruelling Liège–Rome–Liège Rally in 1960. This was a cross-Europe marathon, done with little outside assistance on terrible southern European roads, and without stopping, over four days. It was probably her best event on the European calendar. A good proportion of the European leg of the World Cup Rally was run along a similar route.

By 1970, Pat was winding down her career, but was still active, and her experience made her an ideal candidate for a works World Cup drive. However, Pat herself was not interested.

The South American leg revisited terrain that had been part of the Argentine Grand Prix, confusingly named as it was a rally, not a race. This too had been won by a woman driver, the Swede, Ewy Rosqvist, in a works Mercedes, assisted by Ursula Wirth. Ewy had been a great rival of Pat Moss's for the European Rally Championship (ERC) ladies' prize, finally winning in 1961. She excelled on the toughest terrain and scored top-ten finishes in the Greek Acropolis Rally in

1961 and 1964. This event is still regarded as a car-breaker, even today.

It is unclear whether anyone tried to get her involved again; she retired from the sport in 1967. Another Swedish driver, Sylvia Osterberg, was still active in 1970, driving an Opel Kadett in the Swedish championship. Her career was winding down also, but she had earlier been a skilled gravel driver, finishing fourth in the 1963 Polish Rally, run on mixed surfaces. She was also seventh in the 1972 Olympia Rally, a shorter marathon event celebrating the Olympic Games. It ran between the Netherlands and Germany, via Bulgaria and Turkey. Her car this time was an Ascona.

The final part of the rally passed close to the Pan-American Highway, which ran through Mexico. This had been the scene of a road race, the Carrera Panamericana, in the 1950s. One woman, Jacqueline Evans de Lopez, a British-born, naturalised Mexican film actress, competed five times, normally in a Porsche. In 1953, she drove a 356 carrying a painted tribute to Eva Peron, which was a much-photographed, if not successful, entry. Jacqueline had vanished into automotive obscurity long before the rally was organised, having had to sell her Porsche to pay off debts. However, it is worth remembering that endurance events on roads of dubious quality, sometimes run at very high speeds, were never a male preserve. If anything, female drivers had a history of doing better in marathon events than sprints.

In a rally of this length and duration, sponsorship was incredibly important. A glance at the entry list shows a huge variety of team title sponsors. Jean Denton's car, as mentioned before, carried *Woman* magazine signwriting. Four British newspapers entered cars, as did two British army regiments, the RAF and the navy. Bolivia and Thailand sent government-sponsored teams, in an attempt to promote their countries. Among the most unusual sponsors were USSR Auto Export (the Moskvitch team) and Annabel's nightclub, whose main driver was Innes Ireland.

Tish Ozanne's car carried signage from Marshalls of Cambridge, a garage, but the team had some rather original additional support. A fashion designer got on board, and the three women appeared in specially designed jumpsuits and Courreges-inspired dresses at all of the rally's promotional events. Bronwyn (Bron) Burrell, then 25, had some modelling experience as 'Miss Castrol' 1970. The outfits made for good publicity shots but were exchanged for more practical attire once the rally got started. Rosemary Smith, herself a former fashion designer and model, had started the 'trend' in 1968, when she was supported by the British Wool Board for the London–Sydney. This followed on from her own clothing line, 'Rally Girl' in 1967. When asked about it many years later, she replied that 'they were anoraks. They were terrible.'

Jean Denton's team had another interesting clothing-related sponsor. A company had started manufacturing disposable paper underwear, and each team member received a box of pink paper knickers. The quality of the pants was apparently suspect, but they were free, so they went in the car. This led to a series of jokes about underwear among the girls and their male cohorts, including a story about how the storage net in the back of the Austin, which was for holding crash helmets, was really a rack for knickers.

Jean Denton was a talented businesswoman who would excel in the world of magazines, automotive marketing, and finally, politics: she was a Conservative cabinet minister in John Major's government. She understood that her greatest value to the team was her organisational prowess and her ability to find funding. Friends and colleagues of the time still talk fondly of her (she died in 2002), and there is no suggestion that she was in any way forbidding or 'hard'. Instead, her warmth and humour are always mentioned, as well as her ability to bring people together. She was not above making herself look a little silly in order to publicise her racing and rallying, hence the paper knickers and a series of photoshoots, many of which appeared in *Woman*, involving matching outfits and posing on top of make-believe cars.

Jean's co-drivers were both highly skilled, with international rally experience. Liz Crellin occasionally co-drove for Pat Moss, and Pat Wright had navigated extensively for Nancy Mitchell and Tish Ozanne, so had considerable knowledge of driving in different conditions. The pair had met in 1959.

For most of this book, we have relied on contemporary reports, race and rally results and other 'official' records to piece together stories. For the World Cup Rally, we have some personal recollections, kindly given during an interview at the British Motor Museum in July 2016. Bronwyn Burrell, Tina Kerridge-Reynolds and Pat Smith (Wright) spoke candidly of the difficult conditions they faced, their relationships with the other drivers and teams, and also, many of the more light-hearted incidents that took place during the six-week rally. Being a woman, competing in a marathon rally in a world of men, could be very hard work, but it could equally be incredibly good fun. Some of the anecdotes are not quite suitable for publication, but I am going to attempt to relate the experiences of these three fearless, funny ladies. They still refer to themselves as the 'Rally Girls', even though they are now in their seventies. I have used the term 'girls' here for that reason, as opposed to 'women' or 'ladies'.

As she was no longer here to speak for herself (she died in 2009), I wanted to know more about Tish Ozanne. Bron and Tina drove with her on the World Cup Rally itself, and Pat knew her even better, having been her regular navigator for many seasons.

Tish was very much the leader of the team. She owned the car, paid all of the entry fees, and took on the responsibility of driving all of the primes (special stages). Bron and Tina took over on the road sections. Tish had been running her own rally car for several seasons by that point, after leaving the BMC team. Her main role at BMC had been as a support driver for Pat Moss; the European Ladies' Championship was one of BMC's goals each year, and it entered several all-female crews to ensure that there were enough female drivers in a rally for a Coupe des Dames to be awarded. Once Pat had scored enough points to secure the championship, the other female drivers were often released. Tish took her chances as a privateer.

Much older than her two teammates, at 47, she had had a traditional upper-class upbringing, in 'a family where things were done properly', according to Pat Wright. Having never married, she lived with her widowed father, a retired general in the British army, and acted as the hostess at their home in Surrey. She got into rallying in her thirties, after seeing an advert for 'The Little Rally' which was being run nearby and sounded as though it might relieve some of the boredom she felt.

Her skills in looking after others translated to being something of a mother figure to Tina and Bron, during the rally. She would even check on them in their hotel room, last thing in the evening, and wish them goodnight. According to both of them, 'she kept us in check!' They both remember her fondly, and speak highly of her driving, but Tina also described her as 'bossy' as well as 'brilliant'. That said, both she and Bron credit the discipline of their team to Tish. There was a considerable amount of organisation needed for a trip that passed through so many different countries, and she took it in hand, including obtaining the various currencies needed,

She was always rather 'proper', and normally dressed very respectably in a pleated skirt and cardigan. That said, there was another side to her. As a young woman, she had done some travelling in Australia, and apparently nearly got into a pistol fight over a man. This wild side perhaps came out on the rally stages, where she favoured smooth, twisty tarmac roads. Her favourite rally was the Donegal event in Ireland. Away from rallying, she played the guitar well. One of her co-driver's duties during a stage was to keep her supplied with lighted cigarettes, using an in-car lighter. The girls' World Cup cars were equipped with a dash-mounted bottle opener; Coca-Cola was thought to be a better refreshment whilst driving. The only actual injury sustained by the girls on the rally came when Liz Crellin cut her hand on an exploding Coke bottle.

The first part of the rally route ran between England and Portugal. This was not a straight-line route through France and Spain, but a huge detour through West Germany, then south through Austria and Hungary, and through the Balkans. It turned round in Bulgaria, came back through Yugoslavia again, then passed west through Italy and southern France, through Spain and into Portugal. Only crews who reached Portugal within the allotted time would be allowed to load their cars on to a ship, and start the South American leg of the route. The rally then began again in Brazil, then took a winding route in a roughly northerly direction, through Uruguay, Argentina and Chile, back through Argentina, northwards through Bolivia, Peru, Ecuador, Panama, Costa Rica, Nicaragua, Honduras, El Salvador and Guatemala. The final sections went into Mexico itself, and the finish was at Mexico City. It was a rally that broke cars and people; out of 106 starters, only twenty-six made it to the finish.

Rosemary Smith won the Ladies' Prize. She had been the favourite, and with her London–Sydney Marathon experience, she had an advantage over some of her rivals. She had also taken part in the 1968 Marathon which had crossed the Himalayas and travelled through some quite hair-raising terrain, with unfriendly locals. Rosemary had had to surrender cans of oil to opportunist bandits, who thought it was something they could drink, and were disappointed that she was carrying no jewellery. Her car's engine 'threw a rod' on the Khyber Pass. This serious engine blow-up, where the piston broke through the side of the crank case, meant the car was now running on five of its six cylinders. Badly affected by the oxygen-poor mountain atmosphere, the car struggled to maintain any power. Rosemary ended up driving up part of the Khyber Pass in reverse, in order to obtain maximum traction from the faltering car.

These factors were also a potential problem in 1970, with the additional fear of bandits en route. Before the start, Tish Ozanne and her team were asked if they wanted to carry a gun in their car, for self-defence. They declined the offer.

A danger that the crew decided was worth protecting themselves against was altitude. Much of the South American leg of the rally passed through the Andes, at elevations so high that the air became too thin for breathing. Oxygen tanks, of the kind used by mountaineers, were kept in the car in case of emergencies, although they were a finite resource. Tish Ozanne and her two co-drivers were not immune to altitude sickness, and ended up being treated in local hospitals. The standard treatment involved cocaine, which would result in disqualification now. According to Pat, it was a risk worth taking, as it worked. Jean Denton and her crew ran out of bottled oxygen long before the highest point, having found out that once you start using it, you have to carry on until safely at a lower altitude. Descending the mountains had its own hazards, from the change of pressure. Nosebleeds were a problem.

As well as the danger of drivers passing out from a lack of oxygen, the car had to be guarded from similar problems. Even now, in World

Championship rallies in Argentina and Mexico, drivers have to contend with lowered power on the high mountain stages.

Nowadays, rally drivers watch their diets and eat like athletes. Elite rally teams employ sports nutritionists and specialist medics. The days of driving all night on rendezvous sections are also gone, and this is probably a good thing from a safety point of view. As we might expect, none of these things reached the World Cup Rally's organising team. Packed lunches were provided for crews during primes, and they consisted of a sandwich, a cake and a banana, with a small bottle of Coca-Cola, which would have given a short-term energy boost, if nothing else. There were no nutritionally balanced chicken and pasta meals, sports drinks or protein smoothies. The Russian Moskvitch team was better supplied, and was happy to share their food with the girls.

These problems were not confined to the female drivers. Oxygen deprivation does not discriminate by sex; neither do bad roads, fatigue or hunger. However, one problem that Tina Kerridge has spoken of is one that would be more openly discussed by the women of the rally: guilt over family. Tina had two small children and a husband at home, and during the rally, sometimes asked herself 'why am I doing this?'. She missed the children terribly and felt guilty for abandoning them for six weeks. Neither Bron nor Tish had any children, so they did not have to suffer these guilty feelings. Tish, like her erstwhile co-driver, Pat Wright, had long been involved in the European rally circuit, and had perhaps learned to compartmentalise any misgivings she had about leaving her elderly father.

No-one discusses how these problems may have affected male drivers. Many of them had wives, partners and children at home, but they were not expected to express these kinds of thoughts, whether they experienced them or not.

In the end, it was not the mountains or mentality that did for Tish Ozanne's Maxi, but a less exotic problem: mud. The crew became stuck in a deep trench of the stuff on a long prime on the Argentine pampas, after heavy rain following a long dry period. It was here that Tish Ozanne's independence of mind and natural authority did not serve her well. Tina had competed in many trials and knew what they needed to do to give themselves the best chance of getting through the mud: let some of the air out of the tyres, find something to place underneath the wheels, and push if necessary. Tish, however, was determined to use engine power alone to get out of the mire, and the Maxi's furiously spinning wheels dug themselves deeper in. The rising temperature meant that the mud started to set, the car stuck fast, and the girls went over the time limit, if only by about forty minutes, and were out of the rally.

Prior to the mud incident, the girls had managed mishaps fairly well, especially given their lack of a dedicated service crew. On one prime in the former Yugoslavia, they suffered double punctures, and had to employ their system for replacing them. Tina, the smallest, would retrieve the jack from the boot of the car, while Bron, the tallest, would get the spare wheel down from the roof of the car. Tish and Tina, working together, would change the wheel, for Bron to stow, in the boot or back on the roof. They had practised this routine at Marshalls Garage before the rally, and could do it in a minute and a half.

The works teams had support crews carrying dedicated spares, but the private teams did not have this luxury. They had access to the BL service areas, but had to wait their turn behind the other, higher-priority teams. Bron Burrell related that she had to carry spare parts in her hand luggage on transfer flights, but stressed that most of the drivers did this. Rally drivers carrying steering racks and even body panels on to planes with them was a common sight during the event.

Jean Denton's approach to the rally would have given her a better chance of getting out of such a predicament. She was nominally the team leader, but she took it on herself to be the co-ordinator, rather than the boss. She was not afraid to defer to her navigators' superior experience, or to take advice from others. Jean, with Pat and Liz Crellin, would go on to finish the rally in eighteenth place. Her car was less prone to punctures, which happened, 'but not enough to slow us down,' according to Pat.

The Coupe des Dames was won by Rosemary Smith, and her co-drivers, Alice Watson and Ginette Derolland. All three were regular rally competitors, mainly around Europe. Ginette Derolland had sat alongside some of the leading French lady drivers of the time, including Marie-Pierre Palayer, Claudine Trautmann (then Claudine Bouchet) and Marie-Claude Beaumont. She had also co-driven for Gérard Larrousse. Alice and Rosemary had been a semi-regular pairing for the past couple of seasons, and had finished sixth in the 1969 Scottish Rally, driving a Ford Escort. (Showing how close the British rally girls were, one of Alice Watson's other drivers, Margaret Lowrey, was also co-driven by Pat Wright.)

Rosemary's rally was less tempestuous than before, although she had her fair share of punctures and tricky moments. One modification she insisted be made to her Maxi was the addition of sheepskin seat covers, as they were comfortable for long primes, and warm during cold sections, and at night.

So far, this chapter has focused on the trials and troubles of being one of the World Cup Rally girls, but there were plenty of good times as well. The rally entourage consisted not just of drivers and service crews but of a considerable pack of journalists and photographers, TV crews, spectators, sponsor representatives, team managers, administrative helpers, marshals and other hangers-on. Despite the gruelling schedule of primes and lengthy rendezvous sections, which sometimes meant driving all night, the atmosphere that followed the rally was a lively one. Camaraderie between teams was strong; this was not restricted to the World Cup Rally, as Pat Moss in her later years often suggested that the modern World Rally Championship (WRC) drivers were missing out on this aspect of the sport's earlier days. Friendships forged during the rally, and even a couple of marriages, are still maintained now.

After Tish Ozanne's Maxi was finally towed out of the mud, the girls decided to carry on following the rally, although they were no longer officially taking part. Tina joined up with the army team, two of whose cars had also retired, for the Andes section in Peru. After leaving the army boys, she hitched a ride with the navy team as far as Lima, where she ran into Peter O'Toole at the tiny airport there. Tish and Bron decided to follow the rally route. As they did so, they ended up helping out Andrew Cowan, who had crashed out of the rally, as he was taken to hospital.

Even while they were still active in the rally, the two younger members of the team partied almost as hard as they drove. After Tish had looked round their hotel room door and bid them goodnight, Bron and Tina were free to join in any escapades with mechanics, other drivers and reporters. Some of these high jinks were recorded by Tina on a video camera. Among them is a piece of film of her on a plane between Lisbon and Rio, sitting on the co-pilot's lap, something she claims not to remember even doing. On another plane, on the way home, the pilot had to come out of the cockpit to tell various rally drivers, including Bron Burrell, to sit in their seats properly and stop making so much noise. According to Bron, she was at the back of the plane, singing rude songs with Andrew Cowan, drinking cocktails. It was her first ever international flight.

Tina was ahead of her time with her video recordings, pre-empting social media by about forty years. Her films capture more of the rapport between the crews, including some footage from a beach after the rally had ended, which featured Jimmy Greaves making hand gestures at the camera.

One of the objections to having women involved at the sharp end of motorsport, often more implied than stated, is that their presence puts a dampener on proceedings; for example, it compels men to curb their language and crude behaviour. Women are seen as more easily shocked, conservative and risk-averse, which makes them less fun to be around. Hearing Bron, Tina and Pat talk about their adventures demonstrates that this is far from the truth; rally girls were every bit as fun-loving and pragmatic as their male counterparts. Even Tish Ozanne frequently stayed up until the early hours of the morning on less arduous events, according to Pat.

Decorum was not much in evidence, although the girls were guests of dignitaries including the British Consul on a couple of occasions, and a school in the Andes which was celebrating its twenty-fifth anniversary. Bron and Tish were invited to the party, as the children had never seen Europeans before. Here, even Tish let her hair down, drinking and dancing at many thousand feet above sea level.

In Brazil, Tish Ozanne's team had stopped for a toilet break at the side of the road. Prince Michael of Kent, in his Maxi, was next on the road, and pulled off to check that his 'fellow' drivers had not crashed or suffered a breakdown. He was told in no uncertain terms to leave the scene immediately by the embarrassed girls. He crashed out of the rally the next day, and the girls still jokingly wonder whether the shock had anything to do with it.

One of the other amusing incidents happened quite early on, although details will be deliberately vague, in order to protect the guilty. A man, who will not be identified further than this, had developed a crush on Bron, who was oblivious at that stage. Through a mechanic and Tina, she found out that he was planning to pay her a visit in her hotel room, which she shared with Tina. When Tish came in to say goodnight, Bron was apparently fast asleep, completely under the covers, except she wasn't; she was hiding in the wardrobe, and the shape under her bedclothes was one of the mechanics. When her admirer made his appearance, he got a shock, and the girls got a big laugh. No-one is sure whether Tish was aware of this incident; she had been more laid-back with Pat Wright in the past, who says that 'I could slip out of our hotel room and come back at four in the morning, and she wouldn't bat an eyelid.'

It was a life-changing event for Tish Ozanne's team, in many respects. Tish herself was probably the least affected; she was coming to the end of a long career, and the travel and physical effort was almost familiar to her. Bron Burrell used the rally as a step up in her continuing rally career; she would go on to compete in the RAC Rally in a Ford Escort later in 1970, and in 1971. Her competition career could have gone much further than it actually did, had she not been called back to New Zealand to care for her gravely ill mother. Tina Kerridge's life was affected in a more personal way by her decision to take part; her enforced separation from her husband and children, which she found so difficult, was one more step towards the end of her marriage, she admitted. She and Paul separated, and are now on good terms with one another. Tina eventually married one of the mechanics she had met during the rally, Tim Reynolds, and the marriage is still going strong. Pat Wright too, is still married to a man she met as part of a service crew.

The World Cup Rally was meant to have been Rosemary Smith's last event. She had married in 1969, and her husband was keen for her to stop her 'ego trips', as he called her motorsport activities. Maybe it was the excitement and intensity of the event that made her want to carry on, for her retirement into domesticity lasted less than a year, and the marriage only slightly longer. She was back on the scene in 1971. Jean Denton's husband was involved with motorsport himself, but it worked well with Jean doing the driving, as he suffered from terrible motion sickness. He would work on the cars that Jean drove. Claudine Trautmann, too, had a husband who was also involved in rallying, and who never tried to stop her from competing. Even after she retired from the stages, she worked in management for Bob Neyret's female-centred Team Aseptogyl, having been one of its original stable of woman drivers. Neyret was driving another Citroen in the rally, and could it be possible that he got the idea for Team Aseptogyl by watching the female crews in action?

Claudine's rally had run more smoothly than Tish Ozanne's, which was unsurprising, considering that she was part of a works-supported team, and enjoyed the assistance of her own service crew. Officially, both Claudine's car and that of her husband, Rene, were private entries, but Citroen admitted their involvement in a promotional film which came out after the rally. The film showed Rene and Marlene Cotton, heads of Citroen's motorsport department, performing a recce in South America beforehand. Incidentally, Marlene Cotton would become one of the first women to run a works competition department when Rene died in 1971.

Claudine and her navigator, Colette Perrier, had been comfortably in the lead of the ladies' standings in the latter part of the rally. The car, a DS21, had developed engine problems and was consuming vast quantities of oil, but its drivers and service crew were managing the problem as best they could and were keeping the car going admirably. It ran as high as tenth overall, despite the mounting troubles. Only on the last prime, which ran between Guatemala and Mexico itself, did the Citroen give up, 300 miles from the finish. This sounds like a long way, but in marathon rally terms, was no distance at all. Her retirement handed the Ladies' Prize to Rosemary Smith, who walked away with $2,400.

After the rally had ended, Tish Ozanne's team went their separate ways, and did not meet again for almost forty years. In 2017, Tina and Bron reunited with the Maxi, and took on a classic rally from London to Portugal. They were assisted by Seren Whyte, an experienced competitor in modern historic rallies. The Maxi struggled with hills, lost an exhaust bracket, and broke some wheelnuts, which were nigh-on impossible to replace, but they finally got to Lisbon on time.

Chapter 10

The Real Grid Girls

The 1976 British Grand Prix, Brands Hatch, 18 July 1976

1. Niki Lauda (Ferrari)
2. Jody Scheckter (Tyrrell)
3. John Watson (Penske)
4. Tom Pryce (Shadow)
5. Alan Jones (Surtees)
6. Emerson Fittipaldi (Fittipaldi)
7. Harald Ertl (Hesketh)
8. Carlos Pace (Brabham)
9. Jean-Pierre Jarier (Shadow)

   DSQ James Hunt (McLaren)
   DSQ Clay Regazzoni (Ferrari)
   DSQ Jacques Laffite (Ligier)
   DNF Gunnar Nilsson (Lotus)
   DNF Ronnie Peterson (March)
   DNF Brett Lunger (Surtees)
   DNF Patrick Depailler (Tyrrell)
   DNF Carlos Reutemann (Brabham)
   DNF Arturo Merzario (March)
   DNF Bob Evans (Brabham)
   DNF Vittorio Brambilla (March)
   DNF Henri Pescarolo (Surtees)
   DNF Chris Amon (Ensign)
   DNF Mario Andretti (Lotus)
   DNF Jochen Mass (McLaren)
   DNF Hans-Joachim Stuck (March)

DNF Guy Edwards (Hesketh)
DNQ Jacky Ickx (Wolf)
DNQ Divina Galica (Surtees)
DNQ Mike Wilds (Shadow)
DNQ Lella Lombardi (Brabham)

The 1976 British Grand Prix was the only time that two female drivers competed in a Formula One race weekend. Both Divina Galica and Lella Lombardi tried to qualify but could not make it.

The 1976 season was dominated by the rivalry and close title battle between James Hunt and Niki Lauda, with Lauda's accident at the Nürburgring and subsequent comeback gaining almost as much attention by itself. It could be seen as a season of Grand Prix racing at its most testosterone-fuelled, with fighting spirit, bravery and more than a touch of corporate gamesmanship playing their part. The British race itself was almost boycotted by TV because Alan Jones's Surtees was sponsored by a brand of condoms. James Hunt's disqualification, due to cutting down a service road after his first-lap crash and thus technically jumping the restart, stirred up the British fans. He was reinstated by the stewards and won the race, although protests by the other teams led to him being disqualified afterwards. With this amount of drama, anyone could be forgiven for not paying much attention to the previous day's qualifying sessions.

Into this most masculine of arenas, two women tried to stake their claim.

The Grand Prix weekend was a dry British summer, one with good conditions for racing at Brands Hatch. This was the first time that a Grand Prix had been held since improvements had been made to the circuit, so there was some unfamiliarity for many of the drivers. This was Divina Galica's first attempt at a Grand Prix; Lella Lombardi had raced a private Brabham at Brands in 1974.

Qualifying did not go well for either racer. Divina, as a solo Shellsport entry, was twenty-eighth fastest on the timesheets. Lella, in an RAM Brabham, was thirtieth and last. Her teammate, Bob Evans, managed to qualify in twenty-second place out of twenty-six. He did not finish after the car's gearbox failed on lap twenty-four.

Divina was at the beginning of her brief Formula One career. Lella was coming to the end of hers. RAM was the last team for which she drove, part of a revolving-door series of drivers who usually only made one appearance during 1976. Lella was their second-longest standing driver of 1976, after Loris Kessel. She and Kessel shared the best RAM finish of the year: twelfth, achieved by Lella in Austria and Kessel in Belgium. Their joint appearance at the Osterreichring in August was that year's last race for the team. It was also Lella's final Grand Prix appearance and it was fitting that she recorded a finish, her only one of the year.

The Brabham BT44 was built in 1974. Although its Gordon Murray design was quite technically advanced on its debut, by 1976 it was no longer competitive, the other teams having caught up, and the Brabham team themselves having moved on to the BT45. RAM's cars were sold to them by Brabham once they were surplus to requirements.

Divina Galica's car was a Surtees TS16, which was, like the BT44, from 1974. It was designed by John Surtees and had been bought by Nick Whiting for Divina to use. It was the only TS16 still active in 1976. She was running under the banner of Shellsport, the promotional company run out of Brands Hatch by its managing director John Webb. Webb co-owned the Surtees with Whiting.

This rather futile battle to get on to the 1976 British Grand Prix grid brings us to two very different racers who illustrate the different ways that female drivers have broken into the male-dominated world of elite single-seater racing.

Lella Lombardi is the most successful female Formula One driver to date. She completed most of a season in 1975 with the March team, and became the first woman to score points in a Grand Prix. Her single point for her sixth place in the Spanish Grand Prix was halved due to the race being shortened after Rolf Stommelen's serious accident, but she remains the only woman to get on to the FIA's Formula One points computer.

Today, there is a standard career progression for a Formula One driver: karting from the age of 8 or earlier, followed by whichever junior formula is currently predominant, then Formula Three, perhaps

Formula Two combined with a testing role, then a race seat. In the 1960s, this was less rigidly defined, but a career path still existed. Karting had established itself as a training ground for racing drivers in the 1960s but most still started in club racing, then Formula Junior or Formula Three, pushing as far as their talent and budget would allow. Drivers often gained extra experience, exposure and money by racing touring and sports cars.

Lella Lombardi's early racing career followed that pattern fairly closely. The very beginnings of it are hazy. She was not from a particularly wealthy background; her father was a butcher. She grew up in the Italian village of Frugarolo. According to some stories, her family did not even own a car. Her first experience in a fast car came when she was about 16, and playing handball for her school team. The girl she was marking during the game became frustrated with her and punched her in the face, breaking her nose. After the game, this girl felt guilty seeing Maria Grazia Lombardi, as she was then known, with a nosebleed, waiting for a bus. She took her opponent to the hospital in her Alfa Romeo sports car, sometimes said to be blue. After that, the young Lella became obsessed with fast cars, and decided to become a racing driver.

This story does not quite have the ring of authenticity about it and it is not clear at all where it originated. Perusal of contemporary newspapers reveals that the Lombardi family owned at least one car and also a van used to deliver sausages, which Lella often drove when she worked for her father. Her long-term love of motor cars was well known locally. This and her somewhat masculine appearance were noticed, but she seems to have been generally accepted and liked by her community, even when it became clear she was a lesbian.

Her first racing experiences came not too long after, at Monza. She borrowed money from family members and her partner of the time and started racing in Formula 875. She rapidly showed her talent and her story was picked up by the media. She initially used the name 'Lella' as a pseudonym, perhaps to protect her privacy. In 1967, she raced in Formula Three in Italy, but it was tough going. Her best finish was eighteenth in the Coppa San Piero a Sieve. For the rest of the year, she struggled to qualify her Ford-engined Branca. It was a similar story in 1968 and she was absent from the series in 1969. In 1970, having taken a step back down to Formula 875, she won the championship and added another two wins to her tally of six in 1971.

Another Formula Three season with the Jolly Club team was much more productive. It was not all plain sailing and she had her share of non-qualifications in her Lotus 69, but she managed to break into the top five twice, at Imola and Varano. She was tenth in the championship.

In 1973, her career went international. She raced at the prestigious Monte Carlo Formula Three event and was one of the twenty qualifiers. She finished the race in twelfth place, driving a Brabham BT41 run by Scuderia Italia.

Another tenth place in the Italian championship did not look like progress, but her results were better than ever, starting with a fourth place at Casale. Her best result also came at Casale: a second place.

Away from single-seaters, she won an Italian one-make series for the Ford Escort Mexico, taking six victories.

John Webb and Shellsport join the story here, before he and Divina Galica worked together. He was impressed by Lella's showing at Monaco and invited her to take part in a celebrity Shellsport Escort race, which she won, beating Formula One driver Jacques Laffite.

The support of John and Angela Webb led her to a race seat in Formula 5000 in 1974. F5000 was a series for big single-seaters, usually Formula Two cars with superseded Formula One engines in them. She picked up sponsorship from Radio Luxembourg, then a popular radio station and the first commercial broadcaster to reach the UK. Her racing number was 208, a reference to the station's frequency.

Again, she began strongly with a fourth place. She repeated her fourth place at Monza, her home track, at Oulton Park and at Mallory Park. In the second half of the season, she was consistently in about sixth place. The opposition was strong and included Peter Gethin, Vern Schuppan and Guy Edwards. Her strong finishes were all the more impressive because she tended to struggle in qualifying, leaving herself with a lot to do. She was fifth in the championship.

The time was now right for her to make her Grand Prix debut. Despite Bernie Ecclestone's recent vocal opposition to women in

Formula One, it was from him that she rented her first Formula One car, a 1973-specification Brabham BT42. Jackie Epstein of the Radio Luxembourg team got her a deal with Hexagon Racing to contest that year's British Grand Prix, held at John Webb's Brands Hatch. This would be the first time in fifteen years that a woman had tried to qualify for a Formula One race, after Maria Teresa de Filippis's attempt at Monza in 1959.

Qualifying was once more a tortuous process and her Friday practice was wiped out by a broken driveshaft. In a year-old car and lacking seat time, she did not manage to qualify, missing the time by almost a second. Still, she was not last on the timesheet, and she had recorded faster lap times than her erstwhile F5000 rivals Vern Schuppan and Tom Belsø.

She may not have qualified for her first Grand Prix but her performance was enough to persuade Count Guggi Zanon, an Italian millionaire, to sponsor her for £50,000. She would drive for the March team in 1975, bearing the livery of Zanon's Lavazza coffee brand.

Compared to many others, Lella was quite skilled in getting herself sponsorship, even though she was reserved by nature, did not court publicity and had no desire to be famous. She did not use up sponsor money on personal expenses and when not travelling to race, lived quietly at home in Italy with her partner, Fiorenza.

The Zanon money was enough to support Lella for eleven rounds of the World Championship. Out of eleven races, she qualified for ten, only missing out at Monaco, and finished five. Her season started poorly with a non-finish in South Africa, but her historic sixth place in Spain followed. It was an utter shame that the woeful standards of track safety almost saw the race being boycotted by the drivers – only two attempted to qualify – and that Rolf Stommelen had his terrible accident. Otherwise, notwithstanding the general desirability of a safe and incident-free race, Lella's achievements would be more widely acknowledged. However, I suspect that this was no great personal hardship for her, as she preferred to be seen as a racing driver, not a female racing driver.

Two more DNFs separated Montjuich and her next finish; a fourteenth place at Zandvoort and then eighteenth in France. She did not finish the British Grand Prix, but at the Nürburgring she was seventh, a lap off scoring another point. Robin Herd of March later described it as her best race, especially since she was managing the car with a puncture. Her ability to feel when her car was running with a puncture and act accordingly was one of her strongest skills during her time in Formula One. Although her mechanical sympathy was later praised by the likes of Herd, she often felt that she was not taken seriously in her dealings with mechanics. During the 1975 season, she complained of a traction problem with her car, which began after an accident in Monaco. She described the handling problem to the team, who did not take her word for it and asked her teammate Vittorio Brambilla to test the car. He claimed that there was no problem and the matter was dropped. It was only after Lella's departure, when Ronnie Peterson tested her old car, that the team found that she had correctly identified a serious problem which was caused by a fractured rear bulkhead. Robin Herd, speaking in 2015, believed that Brambilla had not been pushing the car as hard as he claimed. He has felt bad about not believing Lella ever since.

After her German efforts, she was seventeenth in Austria and did not qualify for her home Grand Prix at Monza. At this point the Lavazza money was running very low, and March managed a move to Williams for her for the US Grand Prix. After a string of problems which included her car being impounded by Customs and a breakdown on the warm-up lap, she did not start the race. This was her only outing for Williams. At the start of 1976, she made a final appearance for March in Brazil, before being replaced by Ronnie Peterson, also supported by Lavazza. She then moved to the RAM team.

Divina Galica's route into Formula One was very different, although some of the same players appear in her story. If Lella embodies the traditional career path of a Grand Prix driver, then Divina's route in is an exception. Still, many female drivers up until very recently did not have the support for a lengthy junior career, or did not become interested in motor racing at all until adulthood. Divina was one of these.

Born in 1944 in Hertfordshire, Divina did not race a car until she was almost 30. Her passion for sport and speed was focused on alpine skiing, a sport in which she excelled. Ten years earlier, in 1964, she competed in her first Winter Olympics at Innsbruck. She would return to the Winter Olympics as the British women's ski team captain in 1968 and 1972. Her best Olympic event was the giant slalom, but in the World Championship her best results came in the downhill: two third places. For many years, this was the best result ever achieved by a British skier.

In 1974, John Webb was promoting a celebrity Shellsport Escort series and invited Divina to take part. The celebrity races were run as supports to other Shellsport-promoted events and hosted a mix of TV personalities, journalists, aristocrats and other sportspeople. Divina's first appearance was in a race just for sportspeople, including boxers Henry Cooper and Joe Bugner. She was not the only woman in the field; Ann Moore, a champion showjumper, also took part. Divina surprised and impressed the Webbs and many onlookers, quickly getting to grips with the finer points of racing. She was invited back for other Shellsport events, including the Ladies' Escort Race at Brands Hatch in October. In this race she qualified second and finished second, behind the more experienced Jenny Dell. Interestingly, the previous three Shellsport Ladies' Escort races had been won by Lella Lombardi, who did not take part in the final race.

After discovering her talent in a Ford Escort, John Webb set about tutoring Divina in the art of single-seater racing. She raced a 1600cc Elden Formula Ford in the UK in 1975 and performed well. She was not the only Shellsport female protégée, however. Ann Moore had been taken on by the Webbs and given a more powerful Elden Formula Ford 2000 to race. She found the car difficult to drive and did not make much of an impact on the results lists. After a single season of motorsport, she stepped down, claiming that she had not realised how much time her new racing career would take up. Janet Brise, widow of Grand Prix driver Tony Brise, was another whose career began under the tutelage of the Webbs. She raced sportscars for a season or two in the mid-1970s.

Divina had no such problems and rose rapidly through the single-seater ranks. At the start of 1976, she had left Formula Ford far behind and was busy making her mark on the Shellsport Group 8 International Series, a British-based championship for superseded Formula One machinery. By this time, Nick Whiting had stepped in and provided a Surtees TS16 for Divina to race. She was not quite on race-winning pace just yet, but she was a solid top-ten performer, only finishing outside that bracket once. Her best results were a pair of fourth places at Mallory Park and Thruxton and she was fourth in the championship. It was won by David Purley and Formula One drivers Mike Wilds, Guy Edwards and Derek Bell finished below her in the standings.

In this context, it was not completely surprising that Webb and Whiting decided to take a punt on Divina entering the British Grand Prix. As it was being held at Brands, it was possible for Webb to pull a few strings, and Divina got a wildcard entry as a 'local interest'. She did not qualify, but she was not the slowest on the grid, although her car was old and not prepared to the same standard as some of the others.

The team and Divina did not attempt another World Championship Grand Prix in 1977, but they kept very busy. Divina's main focus was the Shellsport Group 8 International Series. She had a newer car, a Surtees TS19, which she wasted no time in getting to understand. After a false start to the season at Mallory Park, where she was unable to start, she proved her intent with a second place at Snetterton. This was the first of four podium finishes; later in the season, she scored two thirds at Mallory Park and Brands Hatch and another second, at Donington. Only a series of mid-season non-finishes dropped her down the standings and she was sixth at the end of the season. This in itself was quite impressive, considering that drivers of the calibre of Derek Bell were in action.

She may not have entered any World Championship Grands Prix, but Shellsport and Whiting did get Divina one big entry that year, the Race of Champions at Brands Hatch. She qualified and was twelfth overall.

As well as the Shellsport championship, Divina accepted some one-off drives with other teams. She competed in one race in

European Formula Two for Ardmore Racing in a Chevron B39, but does not appear to have made much of an impression. As usual, her car was one iteration behind most of the other Chevrons on the grid.

The end of 1977 marked the end of her involvement with Shellsport. The Webbs, Whiting and Divina had been a good team for the past two years, but it was time to try a new avenue. Divina was approached by James Hunt's brother and manager, David, and picked up some sponsorship from Olympus Cameras, who also worked with James Hunt. Her first race for Team Olympus in the Aurora British Formula One Championship, in her familiar Hesketh, gave her another second place at Zandvoort. Sadly, there was not enough Olympus budget for more Aurora outings. She made another appearance later in the season, driving a McLaren M23 run by Melchester Racing, and was seventh at Thruxton.

The lack of Olympus funds was down to one thing: Divina's second stab at making a Formula One start. The Hunt connections had secured her a temporary race seat at Hesketh in one of their own cars. She was entered for the first two rounds in Argentina and Brazil. Both times, she was bottom of the time sheets and did not qualify.

This was where Divina's Formula One career ended. Despite her obvious talent and ability in Formula One machinery, she never got a chance with a competitive team, so could not make much of an impression. Her relative success in the Shellsport series with Webb and Whiting shows that continued support from a good team can go a long way in getting results, but without resources and capital, it cannot go right to the top.

The story is similar with Lella Lombardi. Count Zanon's support of her for a relatively long time allowed her to build up experience, but ultimately, she never had the machinery to mount a serious challenge. Her problems with the March mechanics exacerbated this.

For both women, the end of their brief Formula One tenure was far from being the end of their careers. Even while she was racing for March, Lella Lombardi was building up sportscar experience. She raced at Le Mans three times, in 1975, 1976 and 1977. The first time was part of a season in the World Sportscar Championship which ran parallel to her Formula One activities. She drove an Alpine-

Renault A441C with Marie-Claude Beaumont, representing Equipe Elf Switzerland (despite neither driver being Swiss). While they were not as quick as the works Alpine-Renault A441C, driven by Jean-Pierre Jabouille and Gérard Larrousse, they were on the pace in the early part of the season, taking sixth place at Mugello and fourth at Monza, this time with a class win. This was their third race together.

Sadly, they did not finish Le Mans itself, a fuel feed failing after just twenty laps. The car suffered further reliability issues later in the year; the rear suspension gave way during practice for the Coppa Florio and a cam belt broke on lap twenty of the Zeltweg race. After that, Lella concentrated on her Formula One season.

According to reports, the relationship between Lella and Marie-Claude was not perfect. It is said that Lella considered herself as capable as any man and had made motorsport her life. Marie-Claude was not quite as sure of her own talents and had other interests outside the cockpit, such as skiing, as well as moving between racing and rallying. Lella was said to have no great interests outside motor racing, apart from occasionally fishing. She is sometimes painted as a rather cold and forbidding person, but those who knew her personally knew that this was a front, constructed for self-defence. Her cars were the only 'things' she was interested in, but she had time for people in her life.

Her choice of team for 1976 showed another side to her. She sometimes claimed that she did not wish to be known as a female racing driver, merely as a racing driver, but this did not mean that she felt alienated from other women. At Le Mans in 1976, she joined Christine Dacremont in a Lancia Stratos, which was run by Team Aseptogyl. Aseptogyl was a French toothpaste brand and the team, normally all-female, was the pet project of Bob Neyret, a dentist and sometime racer. The Stratos was painted Aseptogyl's distinctive pink and red. Previous Aseptogyl drivers had come from backgrounds in other sports and in modelling, but Lella fit right in and finished Le Mans in twentieth place, third in class.

Christine Beckers, her Le Mans teammate of 1977, was also full of praise for her team spirit, kindness and helpful nature. She was eager to pass on her knowledge of driving, and especially car set-up and technical matters. She described her as 'the perfect teammate'.

Lella and Christine drove for the Inaltera-Ford team in 1977. Lella was invited by Inaltera team boss Vic Elford, who had been impressed with her work ethic, mechanical sympathy and stamina. They were eleventh, and this would have been a higher finish had the electrics on the car not malfunctioned, leaving Christine without headlights or engine management.

The Inaltera team also ran her and Christine at Daytona, where they ran as high as fourth before being taken out by a Porsche. This was just one of many big sportscar races that Lella entered between 1975 and 1981. Her sportscar career could be the subject of a chapter by itself, so I will pick out a few highlights.

Her most successful partnership was with the Osella team. In 1979, she won the Pergusa 6 Hours outright in an Osella PA7, with Enrico Grimaldi who was best known as a hillclimber. At the Vallelunga race later in the year she won again, driving with Giorgio Francia this time. In 1981, the same pairing, in a PA9 this time, won the World Championship race at Mugello. These wins were part of a long string of good results, including many podiums.

After 1981, Lella moved into touring cars and competed mainly in Italy until 1988. She normally drove Alfa Romeos, often run by Jolly Club. From 1985, she competed less, before finally retiring in 1988 to run her own touring-car team. The reason for this was ill health; she had been suffering with breast pain since 1985, which turned out to be cancer. She died in a clinic in Milan in March, 1992, aged 50. Her dying wish was that her touring-car team continue after her demise.

Divina Galica took a slightly different route after her exit from the Grand Prix scene. Unlike Lella, who moved into sportscars almost immediately, Divina tried to forge a career in single-seaters by herself. She owned a March 792 which she entered into Aurora Formula One, Formula Two and Formula Atlantic races in 1979 and 1980, the latter in the US as well as the UK. Without the backing of a team, she was unable to contest more than a couple of races in a season and thus could not put any sort of title challenge together. In 1979, she was second in the Hitachi Trophy, behind Norman Dickson in another March. This was her only standout result during this time. In 1980, she picked up some sponsorship with Wendy Wools, who were doing a lot of unlikely motorsport tie-ups, but it was not for a full season.

Shellsport no longer existed in its old form, but John Webb continued to offer Divina the odd drive for Brands Hatch Racing. In 1980, she drove a Tiga SC80 in the Brands Hatch 6 Hours with Mark Thatcher, son of the then British prime minister. They were eleventh overall.

The big Brands sportscar race of 1981 was a 1,000km instead of a 6 Hours, and Divina came back in the same car. She was sharing it with Tim Lee-Davey, and they were sponsored by the Kelly Girl temping agency. The pair were twentieth and fifth in class.

This year was the first big step Divina made in moving the focus of her racing activities to America, much later. She was picked up by Kent Racing to drive their Mazda RX-7 alongside Kathy Rude. They were just about classified in thirty-first in the Sebring 12 Hours in March and they were thirty-sixth at Riverside, not quite finishing.

The US connection continued in 1983, when she drove for Preston Henn's team in the Brands Hatch 1,000km. She and her teammates, David Sutherland and Henn himself, did not finish in their Porsche 956, failing to restart after a spin.

Between 1984 and 1988, she raced in Thundersports in the UK. In her first year in the series, she was supported for part of the way again by Brands Hatch Racing, who put her in a Kelly Girl prototype with Tiff Needell and Tony Trimmer. It was rather a rough-and-ready year in 1984, and Divina only finished once, a fifth at Brands with Trimmer.

In 1985 and 1986 she mostly drove a Shrike, supported by either Gil Baird or the Tech Speed team. She became a regular visitor to the top ten and by 1987, she managed her first podium: a third at Oulton Park. She was driving a Royale for Fulmar Racing by then, with Mike Taylor.

During this part of her career, it is quite obvious that she was a strong team player, who had continuing partnerships with Webb and at least two other teams. After ten years, she was welcomed back to Kent Racing in 1995 to have a go at qualifying for the Daytona 24 Hours in a Chevrolet Camaro. She and Vittorio Brambilla did not make the starting grid.

At about this time, she did at least one season in the British Truck Racing Championship.

The 1990s were a much quieter time for Divina, track-wise. Unbelievably, she started ski training again and made a comeback as a professional, competing in the Albertville Winter Olympics in 1992 in the speed skiing event. This is the fastest of the Alpine skiing disciplines, and was only included once as a demonstration sport. She was nineteenth.

During this time, she had moved to the US and was also looking after her elderly mother. Her only big result was a seventh place in the 1992 Suzuka 1,000km, driving a Spice SE89C for Chamberlain Engineering with Tomiko Yoshikawa and Jun Harada.

During the 1990s, she concentrated more on the business side of motorsport. She joined the Skip Barber Racing School as an instructor and became an important figure in the company on the commercial side, ending up as a senior vice president.

Her other most notable achievement in her later career was her role in the Women's Global GT Series (WGGTS), a sportscar championship for women in the US which used identical Panoz Esperante cars. It ran in 1999 and 2000 and she was the runner-up both years. In 2000, she entered Petit Le Mans at Road Atlanta with Cindi Lux and Belinda Endress, two other leading WGGTS drivers. Their car was a Porsche 996 and they were twentieth overall.

If Lella Lombardi had not had cancer, it is tempting to think of her adding her talent to the WGGTS, if only as a guest driver. The series was mostly contested by American drivers, but some Europeans, like Divina, travelled over, including Lilianna de Menna, who had raced touring cars against Lella.

In their way, the two 1976 Grand Prix women were quite similar. Both were 'no nonsense', practical and pragmatic, and keen to be seen as racing drivers first. However, they both, in modern parlance, 'identified as' female, and happily joined in with women-only races and the sporting opportunities granted to them by John and Angela Webb as part of their 'stable' of woman drivers. Equally, they were happy to encourage and assist other female racers. According to a 2015 *Motor Sport* article, Lella described herself as 'a free and independent woman'.

They were both very private, and wary of the celebrity side of any possible motor racing fame, Lella more so than Divina. While Divina was the archetypal thrill-seeker, who only came to motorsport quite late, Lella ate, slept and drank motor racing, which could sometimes make relating to her a little hard, if one did not share her mindset.

It is not clear how well the two knew each other, although they must have been acquainted at least. I would like to think that there would have been a lot of understanding between them, and that they would have made great teammates, in the right situation.

Shellsport and the Webbs were not finished with their efforts to get a woman into Formula One. In 1980, they nearly succeeded with Desire Wilson.

Desire only appears in the Formula One statistics as a single DNF in the 1980 British Grand Prix, but this is only a tiny part of her story.

Had she been able to put together a sponsorship deal, she would have been able to take up a race seat with Tyrrell in 1981 or 1982, having impressed team boss Ken Tyrrell in the 1981 South African Grand Prix, then being run as a non-championship race due to a row between organising bodies. She spun off after fifty-two laps but had run as high as fifth.

This was not the only time she impressed in a Formula One car. In the late 1970s, she was one of the leading drivers in the Aurora Formula One series in the UK. She had come over to the UK from her native South Africa as part of a Formula Ford young driver programme in 1977, having won the South African championship the prevous year.

Webb saw her skill in a junior single-seater and immediately recognised her promotional value. He got her a seat in a March for the official Formula One tyre tests in 1978. This would function as a test of her abilities as well as a publicity stunt for the British Grand Prix; Webb had no intention of putting her in for a Grand Prix yet. It was a steep learning curve, but she held her own and managed not to spin or cause any incidents. By the end of the sessions, she was twenty-first quickest out of twenty-six cars.

Desire was offered a job in the offices at Brands Hatch and based herself in the UK. Her tyre test and her Brands connections led to a drive in the Aurora AFX Formula One Championship, driving an Ensign for Mario Deliotti Racing. This was a British-based series and far from the Formula One World Championship, but it was experience in Formula One machinery and she learnt quickly. Her best result in her first season was a third at Thruxton. Melchester Racing signed her for 1979 and she advanced further in a Tyrrell 008, picking up four podium finishes and leading a race at Zolder, making her the first female racer to do so. Although she could not hold on for the win due to a spin on the wet track, she fought back to third in the closing stages of the race.

Keeping hold of sponsorship deals was always difficult for her and she was racing Formula Pacific in New Zealand when Teddy Yip offered her an Aurora drive in his Wolf WR4. She repaid his support by winning the second round of the championship at Brands Hatch. Yip had initially been reluctant to back a female driver. The money only lasted for a part-season, but Desire was second at Thruxton and third at Mallory, proving that her success was not a fluke.

Unfortunately, her only attempt at a World Championship Grand Prix was rather a nightmare. Ground effect was the technological talking point of the time and Desire's practice runs were her first experience of a car with sliding skirts, the source of the aerodynamic 'ground effect' that anchored the car to the track. The car was a Williams FW07 run by RAM Racing and she was as high as twelfth place on the time sheets. However, when the race weekend came around, she found the car was handling very differently and that even the seat did not feel right. Later, she found out that it was a different car entirely, one hastily converted from Aurora specification, which did not allow for sliding skirts, to full Grand Prix specification. The aerodynamic devices were not working as they should and she found the car undrivable. She did not qualify for the race.

Desire's pursuit of motorsport success was never entirely fixed on Formula One and it is probably down to this that she enjoyed the long career that she did. Alongside her negotiations with Tyrrell, she was willing to jump into any car she could, often at her workplace of Brands Hatch or as part of a Shellsport promotion, such as the 1980 Talbot Sunbeam ladies' race at Snetterton in which she finished second to Geunda Eadie. At the same time, she competed extensively in Sports 2000 in the UK, with some success, as well as Formula Ford 2000. Her Formula One hopes were over by 1982, but a new chapter of her career was beginning. Alain de Cadenet had asked her to join him in a Cosworth-engined Grid Plaza with himself and Emilio de Villota. The car was quick in qualifying but did not finish. The following year, she drove a Porsche 956 with Axel Planckenhorn and Jurgen Lassig, finishing seventh and recording one of the highest-ever finishes for a female driver.

She proved herself to be a talented and tough sportscar racer, competing in Europe and increasingly America. Although the project ultimately ended without success, she was taken on by Preston Henn for his IMSA team in 1982, driving a Porsche 935 and acting as a driver coach to Henn's daughter, Bonnie. Bonnie Henn left the team at the end of the season and Desire had to look elsewhere.

One of her better years in a sportscar was 1987. She drove a Saleen Mustang and won the Sebring 6 Hours with Scott Pruett, as well as another enduro at Sears Point with Lisa Caceres.

In between, she focused her attention much more on the US and made a good attempt at an Indycar career. She passed her Indianapolis rookie test in 1982 with an eye on the Indy 500.The qualification process started terribly with her teammate Gordon Smiley suffering a fatal accident, then a series of engine failures meant Desire was unable to progress.

The following year, she drove for Rose Wysard's team in a March. Although she was unable to qualify for the Indy 500 that year, she did manage to finish eight other races once the car was updated to 83C specification from 82C. Her best finish was a tenth place at Cleveland.

She made four more Indycar starts between 1984 and 1986, but did not reach those heights again. She never qualified for the Indianapolis 500.

In the latter part of her career, Desire became involved in a number of projects designed to highlight women's participation in motorsport. Her last Le Mans entry was as part of an all-female team in 1991, sharing a Spice SE90C prototype with American Lyn St James and Cathy Muller of France. The car lasted forty-seven laps before its engine blew.

This had followed a time in the PPG Pace Car Team, which was attached to Indycar. A group of twelve or so female drivers, all of whom had competed in motorsport in some way, drove the safety cars for CART and entertained the crowds during breaks with displays of precision driving. Among them in the earlier days were Robin McCall and Patty Moise, who had raced in NASCAR, sportscar racer Margie Smith-Haas and Lyn St James.

Lyn St James had crossed paths with Desire in IMSA sportscar racing as well as Le Mans and would go on to race in Indycar. After she retired from full-time racing, she became one of the leading figures in the Women's Global GT Series, a highly publicised championship for female drivers. By this time, Desire had largely retired from competition and was only active in historic cars.

She was chiefly famous for her attempts at the Indy 500, of which there were nine between 1992 and 2000. Her team was able to put together significant sponsorship from retail giant J. C. Penney and Nike. Lyn qualified for seven editions of the race and had a best finish of eleventh in 1992. Although she did not get the results that Janet Guthrie managed, she was named as Indy Rookie of the Year in 1993, the oldest driver at the time to win the accolade (at 45) and the first woman to do so.

Lyn's career overlapped with that of Sarah Fisher; when they both qualified for the 2000 Indy 500, it was the first time that two women had started at the Brickyard.

The WGGTS was launched in 1999 in a blaze of publicity, a single-make series for selected and invited female drivers in Panoz Esperante sportscars. Despite its entry lists that included the likes of Divina Galica, Giovanna Amati and future Indycar and sportscar racer Milka Duno, it failed to launch any driver into major mainstream motorsport and folded after two seasons. Don Panoz and Lyn had been its main backers but it never had a title sponsor. The 1999 championship was won by America's Cindi Lux and she was succeeded by German Sonja Bayer. Cindi Lux went on to achieve some success in Trans Am racing and enjoyed a lengthy career, but Sonja Bayer disappeared soon after.

Both Desire and Lyn were vocal supporters of the all-female W Series when it launched in 2018.

Chapter 11

Women On Top

1,000 Lakes Rally, Jyväskylä, Finland, 28–30 August 1981

13 Michele Mouton/Fabrizia Pons (Audi Quattro)
36 Carita Ekroos/Eija Seitz (Ford Escort RS2000)
38 Marja-Liisa Korpi/Eija Heiniö (FSO Polonez 2000)
46 Rena Blome/? (Peugeot 104)
48 Waltraud Wünsch/? (Peugeot 104)

The 1981 1,000 Lakes Rally was selected almost at random, from a list of results from one particular female driver (Rena Blome, actually). It was chosen for its five female finishers, listed here with their finishing positions, rather than any specific historical significance.

The abiding image of international rallying in the 1980s is that of the spectacular Group B cars. Group B did not exist as an official class until 1982, but its birth happened at the beginning of the 1981 season, in Monte Carlo, when the Audi team unleashed the four-wheel drive (4WD) Quattro on to the international rally scene. By 1983, top-specification rally cars were all 4WD and packing 300+ bhp. The new regulations had few restrictions on construction materials, power outputs, use of turbos or minimum weights, compared to the old Group 4 rules. Homologation requirements were easier to achieve than before, with only 200 road-going versions of a Group B car having to be built.

The formula got bigger, faster, more powerful and more dangerous very quickly. Just three years later, it was banned by the FIA part-way through the season, following the horrific deaths of Henri Toivonen and his co-driver, Sergio Cresto, when their Lancia Delta S4 exploded after rolling down a steep bank during the Tour de Corse. The construction materials of the S4 were light, but not as flame-retardant as they could be. This, combined with the huge fuel load, turned the car into an incendiary device. Their deaths followed Attilio Bettega's demise one year prior, on the same rally, when his car crumpled upon impact with a tree. Accidents involving spectators also contributed to the decision.

In 1981, this was still far in the future. The first public appearance of the Audi Quattro was on the Algarve Rally in 1980, but only as a course car, driven by Hannu Mikkola. The 1981 Monte marked its competitive debut.

Audi chose the highly experienced and competitive Hannu Mikkola, and the younger Frenchwoman, Michele Mouton as its first works team. There was an element of promotional value in Michele's hiring, which she acknowledges, but she was the real deal as a driver. In 1977, she had been runner-up in the European Rally Championship, mostly driving a Porsche 911. That year, she won the Rally of Spain. The following year, she was victorious in the Tour de France, in a works Fiat 131 Abarth. She used a similar car in 1979, and won the Lyon-Charbonnieres Rally in France. This was quite unusual for the time, as she had only been rallying since 1974, Mikkola, on the other hand, had been active for almost twenty years.

The Quattro's first rally started spectacularly, with both drivers setting very fast times; Hannu Mikkola caught the driver in front, who had set off a minute before him. The car's 4WD system offered superior grip. Unfortunately, Hannu Mikkola crashed out, and Michele also retired after problems caused by sand-contaminated fuel.

Mikkola brought home the first win for the Quattro, in Sweden, but Michele was not far behind. Audi had supported her for the Terre de Garrigues Rally in France in March, which she won. Later in the year, she ensured her place in history by winning the Sanremo Rally, a first for a female driver, the second-ever for Audi and a 4WD car, and its first win on gravel. Michele had now proved herself worthy of a place in the team, and was retained for 1982, after finishing eighth in the WRC standings.

The Quattro was far more reliable during the 1982 season. The Audi team was built around Hannu and Michele, with a series of supporting drivers including Stig Blomqvist. Michele repaid the team's faith in her quickly, winning the Rally of Portugal in March, Audi's first victory of the year. She followed it up with further wins on the Acropolis Rally, and the Rally of Brazil, then a second place in the RAC Rally. In contrast, Hannu Mikkola won two rallies, and Stig Blomqvist, one. Michele was second in the WRC, and actually had the most wins of any driver, but she was beaten to the title by Walter Röhrl, in an Opel Ascona. The two had been neck-and-neck until the Rallye Cote d'Ivoire, which Röhrl won. Michele had needed to win or at least score well to retain a chance of the championship, but she was distracted by news from home that her father was ill, and did not perform as well as she could have done.

Michele continued as an Audi works driver for another three seasons. She did not manage any more wins, but remained competitive on the world stage. Her best WRC finish was a second place, in Portugal. Away from the WRC, she took wins in the Audi Sport Rally in the UK, and the Metz Rallye Stein in Germany, both in 1983. Her final year as a full-time driver was 1986, and she made it count by winning the German championship in dominant style, driving a works Peugeot 205. She won six rallies that year. In 1985, she also travelled to the US to contest the Pike's Peak hillclimb, one of her last drives in an Audi. To the astonishment of many, she won the event outright; it was normally an event for single-seaters and hard-bitten US professionals like Al Unser. Unser was not happy that Michele had won. Her retort to his complaints was said to be 'if you had any balls, you'd race me back down as well.'

In contrast with her American experiences, she was accepted by most of her male teammates, particularly Mikkola. In the early days of the Audi team, he would let her share his car set-up. Michele did undertake some testing, but was happy to have her car the same way as her teammate. A couple of years later, Walter Röhrl, another teammate and serious rival, was asked about women rally drivers. On the subject of Michele, he said that he never thought of her as a female driver, and that he classed her as a man. This was not his most diplomatic statement, but in a way, it was a backhanded compliment from someone who did not rate women as drivers.

There is much more that could be written about Michele's motorsport career, which took in several years of the French championship, a Le Mans class win, fifteen international rally wins, cars including a Lancia Stratos, and a furore over illegal servicing in 1985. Although, until recently, she did not want to be seen as a mouthpiece or example of a female driver, she is undoubtedly the one to whom other women in rallying will be compared.

Who are these other women? 'Where are these other women?' might be a better way of framing the question, and it is not at all surprising that several of them came from Finland, a hotbed of rally talent since the 1960s.

Going back to the 1,000 Lakes in 1981, Carita Ekroos and Marja-Liisa Korpi were obviously not competing in 4WD works cars in the top class. Both were regulars on the Finnish rallying scene. Carita Ekroos had been active since the late 1970s, first in an Opel Ascona, then her Ford Escort. In 1980, she had entered fourteen events, with a series of class runner-up finishes. Her best overall finish was seventeenth, in the Mesikämmen-Ralli in January. She was still driving the Ascona then. Marja-Liisa Korpi was also present that day, and finished fourth overall in her Escort. Marja-Liisa was that year's Finnish ladies' champion, with four wins from five rallies.

Carita and Marja-Liisa were rivals for the Finnish ladies' championship throughout the late 1970s, with the latter winning the title three times between 1978 and 1980. Between 1976 and 1981, Marja-Liisa normally rallied a Ford Escort of some description, and her cars included a Mexico, an RS2000 and a 1300. Despite her loyalty to Ford, she occasionally drove a Saab, or even Eastern Bloc cars such as a Moskvitch and the Polonez. She was a very capable driver, especially towards the end of her career, and she earned at least three top-ten finishes in Finnish rallies: the fourth place mentioned above, eighth in the Kiuruvesi Ralli in 1980, and sixth in the AKU-Ralli in 1981. All of these were achieved in Ford Escorts.

Neither of these two women ever competed in a Group B car, but they demonstrate the strength in depth that existed in women's motorsport in the late 1970s and early 1980s. Sinikka Parkkinen is another name who could easily have appeared on a 1,000 Lakes finishing list of the time; she was another Escort driver who was runner-up in the Finnish ladies' championship in 1977 and 1978. She enjoyed quite a long career, from 1974 to 1987, including a run in the 1,000 Lakes in 1980.

Eine Hukkanen drove a Chrysler Avenger in Finnish rallies between 1976 and 1980, managing to win at least one Coupe des Dames. A little earlier, Marketta Oksala won the 1975, 1976 and 1977 Finnish ladies' championship, and competed further afield in the Monte Carlo Rally and the Tour de Corse in 1977. The list of fast female Finns is almost endless, and goes back to the 1960s, when the likes of Eeva Heinonen, Kirsti Airikkala and many more made their mark, in their own small way, on the famous 1,000 Lakes course. Rauno Aaltonen's sister, Marjatta, was one of these. She entered the 1,000 Lakes at least four times, with a best finish of sixteenth in 1968, driving an Isuzu Sport.

Finnish drivers led the way in the transition of rallying from a discipline with a strong emphasis on navigation and driving tests, to one based on special stages and speed. Women were very much part of this. If any of the female Flying Finns could have picked up that elusive win, it is likely that one of them would have been piloting the nascent Group B Quattro to the first female rally victories of the modern era.

Finnish women continued to have a strong presence in rallying, during and even after the ending of Group B in 1986. Minna Sillankorva drove a Group B Mazda RX-7 for the 1985 and 1986 seasons, supported by Mazda Europe. Her programme took in Belgium, Sweden and the UK as well as Finland. Her best finish in this car was a thirteenth place in the 1985 Scottish Rally. Moving on in 1987, she rallied a Group A Mazda 323 for a few seasons, picking up a couple of top tens in Finnish rallies, before switching to a Group A Lancia Delta Integrale in 1990. She won the FIA Women's World Rally Championship in this car in 1991, with a career-best finish of tenth in the Rally of Argentina, and a point on the WRC tables.

The FIA Ladies' title was taken in 1992 by another Finn, Eija Jurvanen. Her career began in earnest in 1989, after the end of the Group B era, but her first car was an Audi Quattro, retaining some links with the period. Her women's championship was not the most honourable of victories, as she exploited loopholes in the rules to ensure her win. Coupe des Dames hopefuls had to take part in at least one non-European rally, but they did not have to finish it. Eija and her team cut their risks by starting the rallies of Australia and the Ivory Coast, but retiring shortly afterwards. She redeemed herself somewhat in 1993, when she won the Saaremaa Rally in Estonia outright. Her car for both of these seasons was a Ford Sierra Cosworth, and her navigator was Marjo Berglund. Marjo provided another connection to the heyday of the female Flying Finn, having been active since in the mid-1980s as a co-driver, and occasionally as a driver in Finland.

Returning to the 1981 1,000 Lakes, the other two female crews were led by German drivers. Sadly, the names of their co-drivers have not been recorded. In the case of Rena Blome, it was likely to have been Ulrike Dalko or Petra Schuster, both of whom sat beside her that year.

Rena was about the same age as Michele Mouton, and their paths crossed a few times during their respective careers. Rena had begun hers much later than Michele, when she was going into her thirties, but she became quite famous and well-liked in Germany. Her first major season of rallying was 1981.

While Michele Mouton was having her best year as an Audi works driver, Rena also picked up a works drive in her Peugeot 104, supported by the German arm of Peugeot Talbot. Towards the end of 1982, she was finishing just outside the top ten in the German championship, with twelfth places in the Rallye Deutschland and Rallye Vorderpfalz. She got herself a drive in a Group B car in 1983, a Talbot Samba Rallye, still supported for at least some events by the works team. That year, she matched her twelfth place in the Saarland Rally, scored seven class wins, and was eleventh in the German championship. In the same car, she broke into the top ten for the first time in 1984, with eighth in the Saarland Rallye and tenth in the

Hessen Rallye. Her final full season, 1985, gave her a best finish of sixth in the Saarland Rallye, her favourite, in a Peugeot 205 GTi.

Rena's step back from rallying in 1986 meant that she did not get to battle directly against Michele Mouton in the German championship, which Michele won convincingly that year. Michele was another works Peugeot driver, and she also drove a 205, but hers was a fire-spitting T16, a genuine Group B monster that had won the previous year's WRC, driven by Timo Salonen. Rena Blome had negotiated furiously with Peugeot to be allowed to drive one of these; their refusal was one of the reasons she did not compete at all in 1986. It is tempting to think of what a team she and Michele would have made.

Waltraud Wünsch did get to compete directly against Michele again. She had her last major season of rallying in the 1986 German championship, driving an Opel Kadett GSI, running as a Formula Two car. She was not able to challenge Michele for overall honours, but was a strong driver nevertheless. Her best finish that year was an eleventh place in the Sachs Winter Rally.

Waltraud is relevant to this chapter because she, like many of the other women drivers discussed here, flourished during the Group B era. Her best car was a Citroen Visa Mille Pistes, which she drove with the support of Citroen Germany in 1985. Despite some problems with reliability, she was an impressive fourth in the Saarland Rallye, and tenth in the Sachs Baltic Rally. Both times, she won her class; the Visa was a rally-bred Group B machine, but had a smaller engine capacity (1600cc) than the likes of the Peugeot 205 T16 and the Opel Manta 400, which were that year's dominant cars in the German championship. Both times, she was the leading Citroen finisher.

Waltraud's first top-ten finish on a German rally came a year earlier, when she was ninth in the Drei-Städte-Rallye, behind the Audi Quattros of Walter Röhrl and Harald Demuth. Earlier still, in 1983, she was part of an international team of female drivers in Alfa Romeo Alfasuds on the 1983 Monte Carlo Rally. The team was the last big showing for Bob Neyret's team, which had become famous in the 1970s as Team Aseptogyl. Aseptogyl's final hurrah was a nine-car squad, divided into French, German, British, Italian and Belgian teams. Four of these got to the finish, the leading car being driven by Louise Aitken-Walker, followed by Waltraud in fifty-sixth place, seven places behind.

After her retirement from the stages in 1986, Waltraud was a stalwart member of the Rallye Deutschland organising committee, acting as Rally Secretary and helping to guide the event into the World Rally Championship.

The five women who finished the 1,000 Lakes in 1981 were not alone, as we have already seen.

Via the Drei-Städte-Rallye, we come to Susanne Kottulinsky, who was the eighth-place finisher in 1984, one above Waltraud Wünsch. She was from Sweden, and seemed to perform particularly well in Germany, where she often rallied. Surprisingly, she never actually got to drive a Group B car, despite being capable of top-ten finishes on international rallies and having works support behind her at different times. Still, even without Group B power, she was a force to be reckoned with, in a Group A Volvo 240, and later, a Group N Audi 200 Quattro. Her 1984 eighth spot was her first top-ten in the Volvo, and the following year, she would almost match it, with a tenth place. Her career really took off in 1987 and she was third in the West Euro Rally Championship. Her best results were two fifth places, in the Hessen Rally and the Hellendoorn Rally, which was held in the Netherlands. She was also ninth in the International Tulip Rally, also in the Netherlands, and ninth in the Rally of Haspengouw, across the border in Belgium.

Her last season of full-time competition was 1988, when she drove the Audi in the German championship. Her navigator, for the fourth consecutive season, was Tina Thörner, who would go on to compete regularly in the WRC in the 1990s and 2000s, alongside both male and female drivers. She also co-drove on the Dakar for Jutta Kleinschmidt and Colin McRae.

Susanne and Tina scored five top-ten finishes from five rallies that year, the best of those being a fifth place in the Rallye Baden-Wurttemberg. After that, Susanne rallied only sporadically, in Germany and Sweden, although a run in a Mitsubishi Lancer Evo IV in the 2002 Drei-Städte-Rallye proved that she had lost none of her touch: she was eighth overall.

Susanne then retired, having become a mother, but this was not the end of the Kottulinsky name, or its pedigree of female drivers. Both her son and daughter are circuit racers, and Mikaela, her daughter, races touring cars and GTs internationally.

Another driver who came of rallying age in the Group B era, although she rarely drove Group B machinery herself, was Louise Aitken-Walker of Scotland. Just two years before Michele Mouton and the Audi announced themselves on the scene, she was making her debut as part of the Fabergé Fiesta Challenge, a race and rally talent search for female drivers supported by Ford and Fabergé cosmetics. She did not win but used the experience to launch a twenty-three-year career in rallying, in Britain and internationally. Highlights of this included the FIA Ladies' WRC Trophy in 1990, driving a Vauxhall Astra, and an outright win on the British Peter Russek Rally in 1983, in a Ford Escort run by the British Junior Rally Team. Her best WRC finish was tenth, achieved on the RAC Rally in 1991, driving a Ford Sierra Cosworth with Tina Thörner. It was on British rallies that she really shone, having already got national hopes up in 1987, when she retired from seventh place on a snowy RAC Rally, an oil cooler on her Peugeot 205 GTi having cracked. From about 1984 to 1992, she was a regular visitor to the top ten in British championship rallies, finishing fourth in the 1992 championship, driving a works Ford Sierra Cosworth.

Louise retired from regular competition after that, to have three children. It seems that none has followed her into motorsport, although her children's former nanny, Jane Nicol, was encouraged to start her own rally career by Louise, in 2003.

Women rally drivers were far from being just a northern European thing in the 1980s. Their network had a large branch in Italy, the birthplace of Michele Mouton's co-driver, Fabrizia Pons. In the late 1970s, she was a handy driver herself, before joining up with Michele. In 1978, she finished ninth in the Rallye Sanremo, at the wheel of an Opel Kadett.

In 1985, Michele's German championship year, Fabrizia won an event of her own: the Lady Rally dei Castelli Malatestiani. She was driving an Audi Quattro, and defeated Paola de Martini in a Ferrari 308, and Paola Alberi in a Porsche.

Paola de Martini was another driver who made a small impact on the WRC. She scored points in the championship for three years running, between 1988 and 1990. She was driving an Audi 90 Quattro, for the Audi Sport Europa Team. Each year, she picked up a couple of points for a ninth place in the Tour de Corse, and in 1989, this was augmented by a ninth place in the Monte Carlo Rally. In 1988 and 1989, her WRC top-tens were part of a string of strong finishes in international rallies, and in 1988, she won the San Marino Rally outright. This, and two fourths in Bulgaria and Catalunya, helped her to sixth place in the European Rally Championship. She first started driving the Audi in 1986, the last year of Group B, although the car she used was a Group A version.

Paola and Louise Aitken-Walker were rivals for the 1990 FIA Ladies' Trophy, and each had a good chance of winning. Only the superior reliability of Louise's car ensured her victory.

The idea of a ladies' rally in Italy in 1985 showed what strength in depth there was in the ranks of female drivers there. That year, Pierangela Riva made a good showing in the Italian championship, driving a Peugeot 205 and finishing in the top ten four times. At least three of these were as a member of the works team. Had the works WRC team not already had the services of eventual champion, Timo Salonen, and former champion, Ari Vatanen, she might have been in with a chance.

Pierangela Riva's navigator, Mariagrazia Vitadello, was a long-standing member of Italy's rally sorority. Prior to 1985, she was a long-term teammate to Anna Cambiaghi, normally driving a Lancia for Jolly Club, then Paola Alberi, another Jolly Club driver in a Fiat, in 1983. After her year with Pierangela, she was reunited with Anna for a works Peugeot drive in the Italian championship, using the Group B T16. Sadly, they did not finish either of their two major rallies.

Another Italian who slipped through the works teams' nets is Antonella Mandelli. She was another Jolly Club-affiliated driver, who drove a Fiat 131 Abarth and a Lancia 037 Rallye for the team. In the former car, she broke through on the Italian domestic scene in 1980, finishing third in the Rally delle Valli Piacentine. She was not just a domestic flash in the pan either, as she proved the following year, with a second place in the Madeira Rally. She scored five top-ten finishes in Italian and Iberian rallies in 1982, before mounting the podium again in 1983, in the Madeira Rally. This time, she was in the Lancia 037. A final international season gave her a third third place in her favoured Madeira event, as well as a fifth in the Catalunya Rally, which would later be raised to WRC status. She missed out on world championship entries, although some of the rallies she tackled had been part of, or would be part of, the WRC. The 037 was categorically a Group B car, and she proved that she was capable of handling it well.

Mariagrazia Vitadello was then engaged as Prisca Taruffi's co-driver, usually in a Ford Sierra Cosworth. Prisca, the daughter of Piero and Isabella Taruffi, last winners of the Targa Florio, was another proven top-ten finisher in the Italian championship. She competed between 1985 and 1990.

So visible was rallying as a female sport in 1980s Italy, female celebrities even started competing. Cláudia Peroni, a TV reporter, started rallying in a Fiat in Madeira in 1984, before moving on to a Lancia Delta Integrale. Patricia Pilchard, a US-Italian TV actress, drove a Fiat in 1980 and a Peugeot in 1982, sometimes assisted by Mariagrazia Vitadello.

Further to the 1985 ladies' rally mentioned above, at least two initiatives for women in Italian rallying happened during the mid- to late 1980s. LadyRally, which seems to have been related to the original 1985 event, continued in 1986, and a six-woman Ford team was featured in the Italian press at a similar time. Details of these initiatives are quite sketchy, and they were not picked up by the English-speaking press. Many of the drivers above, including Prisca Taruffi and Patricia Pilchard were involved, as well as Marina Perzy, another 'celebrity' driver who had appeared on television, and Daniela Angei, who later competed in rally raids.

In the wake of Michele Mouton and the increasing popularity of rallying, the French motorsport authorities endorsed the Citroen Total Trophy in 1984, a driver search for female talent that Citroen used to promote its rally-bred Visa Mille Pistes model. The Trophy had run as an open event in previous years, with the female angle added in in 1983. This included the revival of the Paris–St Raphaël women's rally. The competition was open to both complete novices and experienced drivers, who had to progress through regional heats first. The winner was Sylvie Seignobeaux, and second place went to Christine Driano. Both won works-supported drives in the French championship for 1986. Christine Driano went on to win the FIA Ladies' WRC award in 1993. Her car was a Citroen AX GTi.

We could go on. A cursory glance at the history of women in rallying in 1980s might look as if it began and ended with Michele Mouton, plus a few pretenders to her crown who lasted a season or two. It is not taking anything away from Michele to state that her achievements, as a female driver, were not as an isolated exception to the rule but as the most successful and fastest member of a large and diverse group of women rallyists, who competed together, shared teams and navigators and probably encouraged one another, too. France and Italy probably had the biggest rally sisterhoods, with Finland, the UK and Germany not far behind. The careers of many of these drivers, like Michele Mouton, began much further back, in the 1970s, and were part of an established tradition.

Women have been winning major international rallies since at least the 1930s. Kitty Brunell was the winner of the 1933 RAC Rally in an AC Ace. Just over twenty years later, Gilberte Thirion won the Tour de Corse in a Gordini-engined Renault Dauphine, in 1956. This was the first running of the Tour de Corse, and a significant win for a woman in a rally still on the international calendar. As rallying moved from navigation and driving tests to special stages in the 1960s, Pat Moss won four events outright between 1960 and 1968, including a victory on the gruelling Liège–Rome–Liège marathon in 1960, in an Austin-Healey 3000. She was a works driver throughout the 1960s, for BMC, Saab, Ford and Lancia.

In the middle of this, Ireland's Rosemary Smith won the Tulip Rally in a Hillman Imp. She took advantage of a handicapping system and terrible weather to earn her win, assisted by Valerie Domleo, an expert navigator who sat beside many British female drivers of the time. A couple of years earlier, and halfway across the world,

Ewy Rosqvist, a Swedish Mercedes works driver, won the Argentine Grand Prix, another long-distance rally.

Donatella Tominz of Italy is another outright winner who often gets overlooked. She took her win on the 1973 YU Rally in the former Yugoslavia, driving a Fiat 124.

The Balkans even produced their own talent. Romana Zrnec won four rallies in Yugoslavia between 1985 and 1987. Her car was a Formula Two Renault 11. Romana's biggest win was probably the 1986 Ina Delta Rally. The year after, she earned a second place in the Saturnus Rally. This was an international event and part of the ERC calendar. She rallied all round southern Europe, as far afield as Portugal and Spain.

Manufacturers and a small number of permitted sponsors used these victories as advertising material, and some of these drivers were well known in the motoring world, and in their own countries. Pat Moss's connection to Stirling Moss, and her previous achievements in showjumping, made her a household name of sorts. However, two factors really benefited Michele Mouton in her rise to become the best known of the rally women: the fledgling WRC, and television.

The World Championship for Drivers was only awarded for the first time in 1979. European, national and other regional titles were contested, as was a manufacturers' championship from 1973, but the WRC gave a clear yardstick for who was the best driver in the world. This was a valuable promotional tool for his or her team. Michele's second spot in 1982 secured her place in both the record books and the history books. Group B and its immediate predecessors provided noise, speed and spectacle, and therefore worked well for rallying as a broadcast sport. Film of Michele powering her Audi through forests and mountain passes is still available to watch now. Her achievements were not just results on a piece of paper; they were visible.

A final note on the Group B era must be to point out the level of danger involved. The accidents to Henri Toivonen and Attilio Bettega have already been mentioned, and there were many others that were not fatal but could have been. It is a common motif in the history of women in motorsports that the more dangerous and crazy the action, the more likely it is that women will be involved somewhere. This goes for Brooklands in the 1930s, the marathon rallies of the 1960s and 1970s, the Carrera Panamericana and 1970s Formula One, as much as it goes for top-line rallying in the 1980s.

When asked why she was retiring in 1986, Michele Mouton stated that she wanted to start a family, and that the death of Henri Toivonen had affected her deeply. After retiring from full-time rallying, she turned her hand to organising the yearly Race of Champions. It is dedicated to his memory.

Chapter 12

The Girls Most Likely To

2 August 1998, Most

Interserie Cup
1. Martin Rihs (Dallara F394)
2. André Fibier (Dallara F395)
3. Dirk Jenichen (Dallara F396)
4. Osmunde Dolischka (Dallara F396)
5. Leos Prokopec (Dallara F397)
6. Claudia Steffek (Dallara F391)
7. Jaromir Zdrazil (Dallara F396)
8. Frank Brendecke (Dallara F393)
9. Christian Eigl (Dallara F394)
10. Hvorje Baric (Dallara F393)

For the race with which to introduce this chapter, I could have chosen almost any Formula Three event held in Austria or Eastern Europe in 1998. There was not only one female driver in European Formula Three but two; two who were rivals and capable of getting on to the podium. Claudia Steffek and Osmunde Dolischka were both battling for the Austrian Formula Three championship, and were also fighting against one another for sponsorship and recognition.

That year in the Austrian championship, Claudia Steffek was sixth and Osmunde Dolischka was third. Claudia's best result was a fourth place at Brno, but Osmunde managed a runner-up spot in the same race.

They drove for different teams and had different cars. Osmunde's team, Fritz Kopp Racing Team, ran a 1995-specification Dallara-Opel. Claudia drove for her own team, and her car was a much older model, an Alfa-engined Dallara from 1991. In that context, her achievements in reaching the top five several times in a season are more remarkable.

Osmunde Dolischka was the older of the two racers. She was born in 1973, making her 25 in 1998. She had been active in senior motorsport since 1995, and took a fairly orthodox route through the single-seater ranks: Formula Ford in 1995, then a season in Formula Three in 1998. The only non-standard factor here was her age; she had only started karting as a young adult, when she was 20, rather than as a child, like many of her male peers.

Claudia Steffek was rather more of an upstart, albeit one on a traditional path. She began her senior career only a year later than Osmunde, in 1996, but she was only 17. After only a year as a single-seater driver, she was trying out Formula Three for size. She moved into the Austrian Formula Three series fully in 1998. Therefore, her career overlapped considerably with Osmunde's, despite the age gap.

Of the two, Claudia seemed the more ambitious and forceful. At the beginning of the 2000 season, she stated to the press that her aim was to be racing in Formula One by 2002. At her rate of progress, this looked to be possible.

Their rivalry continued off the track and into the offices of promoters and managers. At the beginning of 1999, Claudia signed a sponsorship deal with Fujitsu Siemens, who were to support her in the Austrian Formula Three Championship. This was a hammer blow to the career of Osmunde, who had been counting on the Fujitsu money herself, and considered it a done deal. This move effectively pushed her out of single-seater racing. She carried on in one-make saloons, and much later, tried her hand at rallying, but her career never really reached the heights again.

The move paid off for Claudia. She was one of the leading drivers in the series that year, with three podium finishes: two thirds at Rijeka (Croatia) and Brno, and a second at Rijeka. She was third in the championship. At about the same time as she made her announcement about her Formula One ambitions, she signed up for the Italian Formula 3000 championship, having signed a deal with Malta Racing. Formula 3000 was the established last step between Formula Three and Formula One.

If Claudia won the battle of the sponsors in 1999, she lost the war in 2000. Malta Racing turned out to be not what it claimed to be. She was left with no team, no car and no money, having fallen victim to con artists. This was the end of her career. She was 20.

Motor racing is full of stories like those of Claudia Steffek and Osmunde Dolischka. They are not specific to female drivers. Talent can only get you so far without a good team and strong financial backing, as many male drivers have found to their detriment. Among female drivers, the two Austrian women had enjoyed better support than many, having been able to complete whole seasons of racing and apparently do some testing. Their situations made mistakes less critical for them, as they had a full season in which to develop. This is often not the case.

In the early 1990s, when Osmunde and Claudia were both teenagers, they had a possible role model in single-seater racing; this was the last time that a female driver attempted to qualify for a Grand Prix.

Giovanna Amati was hired by the ailing Brabham team in 1992, as a teammate to Eric van der Poele. She had been granted a Superlicence the previous year, following a thirty-lap test in a current Benetton car.

She entered the first three races of the year: South Africa, Mexico and Brazil. For the first two, she was about three seconds off her teammate's pace, but this increased to almost nine seconds at Interlagos. Her inexperience showed, with some embarrassing spins witnessed by journalists. To be fair, van der Poele struggled almost as much to get the car on the grid, but he got to keep his seat, because his sponsorship money was already in place. Giovanna's did not materialise, and she was let go, replaced by Damon Hill on his Formula One debut. He only qualified for six of the eight races for which he was put in and was last each time. The team disbanded at the end of the year.

At first glance, Giovanna's route to her chance at Formula One was quite orthodox. She progressed from Formula Three, where she proved herself capable of winning races, then spent the years between 1987 and 1991 in Formula 3000, the feeder series for Formula One. However, her time as a Formula 3000 driver was a very disjointed experience, undertaking part-seasons for five different teams. The longest association she had was with GJ Motorsport, who ran her in some rounds of British and International Formula 3000 in 1991. She did ten rounds of the International series, qualifying for seven of them, with a best finish of seventh at Le Mans. She was also ninth at Oulton Park. That year, she qualified for more races than almost all of her other Formula 3000 seasons put together.

Giovanna's team-hopping was in all likelihood down to a lack of funding, but it is a common problem for female drivers. Because of their comparative rarity and publicity value, teams are less willing to take a risk on them, without a big injection of sponsor cash. This often means that drivers have to race without undertaking testing, and that they do not get a chance to learn the car and get to know their team properly. We saw this in the case of Lella Lombardi.

As with Lella Lombardi, and probably with Liane Engeman in saloon racing, frequent team moves can give the impression that a driver is 'difficult', and make it harder for them to find another team.

It has been said by other commentators, including the British Women Racing Drivers' Club's (BWRDC) Helen Bashford-Malkie, that women drivers tend to be given less time to prove themselves than their male counterparts, with sponsors hesitant to offer money for full seasons and quick to pull out when their driver is not immediately on the pace. Some of this is due to the visibility of a female driver; one young male driver in a field of many has more latitude to make mistakes early in his career, without them being seized upon immediately as evidence of his unsuitability. There is also a tendency to blame women's mistakes on their being female, rather than a particular lack of technique or temperament. No-one ever comments on videos of Michael Schumacher at his most bombastic that men are dangerous and should not be allowed behind the wheel.

Giovanna's Formula 3000 results are not particularly impressive, but with more continuity and support, they would probably have been much better. At Formula Three level, she won a round of the Italian championship in 1986, and that year, she was a frequent top-five finisher. She was far from being the 'spoilt little rich girl' decried by the press, who had already heard of her due to her having been kidnapped for ransom as a teenager, in 1978. The story was quite a lurid one and was told extensively in the Italian press.

Reputation is another pitfall that male drivers rarely have to manage. Giovanna's Benetton test is widely considered to have come about due to a romantic relationship between her and Flavio Briatore, then the Benetton team principal. She has been accused of sleeping with a number of high-profile personalities within Formula One, although she has claimed that her own dealings with men in the Grand Prix world were quite difficult. Only Ayrton Senna was sufficiently unintimidated by her to give her the time of day.

Despite the media savaging that she experienced, there seem to have been a whole group of young female racers who came in her wake, and were willing to brave the bear pit that was top-line motor racing.

We do not really know how much of an inspiration Giovanna Amati was, but a scan of the records shows that there was a handful of female single-seater drivers who came within touching distance of Formula One. Between Giovanna and Susie Wolff in 2014, there was a long line of women who nearly made it, but didn't.

In Europe, the Austrian girls were not alone. To the north, in Finland, Sanna Pinola was also making her mark on the Formula Three scene. She did her first Formula Three season in 1999, after five seasons in Formula Four in Finland. In 1997, she won at least one F4 race at Hämeenlinna.

In 1999, she raced in the Nordic Formula Three Championship, and quickly got on the pace. She took her first podium finishes at the second meeting, two third places at Anderstorp. The year's best finish for her was a second place at Jyllandsring.

In 2000, despite a less than optimal start to the year when she missed some races, she posted her first Formula Three win at her lucky track of Hämeenlinna. The following year, she won at Hämeenlinna again, en route to winning the Scandinavian Formula Three championship. In 2002, she came close to winning the Finnish Formula Three championship, but a crash in the last round dropped her to second. She scored three wins and two further podiums that year.

Sanna was clearly one of Finland's, and Scandinavia's, best young drivers. She had meant to spend 2003 in the German Formula Three series, which was the premier European Formula Three championship at the time and an acknowledged stepping stone to Formula 3000 and Formula One testing.

Again, Sanna showed that with consistent backing and a continuity of team support, female drivers can be incredibly competitive. There was no 'natural' inferiority for Sanna to overcome, just as Lella Lombardi showed that with decent machinery and opportunities to learn, a woman can drive as fast as a man. The reason that Sanna's career went no further was financial, and the result of criminal behaviour by others. She lost her German Formula Three race seat after her manager embezzled funds meant to take her through the 2003 season. Her story has strong similarities to Claudia Steffek's. Managerial fraud ended both of their careers prematurely.

This is important to consider. The dominant argument for the continuing absence of women from top-line motorsport is that they are not good enough, either through a general lack of ability, or inexperience caused by budgetary constraints. Both Claudia Steffek and Sanna Pinola demonstrate that this is not always the case, and that young drivers (undoubtedly of both sexes) can stop progressing in their careers due to the malicious actions of others.

Interestingly, Sanna is one of a tiny handful of women to have driven a current Formula One car. In 2000, she did some demonstration laps in the driving seat of a two-seater Minardi at Kemora, in Finland. No times were ever published. The two-seater Minardi was slower than the normal car, anyhow. It would be interesting to know what her times in a Formula One car proper would be.

Still in Europe, another female name was linked more directly with Formula One. In 1998 once again, an Irish driver called Sarah Kavanagh was attempting to take a rather unorthodox route into Formula One. She had her first races in the EuroBOSS series, a semi-historic championship for 1980s and 1990s Formula One machinery, with some Formula 3000 and Indycars thrown in. She drove an E-Merge Racing Formula 3000 Reynard, and took the class lap records at Mondello Park and the Brands Hatch Indy circuit. In 1999, E-Merge acquired a 1995 Jordan Formula One car, which Sarah was to race. This made her the first woman since Giovanna Amati to race a Formula One car in anger, albeit in a historic racing context.

It was 2000 when Sarah started racing the Jordan seriously, and 2001 when she made something of a breakthrough with the car. She was ninth in the EuroBOSS championship, and the highlight of her season was a third place at her home track, Mondello Park. This attracted the attention of the motorsport press and began a series of rumours involving Sarah and more than one Formula One team of the time.

The first association was with McLaren. Whispers circulated of a possible testing role or a development deal of some kind. McLaren themselves confirmed that Sarah had undertaken a performance assessment with them, and she had been pronounced fit enough to endure the rigors of the Formula One cockpit. The test was of her physical fitness rather than her driving ability, but it was still a positive outcome.

The following season, Sarah was linked with a number of vacant race seats, both in Formula 3000 and in its successor, GP2. The details were usually vague. Sarah's manager was said to be working on sponsorship packages and developing new racing opportunities. For the next three years, she did not actually race at all, although she retained a media presence and often spoke out about the lack of support for female drivers.

Her name was linked with another Formula One outfit in 2004. This time, it was named publicly: Jaguar. John Allison, the Jaguar chief operating officer, confirmed that talks were underway to add Sarah to the Jaguar driving squad, first as a development driver but with a view to a race seat in the future. The deal would last until 2007. Her development as a driver would be done under the auspices of the Carlin Formula Three team, racing in the British Formula Three series. This would involve 'driving and promotional activities' for Jaguar, as well as Formula Three. He said that Trevor Carlin believed that Sarah had the potential for at least a Formula One testing role, and that a place in the Carlin team was being held open for her.

Sarah did not end up racing for the Carlin team. She was unable to put together the necessary sponsorship package that would have been her part of the deal. Jaguar sources said no more about the affair.

She claimed at the time that other Grand Prix teams were interested in her, but no names were named. She remained in search of a Formula Three or Formula 3000 drive, but this did not happen. She retired quietly from motor racing not long afterwards.

It is difficult to say what went so wrong with Sarah's racing career. Speaking in 2014, she squarely blamed a lack of money for her failure to progress in the way she wanted. The details of her negotiations with Jaguar, and the parties involved, have never been discussed openly. She may have been acting on poor advice.

Did Sarah have the talent to get to the top? This is even harder to judge. Trevor Carlin knew a good driver when he saw one, and his opinion must be taken into account. Going on her race experience, she certainly had the strength and skillset to drive a Formula One car of the modern era; her car for the EuroBOSS series was a 1995 Jordan Formula 1 machine and would have subjected her to considerable G-forces. The chief problem we have with assessing her racing career is that she never stayed in one series long enough to give a reliable idea of her driving style and talent level. Between 1995 and 1997, she raced in Formula Vauxhall Lotus, British Formula Two and Formula Nippon in Japan. For the two latter championships, she used the same Reynard-Cosworth 95D as she used in her first EuroBOSS season. Her Formula Vauxhall results do not seem to be available anywhere, and neither do her Irish Formula Ford and Formula Opel results from 1992 onwards. Her Formula Two season in 1996 consisted of two races. She finished one, coming sixth at Silverstone. Moving to Japan in search of better competition, she did two rounds of Formula Nippon in 1997, finishing once, in fourteenth place, at Suzuka.

Sarah's team-hopping and seeming inability to put a full season together are not particularly unusual among female racers.

At the same time as Sarah Kavanagh was furiously trying to broker a Formula One drive, another Sarah became the first woman to drive a current Formula One car in public since Giovanna Amati. Before the US Grand Prix in 2002, Sarah Fisher did some demonstration laps in a McLaren-Mercedes. The event was more of a publicity stunt than a true test session, with McLaren trying to boost the popularity of Formula One in the US. No times were published, but the drive did its job, being seen by people all over the US and the world.

For a time, Sarah Fisher was touted as a possible Formula One hopeful. She made history in 1999, becoming the youngest person ever to pass the Indianapolis Rookie Test aged 18. She made her race debut that year at Texas Motor Speedway, but did not finish due to a broken timing chain.

She had her first run in the Indy 500 in 2000, driving for Walker Racing. This was another first, as there were two female drivers qualified: Sarah and Lyn St James. Both retired, following accidents. At Kentucky, Sarah earned her first Indycar podium, a third place.

Driving for the same team, she went one better in 2001, finishing second at Miami-Homestead. She qualified ninth for the Indy 500, raising hopes of a strong finish, but did not get to the end of the race.

Sadly, sponsorship difficulties began to plague her career at that point. She only did one more full season, in 2007, driving for Dreyer & Reinbold Racing. After that, it was part-seasons and token appearances at the Indy 500. In 2008, she launched her own team, and in 2010, she retired from the track in order to run it full-time. On track, she never scaled the heights of her early 2000s podiums again, although she did manage some more top-ten finishes. In total, she entered the Indy 500 eight times, qualifying every time. Her best finish was seventeenth in 2009, when she was driving for her own Sarah Fisher Hartman Racing team.

It is not likely that Sarah was ever a serious contender for a Formula One seat. Her background was quarter-midget racing and her expertise was on oval tracks, rather than road courses. With the greater opportunities afforded by the large Indy grids, it made sense for her to stick with what she knew. Again, given a more consistent source of support, she may well have done much better than she did. Her early-career podiums showed flashes of real speed, against tough opposition.

Sarah's achievements have now been eclipsed by those of Danica Patrick, who came on to the scene in 2005. Danica too has been the subject of Formula One-based speculation, but not to any serious degree, and her story does not quite fit in this chapter.

The other half of the American continent had its own female Formula One hopeful in the 1990s. Suzane Carvalho was apparently invited to test a Larrousse car at some point but could not raise the necessary funds. The specifics of this are extremely sketchy; it is not even clear in which year it happened. It was probably while she was racing in 1992, the year she won the Light class of the SudAm Formula Three championship. She was seventh in the championship in 1993.

Suzane Carvalho raced in women's events and in Formula Chevrolet. Her biggest achievement was winning the B class of the SudAm Formula Three championship in 1992. She raced in Formula Three in Europe and Macau at different times, but she was most often seen in touring cars, usually one-make series. Suzane's past as a B-movie actress meant that she picked up a lot of media attention.

Later, after the demise of the Larrousse Formula One team, Suzane returned to Formula Three after a long break in 2011. She proved that she still had her touch, winning a Light race at Jacarepaguá and coming third in another.

Maria Cristina Rosito was a rival of Suzane Carvalho in Formula Chevrolet, and in the one-make saloon series popular in Brazil at the time. In 2000, she took part in SudAm Formula Three. Competing in the Light class, she was eighth. She would return to Formula Three in 2004, and did make something of a name for herself in single-seaters, but it was in saloons, particularly in endurance events, that she really shone. She won the Tarumã 500km outright in 1988, driving a Volkswagen Passat with Paulo Hoher. The same pairing won another race at Tarumã that year, and was second in the Three Hours of Guapore. The following year, they won a regional championship in the Passat. In 2003, just before her second Formula Three season, she raced a Volkswagen Spyder in the Sports Prototype class of Brascar. She and Marcus Peres won at least two races together, at Curitiba and Londrina, and were second in the championship.

On the single-seater side, Maria Cristina won the 1988 Gaúcho Formula Ford championship, for drivers from the Rio Grande do Sul region.

Quite a lot of Maria Cristina's career was spent in the women-only racing series that proliferated in Brazil in the late 1990s and early 2000s. In 1995, she raced in Formula Hyundai Femenina and in 2002 she won the Campeonato Brasileiro Ford Fiesta Feminino, a one-make series for women drivers. This was organised by Maria Helena Fittipaldi, the former wife of Emerson Fittipaldi, who was the chair of AMPACOM, a Brazilian women's racing association. Some of the other women who raced in AMPACOM's championships also tried their hand at single-seaters, although none were linked with a Formula One drive.

Between Giovanna Amati's qualification attempts and Susie Wolff's Friday testing for Williams in 2014, three other female drivers tested Formula One cars in an official capacity. The first was Katherine Legge, a British driver who started her senior career at the same time as Susie Wolff. In 2002, she raised a few eyebrows when she started on pole in a British Formula Renault race (Wolff was also competing that day). Unfortunately, she could not convert her qualifying pace to race wins, and her sponsors soon pulled out. In 2003, she did some British Formula Three races, before focusing on the US single-seater scene as her best chance at a professional career. In 2005, she took part in Formula Atlantic and won her first race, before winning the next two races as well and finishing third in the championship. In the off-season, she was invited to test a Minardi by its principal, Paul Stoddart. She drove a current Minardi at Vallelunga, not without incident; she managed to crash into a tyre wall in front of the press. Undeterred, she brushed herself off and carried on, setting an official lap time of 1:21:17, which was far faster than the official Minardi test driver, Chanoch Nissany, and only sixteen hundredths of a second slower than Juan Caceres, who was a Minardi-affiliated driver. Stoddart said to the press that he was happy with Katherine's performance, but she was not offered a drive, and anyhow, Minardi was sold to Red Bull shortly afterwards.

Katherine went on to race in Champ Car in 2006, with a best finish of eighth, before spending two seasons in the Deutsche Tourenwagen Meisterschaft (DTM), and making a part-time return to Champ Car. She then moved into sportscars, and drove the experimental Delta Wing prototype for three seasons, mostly in America.

Maria de Villota was the next woman to get into a Formula One car. She had been racing in Spanish Formula Three and the Superleague Formula, with mixed results, and her appointment by the Marussia team was widely considered to be an exercise in PR and sponsorship collection. She had initially tested a 2009 Renault Formula One car at Paul Ricard in 2011, as well as doing some demonstration laps at a World Series by Renault meeting. No lap times have ever been published.

She was signed up by Marussia for a testing role in 2012, despite being 32 years old. Her first test session was a straight-line speed test at Duxford Airfield in the UK. This ended in tragedy when the car Maria was driving collided with the tail lift of a team truck. The full details of the accident have never been released. Maria suffered severe facial injuries and lost an eye in the accident. She recovered enough to start making public appearances again, with eye patches that matched her outfits, but the effects of the accident contributed to her death from a heart attack in 2013.

Simona de Silvestro is the only other woman to have driven a modern Formula One car in anger. She was signed as an 'affiliated driver' by the Sauber team in 2014 with a view to a race seat in 2015. She attended one official test in a 2010 Sauber at Fiorano, and completed enough laps to qualify for her Superlicence. No times were ever released, but a Sauber engineer, Paul Russell, said she 'drove well, had a good pace and was consistent'.

Simona was tipped as the most accomplished of the female Formula One hopefuls, with a background in US oval racing. She became the second woman ever to win a Toyota Formula Atlantic race, in 2008, before graduating to the Indy Racing League in 2010. Between then and 2013, she drove for two different teams, and had a best finish of second, in 2013, at Houston. This was the highest finish for a female driver on an Indy road course.

Her career was affected by her team's decision to use the unreliable Lotus IRL engine in 2012.

Formula One beckoned for her in 2015, but it was not to be. Her primary sponsor pulled out at the last minute, and she was unable to raise the funds needed for Grand Prix-level competition. She has since raced in Indycar and Formula E, before going to Australia to race V8 Supercars and back to Europe for GTs.

Another name needs to be added to this list. Carmen Jordá, another Spanish racer, was signed as a Lotus development driver in 2015. Her appointment was greeted with derision; she had been racing in GP3 for three seasons without scoring a point. She did have a good season in Spanish Formula Three in 2007, but that was some time previously.

Carmen mostly worked in the simulator, and did not drive a Formula One car in any official or public capacity. She supplemented her simulator time with some runs in the TCR touring car series, which were not successful, and media work – much of which has not been focused on motorsport.

In 2016, she became involved in a disagreement with another Renault development driver, who claimed that her simulator lap times lagged far behind another driver's, who had been let go by the team. Carmen remained silent. No lap times were ever produced.

A new female Formula One hope appeared in 2017, in the shape of Colombian Tatiana Calderon, who had been competing in the junior European single-seater series since 2012. She impressed onlookers with her run in the 2016 EuroFormula championship, in which she was ninth, with a best finish of third at the Red Bull Ring. The same year, she scored three top-ten finishes in GP3.

She was signed by Sauber, and obviously had a more secure sponsor package than Simona de Silvestro. Her Sauber testing duties ran in tandem with another season in Formula Three.

Women drivers in historic Formula One have been more common. Of course, we cannot compare modern and classic machinery easily, but historic racers have proved that the women are capable of handling the most powerful and temperamental of cars.

The most successful of these historic racers has been Helen Bashford-Malkie, who drove an ex-Elio de Angelis Shadow in the Thoroughbred Grand Prix (TGP) series (now Historic Grand Prix). She was third at Brno during her first season, in 1997. The following year, she nearly made it to the top step of the podium at Spa, but she got tangled up in an accident and was only eleventh at the end.

Helen had been active in motorsport since the late 1970s, having been inspired by Divina Galica to race herself. She was also involved on the management side, maintaining a senior role at the Chevron team, which she now owns, with husband Vin Malkie. She was a long-term chairman of the British Women Racing Drivers' Club.

Lorina McLaughlin, the other female name that springs to mind when discussing historic Formula One, is also a long-standing member of the BWRDC. Like Helen, she began racing in the 1970s, and as Lorina Boughton, was a promising junior single-seater driver. In 1989, she took delivery of James Hunt's title-winning McLaren M23. In this car, she won Class B of the Historic Formula One Championship, with a best overall finish of fourth.

Lorina has raced an Arrows A9 and an ex-Michael Schumacher Benetton B192. She normally uses these cars in hillclimbs, such as the Goodwood Festival of Speed, where she is a multiple ladies' champion.

Less well known, but more recent, are the exploits of Andrea Wessels-Bahlsen, from Switzerland. In 2001, she raced a Tyrrell 008 and a Lotus 81/2 in the TGP championship. She had no previous experience of driving a racing car, but picked it up quickly. She was never a race winner, but she was perfectly capable of holding her own, and was a regular top-ten finisher for the next five years or so.

During her time in the series, Andrea raced against an Austrian driver called Conny Kenner, in a Tyrrell, and Janine Payne, an Englishwoman, in an Arrows A4. Janine equalled Helen Bashford's 1997 record with a third place in 2005. Sadly, neither of these drivers enjoyed a long career in TGP; costs may not be as high as in the Formula One World Championship, but nevertheless, they are very high, and the same problems finding and retaining sponsorship apply.

Conclusion

We have looked at the past, but what of the present and the future?

Since the late 2010s, women in motorsport have been the subject of much speculation and discussion. The idea of a woman racing in Formula One again has been rekindled by the sight of Susie Wolff in a Williams and interested parties have talked about how best to bring this about.

Since Lea Lemoine first jumped astride her tricycle, and even since Giovanna Amati attempted to qualify for a Grand Prix in 1992, motorsport has changed drastically. The path to a Formula One race seat has become standardised, beginning with karting as a pre-teen, through junior single-seaters, Formula 3 and Formula 2. The introduction of the super license for F1 drivers means that sustained success in elite racing over a three-year period is required before a seat for practice can even be considered. The days of plucky chancers sneaking onto the grid on the strength of a 150-lap tyre test and a couple of Formula 3000 races have gone, and with them, the likes of Divina Galica, Desire Wilson and Giovanna Amati.

Women drivers have always been resourceful in the ways they have found to race their cars. They have shared with husbands, family members and each other. They have used celebrity status or success in other sports as a lever to a spot on the grid. Sponsorship deals with feminine hygiene products, bra manufacturers, toothpaste companies and haircare suppliers have funded attempts at rallies, long-distance road races and circuit races up to and including Le Mans. Women have serialised their adventures in newspapers or simply used their own personal wealth to buy their way in.

Now, female drivers have to find a way to make it using standard routes, and these are expensive. Even a fabulously wealthy hereditary peeress, who would have been able to buy herself a blown Bentley and a racing career a century ago, would have to spend millions upon millions over her entire young adulthood to get a chance at an F1 seat. Sponsorship can always help tremendously, but big brands have been slow to get behind motorsport at all, let alone a female driver who will be seen as a terrible risk for bad publicity should something unpleasant happen to her. These problems are not exclusive to women; a top-level motorsport career is out of reach to most men too. However, a man (or even a teenaged boy) crashing a car is not seen as an anomaly or a shock in the same way as a woman doing the same thing would be. Individual men are also rarely held up as examples of the entire male sex the same way that women are.

Increasingly, women-only racing series are being promoted as the solution. This in itself is far from being a new idea; after all, Lea Lemoine was part of a women-only championship in 1897. The W Series, a Formula 3 championship for female drivers which charged no entry fees, was launched in 2019 in a blaze of publicity and some controversy, but by 2022, it appeared to be suffering from the same problems as every other modern single-sex championship: money. The Women's Global GT Series folded at the end of 2001 due to the lack of a title sponsor and W Series had to curtail its 2022 activities when a potential sponsor pulled out at the last minute.

Just after W Series admitted its money worries to the public, the FIA announced plans for its own championship for young female drivers, an F4-based series called F1 Academy. Entrants to this will have to find half of the season costs themselves, with the rest being covered by the FIA.

Critics of both plans included female drivers themselves, including Indycar racer Pippa Mann and F3 and sportscar racer Sophia Floersch, who both want to compete against the best in their chosen field, rather than just other women. Both worry that creating expensive parallel championships takes away potential funding from women wanting to take their chances on the regular single-seater ladder. They and others advocate for female academy seats within established teams and championships.

Supporters of W Series claim that its value will not be seen for at least a few years, when younger girls inspired and encouraged by watching W Series on television start appearing in bigger numbers in karting and the junior single-seater championships. Where this leaves W's existing drivers is unclear.

Of course, away from the pressured environment of F1 and the upper echelons of professional motorised competition, women are still finding ways to compete and to excel. Some of the most demanding and dangerous forms of motorsport attract the most female entrants. The Dakar Rally is one of the longest and most arduous events in the world, passing through hundreds of miles of desert. It is the blue riband event of the cross-country rallying calendar and women drivers and riders appear in all categories, usually in double figures for the whole field. In 2001, German Jutta Kleinschmidt even won the rally outright in her Mitsubishi Pajero. Women excel in drag racing and also in rallycross, where they have been winning titles since 1994, when Susann Bergvall scored her first victory in the European 1400 Cup.

There is also hope in new disciplines involving electric vehicles, especially those outside the traditional four-wheeled box, such as e-scooter racing and airborne racing championships which are only just being developed. The eSkootr championship, the world's first sporting challenge for electric stand-up scooters, had a female winner, erstwhile motorcycle racer Sara Cabrini, in its first year in 2022.

Club racing and rallying have almost never been closed to women. They continue to provide opportunities to women with passion, enterprise and skill throughout the world. If the motorsport authorities want more diversity, they should perhaps be looking at these channels for future talent.

Speedqueens will find a way. Maybe reclaiming their own great, glorious and occasionally tragic history will be another step in the right direction.

Acknowledgements

My first thanks must go to those who shared their stories and research with me directly for this book: Bron Burrell, Tina Kerridge and Pat Wright for their reminiscences, Richard Armstrong for sharing his work on Fay Taylour and John Gabrial for use of his library of race programmes.

Next, the team at Pen & Sword, especially Amy and Gaynor.

There are too many motorsport people to remember individually as so many have given me assistance, information tip-offs or even just encouragement. I'll begin with Jennie Gow and Rebecca Jackson, who both gave me a pep talk at a Dare to be Different event that led to me becoming a professional writer at the age of 37. Next, Matt Beer, formerly of Autosport, who took a chance on me for the Autosport Academy. At Autosport, Stephen Lickorish, Kevin Turner, Matt Kew and Stefan Mackley have all been supportive. The other Academy alumni did a great job bouncing ideas around and reading early drafts.

Many members of the British Women Racing Drivers' Club have been helpful and kind: Lorina McLaughlin, the late Lorraine Gathercole, Sharlie Goddard, Tina Hines, Sami Bowler, Anna Walewska and Charlotte Phelps.

Tara Strong of Motorsport Woman has been amazingly supportive, alongside Ted Pearson, Linton Stutely, Rick Morris, Ben and Lianne Tinkler, the Thurston family, Stuart Kestenbaum, the Grant family, Colin Turner, Andrew and Jackie Smith, Sylvia Mutch, Abi Harris, Jen Ridgway, Alan Morgan, Simon Hadfield, Fraser Collins, Cam Jackson, Benn Simms, Graham Fennymore, Alison Bell, Richard Yeomans, Dick Dixon, Richard Tarling, the Harrison family, John Hayes-Harlow, Drew Cameron, Don Hardman and everyone else who makes life in the paddock more fun.

For inspiration, Mike Jackson and the late Johnty Williamson, Elsa Nystrom, Tamalie and Andrew at the Brooklands Museum, the late Joy Rainey, Anita Taylor, Nina Baker, Pippa Mann, Linda Keen, Anita Latham, Anna Kessel for Dorothy Levitt adventures and Melissa Mallows and Anni Byard for backup.

Last and most importantly, my family for their love and support: Rosemary and Stephen Bichener, Dan, Faye and Beatrice Bichener, Louis, Teddy, Barbara, Julie and Cameron.

Index